1972

Essays on
Music
and History
in Africa

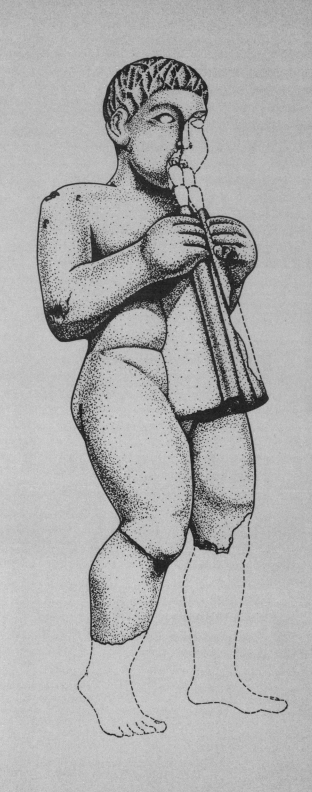

ESSAYS ON

Music
and History
in Africa

EDITED BY

Klaus P. Wachsmann

NORTHWESTERN UNIVERSITY PRESS

Evanston 1971

The drawing opposite the title page is a reconstruction of an *auletes* statue found at Meroë (see Chapters 5 and 6 for discussion). Taken from David M. Dixon and Klaus P. Wachsmann, "A Sandstone Statue of an Auletes from Meroë," *Kush,* XII (1964), 122.

Contents

List of Illustrations

MUSICAL EXAMPLES

Preface

AFRICAN STUDIES IN THE UNITED STATES are no longer merely matters of dispassionate inquiry, and the history of Africa's music is no longer considered a subject fit only for speculation by idle minds. One can make sweeping statements of this kind nowadays because, for Westerners, Africa no longer seems remote—if distance can be measured by the intensity of emotional involvement. For millions of Americans there is an African heritage to be acknowledged and claimed, and this may be true of other cultures too, wherever the African Diaspora has reached.

As for music, it would be foolish to pretend that it stands at the center of the universe of learning. Yet if there is an issue on which musicians and nonmusicians agree, it is that music plays a very important role in the life of an African community. It is interesting to note, for instance, the effect that the African Diaspora had on the societies to which it spread. In the New World, for example, Herskovits gives music the highest score in his Scale of Intensity of New World Africanisms,[1] and in the Old World, in seventh-century Arabia, the singing and dancing of African slaves gave the prophet Muhammad food for serious thought when he found his youthful wife Ayisha watching their performance spellbound. The Prophet's comments on that occasion came to be

1. Melville J. Herskovits, *Cultural Dynamics* (New York: Knopf, 1967), p. 225.

discussed repeatedly in later centuries by theologians and philosophers of Islam.

The precolonial history of Africa was neglected for a long time, largely because the scarcity of written documents was deeply frustrating. But things have changed for the historian; a clear indication of a new interest was the establishment of the *Journal of African History* in 1960. New data were published, new methods led to new insights, and the frustration lost much of its sharpness. But can this also be said about the history of music in Africa? The contributors to this volume have applied themselves to this question. The only common understanding among them of their task was that they would search for musical evidence side by side with archaeological, historical, and similar material; they would correlate these wherever possible; and, in general, they would explore how music and history can mutually define and illuminate each other.

Significantly, the combination of the disciplines of music and history was originally proposed by an expert in the music of China, that field of non-Western music best endowed with an ancient literature. In Africa, musical historical data are notoriously absent. Indeed, before the Symposium on Music and History in Africa and Asia, from which this volume derives, took place, the difficulties confronting the Africanists seemed insurmountable; but the challenge was too provocative not to be accepted.

Opinions on the purpose and the usefulness of symposia of this kind are, of course, divided. Some students value them as opportunities for a personal exchange, but others have more ambitious expectations that meetings between different disciplines may lead to cross-fertilization and thus give rise to new developments.

The essays on Islam and African music by Lois Anderson and Akin Euba were written for the African Studies Association meeting at Montreal in 1969, to be presented at a session under the chairmanship of J. Katz. Through no fault of the chairman or the authors, the papers could not be given at that time. I am indebted to Professor Katz and the authors for permission to include these two essays in this volume, for they help to round out the scope of the book.

Thanks are due to the late Dr. Marion Smith, Hon. Secretary of the Royal Anthropological Institute of Great Britain and Northern Ireland, who keenly promoted the plan to hold the symposium; to Mr. Sam Hileman, who read the completed and edited essays and whose advice has been greatly valued; to Miss Barbara Kellogg, who so efficiently acted as my secretary; and to the Regents of the University of California, for a grant that enabled much necessary secretarial work to be carried out.

My thanks are also due to the members of the Ethnomusicology Committee of the RAI, who ultimately were the driving force behind the symposium, and among them Mr. William Fagg, chairman of the Publications Committee, whose interest in the project was most encouraging. Mr. David Boston, curator of the Horniman Museum, London, bore the brunt of the technical and administrative difficulties that unfortunately prevented the originally scheduled publication of the symposium proceedings in their entirety. Mr. Boston's concern and wisdom gave encouragement to the editor and contributed greatly to the publication of the essays in this volume. It seems that Providence has after all been kind; these essays now appear at a time when interest in African music and history is much more intense than it was in 1962.

KLAUS P. WACHSMANN

West Africa

1.
History and
the Organization
of Music
in West Africa

J. H. KWABENA NKETIA

UNTIL RECENTLY, the historical view of music in sub-Saharan Africa assumed that it was the music of static or isolated societies and that this music represented either the earliest forms made by mankind or forms that could not have departed substantially from those used by early man. Nettl maintains that one reason the music historian should study such music is that "[he] may use it in his efforts to determine the origin of music." [1] In a report on the music of the Basuto, Koole writes:

Like the other Bantu tribes, the Basutos have made practically no cultural progress, although they have been in contact with

1. Bruno Nettl, *Music in Primitive Culture* (Cambridge: Harvard University Press, 1956), p. 2.

Europeans for more than a century. Their music, too, in so far as this has been handed down orally does not deviate from their age-old traditions. This is advantageous to the musicologist, and it enables him to listen to music similar to that which was made by their ancestors in the stone age.[2]

This view of African music is still held by some musicologists, particularly those who look at it only from the perspective of Western art music, of a world history of music, or of the history of Middle Eastern music.

It is clear, however, from what is now known about African history and cultures, that we can no longer maintain such an assumption. We must face afresh the problems of change in the musical traditions of Africa within the larger framework of African history.

MUSICAL CHANGE

Published observations on some aspects of musical change by musicologists in the African field [3] show that historical studies of some depth are needed and that these should be approached not only from without, in terms of distribution studies that link Africa with the rest of the world,[4] but more particularly from within, in terms of what may be discovered about the cultural history of instruments, stylistic changes, and factors affecting the contextual organization of music.

This is not an easy task. It was no doubt an awareness of these methodological problems that led Bukofzer to the hasty conclusion that "a historical study of the styles of non-Western music is at present an unattainable goal," for this music, he continues, "defies the traditional Western forms of notation

2. Arend Koole, "Report on an Inquiry into the Music and Instruments of the Basutos in Basutoland," in *Internationale Gesellschaft für Musikwissenschaft Kongress-Bericht* (Utrecht, 1952), p. 264.

3. See, for example, Klaus P. Wachsmann, "A Century of Change in the Folk Music of an African Tribe," *Journal of the International Folk Music Council,* VIII (1956), 52–56; and J. H. Nketia, "Changing Traditions of Folk Music in Ghana," *ibid.,* IX (1957), 4–9.

4. See, for example, Erich M. von Hornbostel, "The Ethnology of African Sound-Instruments," *Africa,* VI (April–July, 1933), 129–57, 277–311.

and lacks the kind of historical documents we are accustomed to in our normal research." [5]

Naturally, a different kind of approach is required, since we have to proceed to the past from the present. Our data must be drawn not only from structural analysis but also from studies of the interrelations between music and other aspects of culture and from the results of applying distributional criteria to societies that have been in contact or are contiguous enough to permit the assumption of contact. The musicologist has to draw on the work of historians and anthropologists for illumination of his problems, though his studies also provide evidence, as well as problems, that may be followed up by both historians and anthropologists.[6]

Documentary sources on West African music are unfortunately not always reliable where statements about purely musical considerations are concerned. But they do give fair indications of the social context of the music, and sometimes of the relative "age" of a musical instrument or even a musical feature in a given culture. It is illuminating to find references in the works of Barbot (1732) [7] and Bosman (1705) [8] on "the Coast of Guinea" to drums being "generally in consort with the blowing of horns," to men beating drums with "two long sticks made hammer-fashion and sometimes with a straight stick or their bare hands," and to the fact that when drumming "they always set a little boy to strike upon a hollow piece of iron with a piece of wood."

It is similarly illuminating to read some of Bowdich's observations on the music of Ashanti.[9] Describing three-holed

5. Manfred Bukofzer, "Observations on the Study of Non-Western Music," in *Les Colloques de Wégimont*, ed. Paul Collaer (Brussels: Elsevier, 1956), p. 34.

6. See J. H. Nketia, "Historical Evidence in Ga Religious Music," *IVth International Seminary on Ethnohistory of Africa* (London: Oxford University Press, for the International African Institute, 1964).

7. John Barbot, *A Description of the Coasts of North and South Guinea: Churchills Voyages* (London, 1723; reprint ed., London: Frank Cass, 1969), p. 264.

8. William Bosman, *A New and Accurate Description of the Coast of Guinea* (Knapton, 1705), p. 118.

9. T. E. Bowdich, *Mission to Ashantee* (London: John Murray, 1819), pp. 278–81.

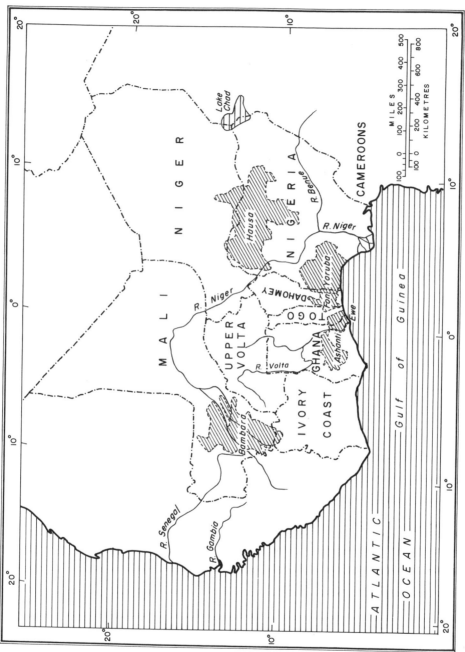

MAP 1a. West Africa

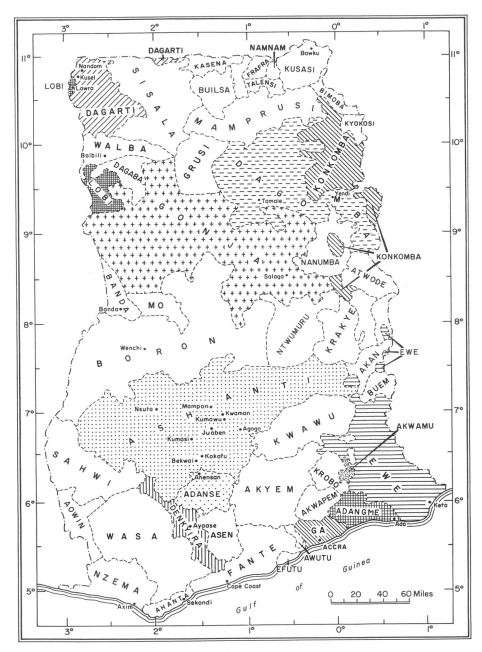

MAP 1b. Ghana Ethnic Groups and Regions

flutes made of "long hollow reed" he remarks that "the tone is low at all times and when they play them in concert they graduate them with such nicety as to produce the common chords. Several instances of thirds occur" [10]—an important characteristic of polyphony in Ashanti music.

In historical studies of African music, one must of course make use of oral evidence when it is available, for in some societies there are oral traditions about the origins of musical types or dances, traditions that associate individuals with particular dances, musical types, or one feature of a musical style. Although some of these traditions should be used with caution, there is no doubt that they can throw some light on stylistic differentiations that may be found in the music of single tribes and also on the way in which such differentiations are linked with contextual distribution. They may also give some indications of the nature and extent of interaction between communities, ethnic groups, and the like in the pre-European period.

It is considerations such as these that have guided this paper. Its aim is to illustrate some of the problems in the music history of West Africa, with particular reference to the factors that governed the organization of music in Ghana and neighboring territories in the precolonial era.

In Ghana and other West African countries today, music is closely integrated with social life. Early documentary references to music in this area—to music performed at the courts of chiefs, to the incidence of music at ceremonies and festivals—emphasize this link. We can thus assume that in the past changes in social life affected the organization of music just as such changes do today and that the history of the development of musical traditions in West Africa must be sought in the social history of the West African peoples.

In the precolonial era, this pattern of organization must have been more rigid than that of today, judging from oral traditions about social control. There was music for individuals and social groups as well as for the institutions that served these groups or the occasions on which such groups

10. *Ibid.*, p. 278

met for the purpose of recreation or ritual. Hence the enlargement of political organization, the creation of new social
groups, the creation of new ceremonies and festivals, and the
adoption of new gods, beliefs, or modes of worship [11] required
a corresponding reorganization of music, both in respect to
the participants and in the provision of appropriate musical
types.

The impetus for change did not always come from within;
the musical traditions of a people's neighbors sometimes
provided the necessary stimulus. But this often depended on
special relationships—relationships defined by cultural affin-
ity, political superiority, mutual respect, and so forth—and
above all on the degree of tolerance that their respective
musical systems provided and which facilitated the adoption
or adaptation of new elements or features.

The factors that appear to have influenced the main lines
of change in musical organization included (1) political factors, such as those that governed or facilitated the creation
and administration of states and empires, (2) the pursuit
of trade, and (3) religion.

THE EFFECTS OF

POLITICAL AND SOCIAL INSTITUTIONS

To some historians, the main lines of development of West
African history in the pre-European period appear to have
been determined by the Mediterranean-controlled trans-Saharan trade routes.[12] When we look at the history of music in
this area, however, we must direct our attention first and fore-
most to the political and social factors arising from the
impetus of trade and the conquest of Islam, for it was the ab-
sorption of new musical elements and ideas into the political
and social organization that tended to determine the directions
of musical development. Borrowed musical instruments only

11. J. H. Nketia, "African Gods and Music," *Universitas*, IV, no. 1
(1959), 3–7.
12. See, for example, J. D. Fage, *Ghana: A Historical Interpretation*
(Madison: University of Wisconsin Press, 1961), p. 10.

became significant when they were integrated into the culture, either through identification with institutions or through adoption by social groups. For example, what makes the ultimate origin of West African xylophones difficult to investigate is the fact that one finds in this area not isolated xylophones but rather "xylophone cultures," into which the instrument has been fully integrated, whatever its origin may have been.

Consider an area like northwestern Ghana—a xylophone-culture area. Here the instrument features prominently in important rites and functions; therefore if the use of an instrument in ritual is an indication of its antiquity, as Hornbostel suggests,[13] we can assume that the adoption and use of the xylophone by the people of this area cannot be recent.

In a recorded interview, the Lawra-Na (chief of one of the "xylophone peoples" of Ghana) stated that when he and his people migrated to their abode in the district of Lawra they brought with them two types of xylophones: the *lo-gu* and the *lo-gil* (small and large xylophones, respectively). Tracing their migrations as far back as he could go, he stated that originally they lived in the Ivory Coast, in a place called Tore. From Tore they went to Gogi, then to Bampo, Bache, and Wable. They crossed "the river" (the Volta) to Kusel, moved to Balbili and then Kuel, and finally settled at Lawra, where they found signs of previous settlement by two groups who are referred to in their tradition as the Dzanni and the Lamba. At Lawra there was a further dispersal. Some went northward to Nandom, others went southward, while still others went back across the river to the Ivory Coast.

The history of the xylophone in this area becomes meaningful when seen against the background tradition of migration [14] and the cultural role of the instrument. Here groups may identify themselves as being either separate or related according to, among other things, their xylophone "tunings" and dances.[15] Xylophones may be consecrated just as drums are consecrated in other regions of Ghana. The repertoire of

13. "African Sound-Instruments," p. 129.
14. For an ethnohistorical evaluation of this, see Jack Goody, *The Social Organization of the Lowiili* (London: H. M. S. O., 1956), pp. 7–16.
15. *Ibid.*, pp. 21–24.

xylophone music is contextually distributed, and we find this use of the xylophone to be parallel to the use of drum language in other areas. For example, different pieces are played to announce a death, according to whether the deceased was a man or a woman.

THE BAMBARA

There is an interesting example of this kind of problem among the Bambara, in the way in which some musical instruments are integrated into their political and religious systems. An account of two of these, the *tabale* drum and the *ngoni* harp-lute, embodied in a communication by Dieterlen, is given by Viviana Paques in her ethnographic survey of the Bambara.[16]

According to Helen Hause, thc *tabale* is of Arabic origin.[17] A drum bearing this name, or a variant of it, is either cylindrical, spherical, or in the shape of an hourglass. It has a widespread distribution in the Sudanic area, where it is a symbol of kingly command. This function of the drum is reflected in its use by the Bambara, who reserve it for royalty and chiefs.

The Bambara *tabale* is encased in copper—a practice that, incidentally, one finds also at the courts of some of the paramount chiefs in the Akan area of Ghana.[18] Around this instrument has grown an elaborate symbolism in keeping with the metaphysical system and religious outlook of the Bambara. Not only are the various parts of the drum interpreted symbolically, but even the drumstick shares in this symbolism. The stick is unusually long and, we are told, anthropomorphic in form. It has a bell attachment at the end, representing Koumabana, the giver of speech, the first of the eight ancestors in the Bambara ancestral pantheon.

The *ngoni* harp-lute of the Bambara—an eight-stringed instrument—is similarly regarded. The rectangular sound-

16. *Les Bambara* (Paris: Presses Universitaires de France, 1954), p. 106.
17. Helen Engel Hause, "Terms for Musical Instruments in Sudanic Languages," *Journal of the American Oriental Society*, LXVIII, no. 1 (1948), Supp. 7, pp. 9–13.
18. See J. H. Nketia, *Drumming in Akan Communities of Ghana* (Edinburgh: Thomas Nelson, 1963).

box of the instrument represents the mask of Koumabana; various parts of the instrument represent his eyes, nose, mouth, and teeth, while the strings represent his speeches. The instrument is also an image of his tomb, and the two sticks that lie across the sound-box represent the second and third ancestors. It is by means of associations such as these that the instrument becomes both a religious symbol and a symbol of royal authority.

It was not only because the possession of single instruments provided religious sanctions for political office that West African kings were interested in music. There is evidence in oral traditions to show that the kings of some of the states of West Africa, such as those of the forest regions of Ghana and Dahomey, were patrons of music and that some of them went out of their way to encourage the creation or adoption of new royal orchestras, new musical types, or sometimes a feature of another musical style.

THE FON OF DAHOMEY

The traditions of the Fon of Dahomey appear to be precise in this regard. The names of kings responsible for various orchestras, and sometimes the names of those who led these orchestras, are remembered. Examples are given by da Cruz in his work on the musical instruments of Dahomey.[19]

One Dahomean king whose reign saw many new musical creations and adoptions was Ouegbadja (Akaba), who reigned from about 1679 to 1708. He introduced the *kpanligan*, praise poetry recited with the accompaniment of double bells; the orchestra *abidondon*, or *hougan*, which is played behind the king to proclaim victories of the royal army; the *gohoun* orchestra; and the *ako, hounvla, adjakpete, adjoguin, dogba,* and *ado* orchestras.

King Tegbouesson's reign, which da Cruz dates as 1732 to 1775, was equally productive. He is associated with the *agbadja* orchestra, and the *hanhye, gokoe,* and *gbolo* orchestras.

King Guezo, who reigned from about 1818 to 1858, is

19. C. da Cruz, "Les Instruments de musique dans le Bas-Dahomey," *Etudes dahoméenes,* Vol. XII (1954).

associated with *agbessissohoun, bloukpete, kantanto,* and the revival of *gohoun* created during the time of Ouegbadja.

The keen interest that Dahomean kings showed in music may be interpreted against the social background into which the organization of musical types fitted. There were ceremonies to be performed, funeral rites to be celebrated, special agricultural and purificatory rites to be observed, and the great festivals, which have been described in some detail by observers like Burton,[20] to be held.

But there was also a daily round of music at the king's court that required the services of a large number of musicians— musicians who extolled in song the might and majesty of the reigning monarch or who recalled the lofty deeds of the royal dead. There were the musicians who recited the strong-names and attributes of kings to the accompaniment of the double bell. Some of the appellations of ancestor kings are given by Burton.[21] For example, the strong-names of King Ouegbadja (Akaba) were:

1. He flung a cutlass, and the owner of the country resigned to him his lands (alluding to his throwing a sword at Yaghaze, the conquered king of Weme).
2. A big club as he is, he will break down all the surrounding thorns.
3. He was not before Death (i.e., he was not born before Death came into existence), or he would not have allowed it.

A description of the daily round of music at the court today (given by da Cruz) is illuminating.[22] There is a concert of *dogba* music before the king arises in the morning, and this goes on until about 9:00 A.M. The musicians go round the palace as they play. The music of *hanhye* follows this for about an hour and a half. *Gbolo* follows and is played until midday, when the reciters of praise poetry take over. Later in the day

20. Sir Richard F. Burton, *A Mission to the Gelele King of Dahomey* (London: Tinsley Brothers, 1864).
21. *Ibid.,* pp. 376–409.
22. "Les Instruments dans le Bas-Dahomey."

the orchestras *gokoe* and *agbadja* are played in succession. Trumpets are played at nightfall, and the round ends with the music of *ako*. It is probable that this practice was followed in the past.

ASHANTI

A similar situation existed at the court of the king of Ashanti. Special music was played at various times of the day, as well as for particular occasions. As in Dahomey, oral tradition associates reigning chiefs with musical instruments, orchestras, musical types, or singing styles. Such traditions are found in all Akan areas. The *nkofe* horn ensemble is attributed to King Osei Kwadwo (1764–77).[23] The *ntahera* horn ensemble and *kete* are associated with Osei Tutu, the founder of the Ashanti kingdom (d. ca. 1712).[24] *Mpebi* and *nkrawiri* drums are attributed to the successor of Osei Tutu, Opoku Ware (ca. 1712–50).

Reindorf similarly attributes the *kwadwom* to Boa Ampɔnsɛm of Denkyira;[25] Christaller ascribes its creation to Akafo, king of Denkyira (ca. 1650–70), predecessor of Boa Ampɔnsɛm;[26] while Kyerematin adopts the tradition of Kumasi, which associates it with Osei Tutu. It is likely, however, that this is one of the contributions of Denkyira to the music of the court of the king of Ashanti. (*Kwadwom* is a kind of dirge, sung nowadays by male minstrels attached to the courts of great chiefs. It is sung with a nasal voice quality.) There are references in Rattray's *Ashanti Law and Constitution* and in the *Sunlight Magazine of History* to the practice in Denkyira of cutting the noses of slave girls in order that they might sing "sweet dirges to the King."[27] The same area is associated

23. A. A. Y. Kyerematin, *Regalia for an Ashanti Durbar* (Kumasi: A. A. Y. Kyerematin, n.d.).

24. The revised chronology of Ivor Wilks and Margaret Priestley is used in this paper for the dates of the reigns of Ashanti kings. See "The Ashanti Kings in the Eighteenth Century: A Revised Chronology," *Journal of African History*, I, no. 1 (1960).

25. C. Reindorf, *A History of the Gold Coast and Ashanti* (Basel, 1895).

26. *Dictionary of the Asante and Fanti Language.*

27. R. S. Rattray, *Ashanti Law and Constitution* (London: Oxford University Press, 1929), p. 278; *Sunlight Magazine of History*, III (July, 1926), 61.

with the use of the gourd drum, *mpintintoa* (a drum of non-Akan origin), in the reign of Boa Ampɔnsɛm. Both Kumasi and Denkyira suggest a northern influence on the musical style of Ashanti in this period and make the Denkyira the more plausible of the two traditions about the *kwadwom*.

A few references to musical creations attributed to kings occur in song texts, and I would like to quote one or two examples of these from my collection of funeral dirges of the Akan people.[28] The first three refer to the *apirede,* a drum orchestra found at the courts of paramount chiefs in the Akan area of Ghana.[29] It is used primarily in connection with stoolhouse ceremonies. Accordingly, *apirede* used to be described as the dance of the departed (*nsamanfo agorɔ*) and as a fearful dance both on account of this and the heroic practices associated with it. If a commoner danced *apirede* and could not stop at the appropriate moment simultaneously with the drums, he got into trouble.

> Your grandmother is Amoaa Awisi,
> The woman who had many children
>   but reared those of others as well.
> It is Amoaa that hails from Hwerebe Akwasiase.
> Awisi's grandchild comes from Anitibanso,
> Where skulls are used in the *apirede* dance.
>
>   . . . .
>
> We say "Excuse us" to our grandsires.
> We say "Excuse us" to our fathers;
> For in the olden days if you had something hard to say
> And you asked to be excused, you got away with it.
> For in the olden days when you were going to
>   Grandsire Kusi's house,
> You would stumble over skulls.
> You would stumble over jaw bones.
> Flies buzzed round you as if to pity you.
> Old Kusi built his palace and his storeyed building.
> Old Kusi's grandchild hails from Hwerebe Akwasiase,
> Where mere women play the *apirede*.
>
>   . . . .

28. J. H. K. Nketia, *Funeral Dirges of the Akan People* (Legon: University of Ghana, 1955).
29. See Nketia, *Drumming in Akan Communities of Ghana.*

Apea Bosompem Booban
Who created the *Apirede* orchestra,
If anyone forms such an orchestra,
He does so after his example.
Apirede, whose strong name is Yɛmmɔsoɔ,
It is grandsire Bosompem who created it.

Some Kumasi traditions attribute this orchestra to one of
the kings of Ashanti. But it was most probably the Adanse
contribution to the music of the Ashanti court. In Adanse,
where these dirges were taken down, I was told of chiefs who
obtained formal permission from the chief of Ayaase to adopt
the dance. *Apirede* has a very limited distribution in the Akan
area. In the states of Juaben and Nsuta, for example, it does
not appear to have been in use before the Ashanti-Denkyira
struggle at the close of the seventeenth century. (Denkyira
was defeated by Ashanti in 1701.)

The next two examples refer to the hourglass drum, *donno*,
which undoubtedly came to Ashanti from the north. Its introduction is attributed to Atakora of the Mampɔn Biretuo clan.
Accordingly, it is incorporated into the dirges of the Biretuo
of Mampɔn and of Ahensan, one of the places in Adanse from
which the Biretuo people of Mampɔn migrated.

Akuɔko Tɔntɔntɔn,
Who made the *donno* drum enjoyable,
Akuɔko's grandchild who comes from Nwerɛmu in Adankrannya.

.   .   .   .

Konadu of Botodoase in Mampɔn,
Konadu the flighty bird
That made the *donno* drums enjoyable.
You hail from Botodoase in Mampɔn
Where the path to the grave goes through the Ancestor's chamber,
Where the Osensiasɔ bird cries in the heat of the day.

My last example is a dirge that refers to the use of "twin"
horns, two horns playing in a kind of call-and-response pattern. The interesting point here is stylistic. This dirge indicates that such use of horns is not a recent innovation, since
the reference is to the early period in the formation of the
Ashanti kingdom.

It is Saben, grandsire Kurofa Ntim,
The valiant that bears the brunt of war.
It is grandsire whose twin short horns say:
"If battles were hard and dangerous, ɔsaben would die in battle."
Grandsire Saben never failed his admirers.
Grandchild of the Valient hails from Akyerɛmade Nitibanso.

The technique of using two horns in a call-and-response pattern is restricted to paramount chiefs. Indeed, in Ashanti it used to be the prerogative of the Asantehene.

The motives that inspired the creation or adoption of musical instruments were not always musical. The number of musicians attached to a king's court and the variety of his musical instruments and ensembles seemed to be an index of a king's greatness. In Ashanti, for example, the hierarchical structure of chiefs was also reflected in the organization of music. The higher chiefs were permitted drums and other instruments that junior chiefs could not keep. Short horns were reserved for chiefs, but only paramount chiefs could own ensembles of trumpets. The local histories of Ashanti political divisions, as recorded by Rattray,[30] and the traditions included in Reindorf's work [31] give instances of chiefs who asked permission to own particular instruments or ensembles and of chiefs who were elevated and given presents of musical instruments befitting their new rank.

Territorial expansion of states by conquest often led to the enlargement of the musical organization of the court, in respect to both numbers of musicians and new musical types. At the height of the Ashanti expansion that extended eastward beyond the Volta, westward into the Ivory Coast, and northward to the Gonja and Dagomba areas,[32] the music at the court of the king of Ashanti included contributions from various regions that were modified or re-created to suit Ashanti tastes. They included the traditions of Denkyira,

30. *Ashanti Law and Constitution.*
31. *History of the Gold Coast.*
32. See Ivor Wilks, *The Northern Factor in Ashanti History* (Legon: Institute of African Studies, University of Ghana, 1961); Ivor Wilks, "The Rise of the Akwamu Empire, 1650–1710," *Transactions of the Historical Society of Ghana,* III, pt. 2 (1957), 99–133.

which had been built on the foundations of the earlier kingdom of Adanse.

The Adanse contribution included the *apirede,* and the Denkyira contribution the *kwadwom.* Bekwai tradition states that, after the Feyiase battle in which Denkyira was overthrown, Mampɔn, Asumegya, and Dwaben were "permitted by Kumasi to copy the regalia of Ntim Gyakari, e.g., his *fɔntɔmfrɔm* drums and horns." [33] It seems probable, however, that these orchestras were already known in Ashanti, for in the early period of the formation of the state of Ashanti, Osei Tutu is said to have captured the *fɔntɔmfrɔm* and the *ntahera* trumpet ensemble of the king of Tafo, near Kumasi.[34] It is likely, however, that the ensembles of a great state like Denkyira were better designed or had a more interesting musical repertoire, which the Ashanti wanted to adopt.

There were contributions also from the northern region to the music of the Asantehene's court. Hourglass drums came to Kumasi via Mampɔn, and slaves from the north were at first the chief musicians for the *mpintin* orchestra.

The music of the chiefs of the various territorial divisions of Ashanti was similarly enlarged. Many instances of this are to be found in Rattray's account of Ashanti oral tradition,[35] and I would like to quote a few of these by way of illustration.

As a reward for his services in the Banna war, the Asantehene presented the chief of Kokofu with the Queenmother of Banna's mpintini drums [p. 201].

At the battle of Feyiase, the Nsuta captured the Head of the Denkyira horn blowers and his descendents are in Nsuta today [p. 258].

About this time there was a chief called Atada Affram who lived in the Affram plains. Kumawu, Kwaman and Agogo went to war against him. . . . Atada Affram eventually fled and drowned himself in the Volta. Nsuta was given his *ntahera* horns [p. 258].

33. Rattray, *Ashanti Law and Constitution,* p. 132.
34. *Ibid.,* p. 275.
35. *Ibid.* Subsequent page numbers in the text refer to this work.

During the reign of Opoku Ware (1712–50), Opoku Kwabon of Bekwai "fought against Akroma Apim of Nyame Duaso defeating him and capturing his *ntumpane* drums."

Osei Kojo of Bekwai helped King Kwaku Dua I (1834–67) in a civil war against Juaben, in the reign of the Juaben chief Boaten. A battle was fought at Nkateso. The Bekwai captured all the Juaben fɔntɔmfrɔm drums and umbrellas [p. 150].

Although Ashanti gained musically from its territorial expansion, it also left its influence on some of the areas with which it came into contact. One may cite, for example, the Ashanti talking drum, *atumpan*, which is now found in northern Ghana and which is still played in the Akan language; there is also the creation of *kambonwaa* in the Dagomba area, or *agorɔ* in Gonja, both types in imitation of the music of the Ashanti.

Beyond the Volta, the interaction of the Ashanti with Dahomey is seen in a number of common musical types or instruments; these constitute evidence of more intensive contact between the two kingdoms than has been generally described. There is the orchestra called *kantanto*, listed by da Cruz,[36] which Dahomean tradition attributes to Ashanti, and there is the talking drum *atonkpanli*, played in Athieme, which is probably of Ashanti origin.

There are other orchestras and musical types found in both Dahomey and Ashanti for which there is at present no evidence of origin: *akofin* (trumpet ensemble) in Dahomey; *nkofe* (trumpet ensemble) in Ashanti, attributed to Osei Kwadwo (1764–77), whose predecessor Kusi Obodum sent a mission to Dahomey; *kpetehoun, ketehoun,* and *bloukpete* orchestras (of drums and flutes) in Dahomey;[37] and the *kete* orchestra (of drums and flutes), which in Ashanti is attributed to Osei Tutu.

THE EWE

Musically, the Ewe on the eastern side of the Volta were wedged between Akan influence, through Ashanti and Ak-

36. "Les Instruments dans le Bas-Dahomey."
37. *Ibid.*, p. 49.

wamu, and the influence of Dahomey. Accordingly they now belong to two distinct musical groups: the coastal Ewe, of the Anlo-Tongu, and the Ewe of the hinterland. Both of these had contact with the Akan, and this is evident in the music of warrior organizations (*asafo*), songs of exhilaration, and music of the court—the *timpani*, *vuga*, and *bomba*, and the music of horns, which may have either Ewe or Twi basis. Contact with the Akan was more intensive in the north than in the south. Songs in both Twi and Ewe are sung, and there is a complete changeover from the Ewe singing style, based on some form of pentatonic or hexatonic foundation, to the heptatonic forms of the Akan and to singing in parallel thirds.

On the other hand, the Anlo-Ewe appear to have drawn their influences more from the east than from the west—particularly in the field of cult music and social dances. Some of the Dahomean musical types listed by da Cruz [38] appear to be the same as those found among the Anlo, but this has yet to be confirmed from actual recordings of Dahomean music.

While the Ewe idiom of the Anlo was lost in the hinterland Ewe areas, both Akan and Ga-Adangme musical styles have survived [39] in the Ga-Adangme area, where Akan influence extended as a result of the Akwamu conquest [40] in the seventeenth century. The styles are, however, used in different contexts. Here again, we have the music of Akan courts and the music of warrior organizations (whose songs are sung in Twi).

The Akan influence was greater in the Ga area. While the Adangme did not lose their own style (which is now used in music of recreation and worship), the old Ga style was preserved only in *kple*, *oʃi*, and a few other forms of old Ga ceremonial music. Recreational music began to be practiced, as it still is, in the Akan idiom and sometimes in a mixture of Twi/Fante and Ga.[41]

A similar picture of the musical results of territorial ex-

38. *Ibid.*
39. See J. H. K. Nketia, "The Organization of Music in Adangme Society," *Universitas*, III (December, 1957), 9–11.
40. Wilks, "The Rise of the Akwamu Empire."
41. See J. H. K. Nketia, "Traditional Music of the Ga People," *Universitas*, III (June, 1958), 76–80.

pansion or conquests by migrating groups can be found in other areas.

Elements from Konkomba dances were, according to David Tait, absorbed into the musical organization of the Dagomba when the Konkomba were conquered. The triumphant *zem* dance is said to be connected with the Konkomba *ndzee* dance.[42]

THE EFFECTS OF TRADE

The oral traditions that I know of do not say very much about the musical results of the trade that linked West African states with one another and with the outside world, trade carried along trans-Saharan routes or routes that linked the Gulf of Guinea to the Niger River long before the arrival of the Portuguese in the fifteenth century.[43] It is easy to imagine that the contacts resulting from this kind of activity probably enlarged the experience of traders, who carried back musical ideas and even instruments to their homes. Such an assumption seems all the more probable when we learn that in Ashanti, for example, chiefs carried on their own trade, and those who traded for them included the *asokwafo* (the musicians who played the trumpets) and the drummers. The informants of Rattray stated that

[these musician-traders were] sent to the coast to buy cloth, beads, salt, and these articles were sent to Bontuku (Ivory Coast) and Salaga and sold for cowries with which were bought slaves, shea butter, *kyekye* (blue cloth woven with the indigenous cotton) and cotton thread. These articles were again retailed in Ashanti and the profits made went to the stool. Bekwai had not any trade in Kola. These Asokwafo who traded for the Chief were never fined, but they might be whipped. They were not paid but made their own profit on each transaction. They often became rich.[44]

42. David Tait, "History and Social Organization," *Transactions of the Historical Society of Ghana*, I, pt. 5 (1955), 205.

43. See Ivor Wilks, "A Medieval Trade Route from the Niger to the Gulf of Guinea," *Journal of African History*, III, no. 2 (1962), 337–41; reprinted in *Problems in African History*, ed. Robert O. Collins (Englewood Cliffs, N. J.: Prentice-Hall, 1968), pp. 312–15.

44. Rattray, *Ashanti Law and Constitution*, p. 161.

It is possible, however, that musical considerations were not always uppermost and that this merely reflected the class of people from whom musicians were recruited to serve a chief. Slaves attached to a court could not be sold. "A chief who bought slaves and sold them again on the Coast would have been destooled for a chief's slaves were *agyapadeɛ* (heirlooms)." [45] The slaves of the court invariably included musicians of vanquished states who continued to play for their new masters and to perform other duties at the court. The evidence in oral traditions on the question of musical elements brought back to various states is quite thin and requires further investigation.

It is possible, alternatively, that the presence of foreign traders in the forest states of Ghana—particularly Mande traders—made a definite impact, which was strengthened by the experience of those who traveled out of the state. Denkyira, for example, lay on one of the great northern trade routes. It was a rich area for gold and probably attracted a great number of those engaged in the trans-Saharan trade. The tradition about the gourd drum in the reign of Boa Ampɔnsɛm and *kwadwom*, the dirges of minstrels, suggest that the northern influence represented by Mande traders was strong enough for a new stylistic feature in singing to be adopted for restricted use at the courts of chiefs.

THE EFFECTS OF RELIGION

This leads me to the last of the historical factors in the development of music in West Africa—religion. So far as Islam acted as a carrier of Arabic musical traditions, the extent of change that can be attributed to it varies considerably—from areas in which Islamic conquest was complete, both culturally and politically, to areas in which Islamic agents provided services but failed to conquer or convert to Islam. [46] The fur-

45. *Ibid.,* p. 111.
46. For an account of an area of Muslim penetration and influence which was not converted, see Wilks, *The Northern Factor in Ashanti History.*

ther north one goes, to the Sahara and beyond, the greater has been the Islamic impact.

In the Sudan, according to Fage, "[Islam] was never wholly assimilated by the Negroes. . . . The mass of the people preferred their own religion, culture and way of life." [47] This is reflected in the musical situation, which shows both the effect of Islamic penetration and the residual culture of the mass of people who did not embrace it. Here I would like to refer to the lexicographical inquiry of Helen Hause into the terms for musical instruments, which gives a fair indication of the musical situation.[48]

South of the Sudan, more particularly in Upper Volta and Ghana, the contribution of Islam is not so rich. The music of states in northern Ghana, in particular Gonja, Mamprusi, and Dagomba, was only partially Islamized through Mande and Hausa immigrants.[49] The one-stringed fiddle and the hourglass drum, two important musical instruments in the Dagomba area, betray the Hausa affinities of the immigrants who founded this state. One not only hears music played on these instruments in a fashion similar to Hausa style, but also one sometimes finds song and drum texts in Hausa. Praise-singing by wandering musicians is an important part of the tradition here, and it is organized on more or less the same pattern one finds in Hausaland and Yorubaland. There are a few musical types common to Dagomba and Hausa, such as *Damba, tora,* and *lua,* but there are also other musical types that belong solely to the Dagomba area. Fewer instruments of Arabic origin are used by the Dagbani than by the Hausa. According to Dagbani traditions, their instruments are importations from Hausaland.

Though the people of the forest states of Ghana were exposed to Islam and had many Muslims living among them, they preferred their own culture and looked to Islam only for help in political advancement. The adoption of Islamic musi-

47. J. D. Fage, *Ghana* (Madison: University of Wisconsin Press, 1961), p. 18.
48. "Terms for Musical Instruments in Sudanic Languages."
49. See Fage, *Ghana*, p. 22.

cal features was slight and restricted to categories of minstrelsy already referred to.

Indigenous African gods sometimes migrated, taking with them their music and forms of worship. In Ga society, the adoption of gods of Akan origin for worship meant also the adoption of the appropriate Akan musical types. These have survived and are now regarded as an integral part of the Ga musical tradition.

CONCLUSION

It is in the light of evidence such as I have presented here that I think studies of some historical depth are needed in African musical studies, for, although music in the precolonial period was practiced on a "tribal" basis, the traditions of the "tribes" were exposed to influences leading to change.

The rate, extent, or direction of change in music practiced by oral tradition cannot, of course, be the same as that based on written tradition. Nevertheless, such changes may be historically significant within the African context and should not, therefore, be overlooked.

As we have seen, the effects on music of contacts in the precolonial period resulted in differing stylistic characteristics. In some cases, such as among the Ga and the Ewe of the hinterland, it led to the smoothing-out of the rough edges of their musical idiosyncracies and to the widening of the Akan musical area, as characterized by its emphasing the heptatonic, by singing in parallel thirds, by introducing heavy drum ensembles, and by using language as the basis of complex musical rhythms. The widening of this area was the outcome of territorial expansion backed by efficient militarism and diplomacy. Music was an important ingredient in the territorial organization. Wars were fought with music—with the drums that kept up morale and gave directions and with the songs that roused the various companies into which men were permanently organized or the divisions to which towns and villages were assigned.

There were also areas such as Adangme, where contact led to partial assimilation, as well as areas like Dagbon, where it led to creative additions and the widening of the scope of music but not to *radical* stylistic innovations.

Musical influences sometimes impinged directly, as in the case of active occupation of a conquered territory. Sometimes they passed through intermediaries or contact agents, such as Mande traders and slaves. Sometimes they followed the voluntary adoption of new institutions carrying their own music, or the reorganization of old institutions on models from the outside. These were the trends of historical development in the precolonial era. The colonial period only brought a new impetus and a new source of change to a historical process that was already operating in West Africa.

2.

Court Songs
and Traditional History
in the Ancient Kingdoms
of Porto-Novo and Abomey

GILBERT ROUGET

INTRODUCTION

ALTHOUGH THERE ARE NO LONGER any reigning kings in Dahomey, royal courts still exist there, in more or less decaying
form. Of the different kingdoms still surviving in the southern
part of the country, Abomey, which rules the Fon people, is
best known to anthropologists; Porto-Novo, which is less well
known, rules the Gun people. Both are branches of the same
vine, the ancient kingdom of Alada, from which they originated at the beginning of the seventeenth century.

The court songs of Abomey have been described as the primary means of keeping oral historical traditions alive in the

The author wishes to acknowledge gratefully the help he received
from Mrs. Barbara Bentley and Mr. John Wright in preparing the final
English text for publication.

kingdom. The question arises whether the same holds equally true for Porto-Novo; judging by the documents I recorded there, such is not the case.

Turning then to what is known about Abomey, we shall discover that a certain nuance must be added to what has already been written concerning the historical substance of the Abomean court songs. Next I will try to point out the real role played by court songs in the general process of keeping Dahomean history alive. This role will be seen to be complex, connected in its different aspects with the various poetical genres making up the repertoire. Finally, we shall see that music has to be integrated into the definition of these poetical genres and that consequently the typology of oral tradition, considered from the point of view of its value for history, could perhaps be refined by the addition of purely musical criteria.

At Porto-Novo, as well as at Abomey, the king is someone who is naturally exalted above every other living creature; in this way he is unique. His palace and court have no equal. It nonetheless remains true that the chiefs of the other houses of royal lineage behave, in their own households, somewhat like kings. Around them, wives, relatives and servants form something comparable to a small court. One can say as much for the chiefs of certain other clans, and, in the kingdom of Porto-Novo, for petty kings subject to the monarch.

The completely unique character of king and royalty pertains to only part of the person and the institution. Between the king on the one hand, and the princes, ministers, and subjugated kings on the other, there exist many common traits. From certain viewpoints, there is only a difference of degree between his house and theirs. Therefore, it would be misleading to take only palace music into consideration here; of all the musical ensembles to be heard in the palace, very few are really peculiar to it. Most of them are found among the princes or ministers as well. Thus, the title of this chapter refers to *court songs,* not to *palace songs.*

At the same time, this title refers to *traditional* history rather than to history alone, to show that we have in mind history as it is understood in Dahomey, or at least as we think it is understood. Let us say that traditional history could be defined, in a schematic way, as the sum total of knowledge the group possesses concerning its past. For the group it is essentially a factor of cohesion. Thanks to history, the group can identify with itself and with others. This history justifies the position of the group in society and provides it with the basis for its rights. It is the property and the secret of the group.

Thus, it is treason to speak to a foreigner of the history of one's own group and indiscretion to speak to him of the history of another. At least, such is the traditionalist attitude. (Nowadays things are changing; among other things the recent distribution at Porto-Novo of a printed leaflet concerning the history of the Akplogan bears witness to this.)[1] The result is that, on a traditional level, there exists for neither the kingdom of Porto-Novo nor the kingdom of Abomey a *general* history of the society. Each of the groups constituting it has its own particular history. These histories coexist, are juxtaposed, but never form a whole. Or, rather, this whole always remains theoretic.

Nevertheless, since the two kingdoms are centralized states (Abomey more so than Porto-Novo), the history of the kings subsumes the other groups living therein, and in this way the history of the kings is identified with that of the country. By giving an account of the origins and establishment of the dynasty and by recalling the succession and great deeds of the different monarchs, history legitimizes the ruling power. Thus, the history of the kings is relatively well known to everyone, especially to foreigners. Nonetheless, it remains the history of one clan among many.

According to Le Herissé, a few chroniclers, carefully chosen among the brothers or the sons of the reigning king, were the depositaries of the "general history of Dahomey" (i.e., of Abomey), which Le Herissé himself records in his twelfth chapter.[2] But it is clear that this "general history" is in fact the history of the royal clan.

The transformation of traditional history, as we have de-

1. At Porto-Novo, Akplogan (spear-chief), "Chief of the spear," is one of the principal ministers of the king. He is in charge of all the vodun cult affairs.
2. A. Le Herissé, *L'Ancien royaume du Dahomey* (Paris: Emile Larose, 1911), p. 271.

scribed it, into history as it is understood in the Western world —tending, or purporting, to be an objective science—poses the problem of integrating the diverse materials provided by oral tradition. Jan Vansina has devoted a book to this problem; in its essentials it must be considered definitive, so we will not return to the subject again.[3]

HISTORICAL SONGS

At Porto-Novo Palace, the court music most frequently heard is performed by the wives of the king—let us say, the queens—and is called *ajogã* (ajogan).[4] This music is also heard at the houses of other lineages of the royal clan. In addition, some ministers have fairly recently been given the privilege of having this music performed at home by their own wives; others have simply taken it.[5]

At the palace, as well as in these different houses, the king's or chief's wives, under the leadership of an elder, form a group in charge of ajogan music. For the performance, eight to ten of the wives remain seated and beat drums and iron bells. One of the "drums" is the large vase-drum, *livi* (livi), an earthenware pot that is tapped on the open mouth with a sort of

---

3. Jan Vansina, *De la tradition orale: Essai de méthode historique*, Annales du Musée de l'Afrique Centrale, Vol. XXXVI (Tervueren, 1961); *Oral Tradition: A Study in Historical Methodology*, trans. H. M. Wright (Chicago: Aldine, 1965).

4. Vernacular words are spelled phonetically at their first appearance but are thereafter transliterated. Proper names have been transcribed in the traditional Dahomean way (inherited mostly from the French), leaving out tones and marking a nasal vowel by means of an *n* following the corresponding oral vowel; thus ɛ̃ is always transcribed *en*, and ĩ is *in*. Unlike French usage, the closed back vowel *u* is written *u* and not *ou*, the affricate *j* is written *j* and not *dj*, the semi-vowel *w* is written *w* and not *ou*. For proper names of persons, closed and open *e* and *o* have always been transcribed respectively *é* and *è* (for *e* and *ɛ*) and *ó* and *o* (for *o* and *ɔ*). The voiceless back fricative *x* is transcribed *kh:* thus *Xɔgbónu*, the Gun name for Porto-Novo, is written Khogbônu.

For texts in Gun the generally accepted transcription for African languages has been used. There are two distinctive tones. The high tone is marked [']; the other tone is not marked. Except for slight modifications, my transcription follows Westermann's *Wörterbuch der Ewe-Sprache* (1954), as my *Description phonologique du parler Gun de Porto-Novo*, to be published in 1971, will make clear.

5. The fact that ajogan is also performed in other clans of Porto-Novo (the Dravonu, in particular) raises problems, which however it is not necessary to examine here.

leather or basketry fan.[6] Four wives, chosen from among the youngest, stand in front of the others and sing and dance. Each one carries a rattle staff, *alūlū* (alunlun), which is made of metal and carries rings which rattle as the staff hits the ground. The wives hold their staves by the handle and lean on them while they dance, stamping the ground in measured time all together, as they go to and fro.

These dances and songs are performed on such ceremonial occasions as feasts for the ancestor cult, or simply at the king's pleasure. Certain formal patterns are characteristic of the songs, which are carefully memorized and rehearsed. It is not necessary to specify the patterns here, but it is important to emphasize that every stanza is repeated twice, sometimes three times, in order that every single word be perfectly understood by the audience. The music is homophonic. In a good performance the unison realized by the four women singing together is nearly perfect. Thus, we are dealing with music that is made to be listened to, that carries a message meant to be thoroughly understood, and whose main interest lies, consequently, in the meaning of the words.

I recorded a number of such songs at King Gbèfa's court in 1952 [7] and in the families of different princes and ministers in 1958. These recordings were made mainly for musicological study. The texts of the songs recorded at the royal palace, hastily transcribed at the time, turned out to contain a large number of words closely related to the history of Porto-Novo.[8]

---

6. In Dahomey, depending on the type of ensemble involved, the vase may be made either from pottery—empty or filled with water—or from a big calabash.

7. A short sampling of ajogan music has been published in a record entitled *Guinée, musique malinké. Dahomey, musique du roi*, recordings, notes, and photographs by G. Rouget, Vogue-Contrepoint MC 20.146, Collection du Musée de l'Homme, 1958.

Concerning the first piece—maledictions shouted against the king's enemies—note that the king's chanter, his *gbesatɔ́* (voice—to attach—one who does), "the one who attaches the voice," has been wrongly identified as his diviner *bokɔ́nɔ*).

A book entitled *La Musique du palais dans l'ancien royaume de Porto-Novo*, accompanied by records, is in preparation.

8. I gratefully acknowledge the help I later received from Jack Berry while he was professor at the School of Oriental and African Studies in London. His advice to me as a beginning student of the Gun language has been most valuable.

Constant references were made to Alada, the place of origin of the Gun dynasty. Names of other places more or less remote from Porto-Novo appeared in every song. Names of kings were often heard, among them Tè Agbanlin, founder of the dynasty, and Dé Tofa, last king in the real sense of the word; names of persons who figured in the traditional hierarchy also occurred. One of the songs—the longest—was inspired by incidents that occurred at Porto-Novo in 1950: a riot and the sacking of the royal palace. Except for this one, all the songs recorded in 1952 had been sung at King Gbèfa's coronation ceremonies in 1948. Given what had been written about similar songs from Abomey—quotations will be found below—these facts seemed to justify, at the time, a simple labeling of these songs as *historical*.[9] Closer examination of the texts led me to question this comfortable assumption and to reconsider the problem of the value of this repertoire for history.

During the years following the recording of the songs, I asked several persons from Porto-Novo to listen to the tapes. They could easily understand words and sentences, but they could make practically no sense of any song as a whole. I was astonished to see that on hearing the song concerning the riot of 1950, the Porto-Novians were unable to connect the text with the incidents, even though they might have witnessed the riot or even taken part in it. As soon as they were told what the song was about, however, everything became clear to them. All the details which had thus far been unintelligible were then easily interpreted.

It became more and more evident that these songs were difficult for anybody to understand, and, finally, that this was due to their particular style, which was deliberately allusive, even hermetic.

Names of kings, as well as other personal and place names, turned out to be used only allusively. Avadjo Adimula, for instance, well known to historians of the ancient kingdom of Dahomey and hero of various stories belonging partly to history and partly to legend, is named in one song. But he is mentioned only in order to recall his presence at the origin of

9. *Historical* in this context does not refer to a historical date or event but to the process of memorizing history.

the royal dynasty and thus to guarantee the legitimacy of the present king's reign. Tè Agbanlin (1688–1729) [10] and his successor Dé Khakpon (1729–39) are mentioned in other songs in a similar context. The name of King Dé Sôdji (1848–64) [11] appears elsewhere, but only as one whose activities in the slave trade were famous. Reference is made to him with the intention of insulting the Yoruba of Porto-Novo by recalling the fact that they are descendants of his slaves. In another song, following a proverb which means that hatred is not easily forgotten, the name of King Dé Mikpon is mentioned in connection with an obscure story about a broken bottle.[12] The allusion serves as a warning to enemies. It refers to a historical incident certainly known to a few people versed in matters of customs and proverbs, but for most of the people it would have no meaning.

Much the same can be said for all the names, of persons as well as of places, mentioned in the different songs I collected and translated.

Briefly, the substance of ajogan repertoire finally emerged as a mixture of praise and defiance—praise for the master of the house (king, prince, or minister) and defiance against his enemies—expressed in an allusive way, mainly using images and proverbs, often referring to historical data, and sometimes having an anecdotal content.

Thus, the second stage of my investigation showed that the historical information conveyed by these ajogan songs was scanty, and that these data were almost without value unless they could be related to a preexisting knowledge of local history.

In 1964, I recorded a more private, and at the same time more complete, performance of the queens' songs and dances in King Gbèfa's palace. This took place on the occasion of a yearly ceremony called *tanúwiwa* (head—thing—the making),

10. These dates follow Adolphe Akindélé and Cyrille Aguessy, *Contribution à l'étude de l'histoire de l'ancien royaume de Porto-Novo*, Mémoires de l'Institut Français d'Afrique Noire, no. 25 (Dakar, 1953), p. 65. The dates given by Edouard Foà, *Le Dahomey* (Paris: A. Hennuyer, 1895), p. 38, are different.
11. Akindélé and Aguessy, *Contribution à l'étude*, p. 75.
12. *Ibid.*

"The ritual of the head," which consists in the king "feeding his head." Ajogan was at that time preceded by a suite of four dances called jɛ̃glɛ̃ (jenglen).[13] While ajogan is sung and danced, as has been said, not only at the royal palace but also at the houses of princes and ministers, jenglen belongs exclusively to the royal court repertoire.

The music and choreography of these four dances differ from ajogan and also from one another. Each dance has its particular name. One was danced without any singing at all, while another was danced to sung texts, made up of stanzas enumerating the kings who have reigned over Porto-Novo. One of these songs is as follows:

> Axɔ́lú Gbɛfá xwé sĩ hɔ́nu ma nabɛ
> Xwénɔ Gbɛfá wá zé mi sɔ́ yi jɛ kpóló jí
>   asúe, asúe sĩ hɔ́nu ma nabɛ
>   wã̃ zé mi sɔ́ yi jɛ kpóló jí

> Axɔ́lú Gbeñɔ́ xwé sĩ hɔ́nu ma nabɛ
> Xwénɔ Gbeñɔ́ wá zé mi sɔ́ yi jɛ kpóló jí
>   asúe, asúe sĩ hɔ́nu ma nabɛ
>   wã̃ zé mi sɔ́ yi jɛ kpóló jí
> Axɔ́lú. . . . (etc.)

At King Fresh-Life's door one never keeps silent [14]
Lord Fresh-Life, take me and put me on the bed
My husband! at my husband's door one never keeps silent
            take me and put me on the bed

At King Good-Speech's door one never keeps silent
Lord Good-Speech, take me and put me on the bed
My husband! at my husband's door one never keeps silent
            take me and put me on the bed
At King. . . . (etc.)

In the first stanza, the queens addressed themselves to their actual husband, axɔ́lú Gbɛfá, King Gbèfa, "King Fresh-Life," the reigning king. In the second stanza, they named King

---

13. A synchronized 16 mm color film of the successive parts of the two "suites" (jenglen followed by ajogan) was made by Jean Rouch and myself at the end of 1969.

14. Literally, "no one ever ceases speaking," which means that the place is never still, that there is always life and movement.

Good-Speech, the sixth king of Porto-Novo, who reigned, according to Akindélé and Aguessy, from 1761 to 1775.[15] In another version of the same song they named another king, but he too was one of the early rulers. In a third version, the queens addressed themselves to yet another king. However, all versions had a common structure: the first stanza was addressed to King Gbèfa, the present king; the second was addressed to a king of olden times; the following stanzas were addressed in turn to other kings, named in more or less chronological order. The lists of kings thus obtained from different versions of this and other comparable songs, all of which were related to the same dance, were different each time. They were all far from complete.

Here again, the point to be remembered is that the song, despite appearances, does not carry any really substantial historical matter.

Ajogan songs, it has already been noted, make use of a strongly allusive style. Allusiveness is well known to be a customary feature of African traditional literature. But what interests us here is that the way it is used in the repertoire is closely related to the structure of Porto-Novian society. Texts of ajogan songs are composed of a blending of praise and defiance—praise for the master of the house where they are sung, and insults for his enemies. Praise and insults are respectively expressed in different rhetorical ways, but both have in common the requirement that they not be spoken outright. The more allusive they are the better they are and the more highly they are praised by connoisseurs. The best mockery is made in the presence of the person who is being mocked, without his being aware of it.

Allusion must be as hermetic as possible. Why? Apparently because in this way it will be understood by very few people, most of them old; in the case of the royal affairs, only by the aristocracy or members of the king's entourage. If one considers that the ancient kingdom of Porto-Novo was made up of communities (clans, lineages, families) eager to preserve their own identities, ruled by old people, divided into different

15. Akindélé and Aguessy, *Contribution, à l'étude*, pp. 65, 72.

social strata, and governed by kings, it is easy to understand why allusions to historical data provide ajogan songs with a great part of their substance. Ajogan has largely to do with prestige, prestige is the affair of the lineage, and the lineage is ruled by old people "who know" and are the real "keepers of the records." By means of the historical background implied in the songs, ajogan reinforces their power. On the other hand, ajogan is performed publicly. Its songs are nourished by traditional knowledge, but, being hermetic, they do not give away traditions freely to anybody. To know history— and particularly the not too glorious aspects of the history of *others*—is to hold power. Nowhere is power or knowledge given away for nothing. Such is the way, it seems to me, in which the choirs of the queens (or the princesses) of Porto-Novo help to keep history alive: indirectly, by recognizing its value; not by preserving or transmitting it.

The metal ringed staves (alunlun), characteristic of Porto-Novo ajogan, are unknown at Abomey and Alada (where ajogan is pronounced *ajogɛ̃* [ajogen], a dialectal variant). If we are to believe E. Dunglas—not always an entirely reliable source—ajogen was taken away by Tè Agbanlin when he left Alada to undertake the long journey which ended in his founding of Khogbônu (Xɔbonu), later named Porto-Novo.[16] This might well be the reason why the alunlun are found neither at Alada nor at Abomey. Be that as it may, in the works of Clément da Cruz, ajogen figures among the "orchestras in the Service of the Kings for the great funeral feasts."[17] According to information I collected at Abomey, which finds confirmation in da Cruz, ajogen is an ensemble of iron bells that does not include drums. All I know of either ajogen songs or dances at Abomey is that they are performed by the queens in an interior court of the palace.

One of the best-known musical instruments at Abomey

16. Edouard Dunglas, *Contribution à l'histoire de Moyen-Dahomey: Royaumes d'Abomey, de Kétou et de Ouidah,* Etudes Dahoméennes, Vols. XIX, XX, XXI (Porto-Novo: Institut Français d'Afrique Noire, 1957–58). Dunglas mentions ajogen in Vol. XIX, p. 83.

17. Clément da Cruz, *Les Instruments de musique dans le Bas-Dahomey,* Etudes Dahoméennes, Vol. XII (Porto-Novo: Institut Français d'Afrique Noire, 1954), pp. 41–45.

Palace is the *zɛlí* (zenli), a vase-drum. Some very fine glazed pottery zenli, made in Europe (Portugal?) and dating from the time of the ancient kings, are on display in Abomey and Ouidah museums. These imported vase-drums were the instruments par excellence of the queens and were only found at the king's palace. At Abomey, as well as at Porto-Novo the vase-drum is but one element in an instrumental ensemble. At Abomey, apart from the zenli, this ensemble consists of two membrane drums, rattles, and, according to da Cruz, an iron bell.[18] From what I have been able to find out for myself, at Abomey the palace zenli has not just one but seven iron bells, the same number as the ajogan bells at Porto-Novo Palace (seven being the number associated with womankind). Anyhow, at Abomey, zenli as well as ajogen was played by the queens in one of the palace courts.

Clément da Cruz classifies ajogen and zenli among the orchestras used at the palace for the "great funeral feasts," that is to say, for the "Annual Customs" (abundantly described by travelers) which were organized by the king in honor of dead sovereigns, especially his immediate predecessor. Thus ajogen and zenli are indeed types of music played for rituals concerning the dead. However, strictly speaking, we are not dealing with funeral music, since there is nothing funereal about it.[19]

At Porto-Novo, the queens, whenever questioned on this subject, always categorically affirmed that the ajogan vase-drum, played at the palace under the name livi, had nothing to do with the zenli vase-drum, played everywhere else on the occasion of a death. Everything connected with death is rigorously banned from the palace. The zenli songs, which are never played at the palace for the reason just mentioned, are in no way concerned with history, as the recordings that I made at Porto-Novo during funerals have shown. Herskovits has a great deal to say about the zenli music and vase-drum

18. *Ibid.*, p. 43.
19. For funeral music and the diverse musical genres which are sometimes mistakenly grouped under this term, see "La Musique funéraire en Afrique Noire: fonctions et formes," Round table, *Bericht über den Neunten Internationalen Musikwissenschaftlichen Kongress, Salzburg, 1964*, II, 143–55.

and the essential role they play in the funeral rites at Abomey.[20] Nothing in his writings leads one to believe that these songs make historical references.

At any rate, he says nothing about the zenli played by the queens at the palace. Unfortunately, I am unable to say anything about it either. Let us be content with the statement that at the palaces of both Abomey and Porto-Novo, the queens play a certain kind of music, characterized by the use of a vase-drum beaten with a fan, and connected with ceremonies dedicated to the dead kings.

However, two facts have come to light. First, whether we are speaking of Abomey or Porto-Novo, the music called zenli is not of the kind which uses historical songs. Second, at the palace of Porto-Novo, the music which uses vase-drums, called ajogan, has only a very relative historical interest. Thus, we have the right to presume that at Abomey, as at Porto-Novo, the ajogen and zenli music played in the palace does not constitute a historical genre.

Yet the songs of the queens and the Amazons—the distinction has not always been clearly made—have time and time again been made out, by different authors describing the kingdom of Abomey, to be historical songs par excellence. So too were the songs of the singers seen at the court who were said to be "bards" and "chroniclers." Summing up his own observations and those of his predecessors at Abomey, Herskovits writes that "songs were and are the prime carriers of history among this non-literate folk." [21] This statement covers what is in fact a complex situation. Quoting a few texts is the best way to make this clearer. I will present the quotations in chronological order. Keep in mind that the first three authors quoted—Forbes, Burton, and Skertchly—are describing the famous Annual Customs of Abomey, to which I have already referred above.

In the center of each circle are two bands and two of the royal troubadours, who take in turn to sing the praises of the Dahoman monarch.

20. Melville J. and Frances S. Herskovits, *Dahomey: An Ancient West African Kingdom*, 2 vols. (1938; reprint ed., Evanston, Ill.: Northwestern University Press, 1967), I, 305.
21. *Ibid.*, II, 321.

Dressed in very gay attire and holding in his hand a blue crutch stick, one of these troubadours recited the military exploits of Gezo. . . . His song commenced with a general view of the royal conquests, and then recited a romantic account of the late war. . . .

These troubadours are the keepers of the records of the kingdom of Dahomey, and the office, which is hereditary, is a lucrative one.

Among the crowd of amazons were planted twenty-eight crutch sticks. . . ; these were the sticks of office of the female troubadours, and each, in her turn, had to sing the romance of the history of Dahomey.[22]

Bards who, in Dahomey, preserve all history . . . are of both sexes, and the women dwell in the palace. These chroniclers and narrators of native tradition are here called "Wenukhodoto." [23]

Court singers, or *Ahanjito* [24] . . . are the bards of the country, to whom is entrusted the history of the past; for the Dahomans, having no written language, commit every great action to memory through the media of songs. There is a quaint, sad melody in their monotonous chant. . . .

A company of Whenukhodotoh, or singers, . . . then sang and danced before the King, the leaders with horsetail flyflappers, which they waved to and fro in time to the tune.[25]

From the point of view of musical style, the most striking are undoubtedly those songs which glorify the names and deeds of the dead kings and living chiefs. Here is no impromptu performance, but rather singing of a quality that can only result from long periods of rehearsal. One ritual occasion on which such songs were heard has been described, in connection with

22. Frederick E. Forbes, *Dahomey and the Dahomans* (London: Longman, Brown, Green, and Longmans, 1851), II, 12–13, 13–14, 21.

23. *hwenuxódɔtɔ* (old—time word—say—one who does), one who says stories of the old times, a "story teller." Captain Sir Richard F. Burton, *A Mission to Gelele, King of Dahome*, Memorial ed. Vol. II (London: Tylston and Edwards, 1893), p. 11.

24. In fact, the word is *hãjitɔ* (song—give birth to—one who does), "singer." But *hãjitɔ* means only someone who sings. The singer who performs publicly is called *hãsinɔ* (song—belonging to—one who usually does) at Abomey (cf. da Cruz, *Les Instruments de musique*, and n. 52 of this paper) as well as at Porto-Novo.

25. J. A. Skertchly, *Dahomey As It Is* (London: Chapman and Hall, 1874), pp. 135–36, 247.

the worship of royal ancestors, where the chorus of wives of
the chief, representing the ancient "Amazons," knelt before
the royal couch and summoned the chief to dance. These songs
were also heard and recorded in the compounds of a number of
chiefs in and about Abomey. The choruses, which are formed
of the younger and more attractive wives of a chief, consist of
from fifteen to forty women. . . . The songs themselves are of
many stanzas, and the words are characterized by extravagant
metaphor. These songs are sung in unison to the accompaniment of only a gong, and to the European ear, the tessitura is
almost incredible, particularly in view of the length of the
skips, which take the singers abruptly from the highest to the
lowest tones of their range. The training of the chorus is also
to be remarked, for judged by any standards of *a capella* singing, the technical proficiency of these groups of women in
unison of attack, and in dynamics of shading, is of the
highest.[26]

These songs "glorifying the deeds of the kings" are doubt-
lessly those whose performance is the most refined. They are
minutely rehearsed: one must not forget that they represent
a great part of the historical archives of the kingdom. We
heard them many times, sung by choirs of chiefs descended
from the ancient kings.[27]

From these texts let us first grasp the following points:
singers described as bards, chroniclers, or troubadours carry
either a staff or a horsetail fly-whisk; they are of both sexes,
the females being Amazons, chief's wives, or queens.

During the Annual Customs thousands of people gathered at
Abomey, and feasts went on for weeks; the rites performed
daily were extremely numerous and varied and, for the most
part, accompanied by music of some sort. Descriptions of these
ceremonies could not give a detailed account of the music. I
will try to elucidate a few points that are important for my
argument by using complementary sources, including my personal experiences at Abomey, where I saw, in company with
Pierre Verger in 1952, a small part of that ritual as it is
performed nowadays.

Amazons were warriors. They had to be absolutely chaste,

26. Herskovits, *Dahomey*, II, 321–22.
27. Paul Mercier, *Civilisations du Bénin* (Paris: Société continentale
d'éditions modernes illustrées, 1962), p. 209. Translation is mine.

but they were not considered the king's wives and, except for those who were part of his personal bodyguard, they did not dwell in the palace. Naturally, their songs were about war. In the form either of praises or of anecdotal accounts, they sang about the king winning battles and themselves fighting them. As one might expect, their songs were also encouragements to war.[28]

No doubt the Amazons also sang, among other things, accounts of battles—which were certainly as allusive as those sung by other singers, as we shall see below—but for all that they were not "bards preserving all history." The following text, taken from Skertchly, shows the kind of song they sang.

A group of Amazonian singers (Wenukhodoto) distinguished by their crossbelts of white beads and their kpogi, or staves . . . then started up, and giving a few preliminary beats with their wands, commenced the following song:
We ask King Gézu to teach us to dance
For if we are not good dancers we shall
                                                  disgrace him.
Why should he not therefore show us how to do it?
As these bards sang their ditty, they waved their batons in time to the measure. . . . At the end of the song they commenced their Terpsichorean exercise.[29]

As one can see, there is no reason to credit these "bards" with historiography.

Traditionally the ceremonies of the *nɛsúxwé*, vodun of the royal and princely families, are carried out each year at Abomey. They take place immediately after the ceremonies for the ancient kings;[30] it is therefore likely that they formed part of the Annual Customs (*xwetanú* [khwetanu]) described by the above-mentioned authors.

Claude Tardits has shown what these ceremonies mean for

28. See Burton, *A Mission to Gelele* (notably II, 9, 151); and Maximilian Quenum, *Au pays des Fon (Us et coutumes du Dahomey)* 2d ed. (Paris: Emile Larose, 1938), pp. 57, 162.

29. Skertchly, *Dahomey As It Is*, p. 214.

30. Pierre Verger, *Notes sur le culte des Orisa et Vodun à Bahia, la Baie de tous les Saints, au Brésil et à l'ancienne Côte des Esclaves en Afrique*, Mémoires de l'Institut Français d'Afrique Noire, no. 51 (Dakar, 1957), p. 552.

history as it is lived by the Dahomeans themselves.[31] One part of this ritual is concerned with the *tɔxɔ́sú* (tokhosu), water-king, the "kings-of-waters" of the kings, i.e., the abnormal children they have brought into the world who, like all children of this sort, belong to a certain category of traditional divinity in Dahomey. This festival of the tokhosu has been described by Verger.[32] The drummers are men, but the dancers, who are the principal actors in the ceremony, are women. Those reincarnating the "kings-of-waters" are recognizable by their headdresses of snail shells dyed violet. All are magnificently dressed. Most of them carry wooden staves with crooked handles and a hook on the side if they are very long. It is clear that these are the "staves" and "crutch sticks" that Forbes spoke of. Some of them carry a fly-whisk in place of a staff. For certain dances in the ceremony, which consists of numerous episodes, some of them carry sabres, thus showing that they reincarnate dead warriors. The music is extremely varied and naturally changes with each type of dance and each episode of the ritual.[33]

While in the temple of the "kings-of-waters," whose feast day it is, or while coming out to meet at the ceremonial place, thus forming a long procession, or while returning to the temple in the evening, the priestesses sing a very particular kind of song, a song of rare beauty, which corresponds in every detail to the description by Herskovits.[34]

It is reasonable to assume that this is the type of song to which Paul Mercier alludes in the quotation given above (see p. 40). The best-known stanza in this song of the vodun and water-king is the following:

31. Claude Tardits, "Religion, épopée, histoire," *Diogène*, XXXVII, (Paris: Gallimard and UNESCO, 1962), 17–28. Special issue on the Black World.

32. Verger, *Notes*, pp. 552–60 and photographs no. 136–48.

33. See the LP record, *Dahomey, Musique des Princes. Fête des Tohossou*, recordings and notes by G. Rouget, texts and photographs by P. Verger, and illustrated sleeve-notes, Vogue-Contrepoint MC 20.093, Collection du Musée de l'Homme, 1955. This record was issued in the U. S. as the third disk of an Anthology of Music of Africa (Everest 3254/3, record 3. 12"), under the title of *Music of the Princes of Dahomey, Festival of the Tohossou*, without the illustrated sleeve-notes.

34. Herskovits, *Dahomey*, 321–22; see quotations above, p. 39. Two of these songs are featured in the above-mentioned record, bands 1 and 12.

> You are trying to find out what the vodun is
> That would be the end of the world.[35]

Thus the general sense of this verse is defiance against one who would try to penetrate the secret of the vodun.

Herskovits characterizes the style of these songs in few words but in a very appropriate manner: wide ambitus, very disjoined melodic degrees, quality of unison singing, large number of verses, *a cappella* singing to the accompaniment of one bell. In fact this instrument is a double bell, or twin bells, one decidedly smaller than the other, which are beaten with a stick. The use of the double bell is, most of the time, connected with religious music. *Nɛsúxwé* and tokhosu are indeed vodun. The grand airs, sung by the priestesses at the top of their voices while they are walking in procession or leaning on their staves,[36] are intoned in a special way, characteristic of the vodun songs,[37] which may be distinguished by the timbre, which differs from that of profane songs.

Thus, the songs in question are not of the historical kind, but rather of the religious kind. A song about Zomadonu, first of the royal "kings-of-waters," is quoted by Dunglas.[38] It recalls, in an allusive manner, an episode in King Gézo's wars against the Mahi, and it quotes a moral in the guise of a proverb. Praises, defiances, allusions to history, proverbs, "extravagant" metaphors, as Herskovits puts it—we find here all the components of the ajogan songs of Porto-Novo, even the staves upon which the singers lean.

At Abomey, as at Porto-Novo, the staff appears to be an essential accessory of the singer who sings long songs called *hāga* in public. The word *hāga* stands for a relatively long sequence of stanzas sung slowly. It can apply to religious as well as to profane songs, and it designates the movement or

35. Verger, *Notes*, p. 557.
36. *Ibid.*, photograph no. 137.
37. For certain aspects of this, see Gilbert Rouget "Un Chromatisme africain," *L'Homme*, I–III (1961), 32–64.
38. "During their ceremonies, the Zomadonu fetish-people sing a liturgical song," writes Dunglas (*Contribution à l'histoire*, XX, 67), but he does not state whether this is the song sung by Zomadonu herself, or rather a different song sung by the men surrounding the drummers who make her dance. The two types of songs are completely different.

section of a song, not its type. The *long song* is often performed by two singers in turn, who stand side by side, leaning on their staves. This way of singing, still very much alive at Porto-Novo and Abomey, corresponds to that described by Forbes when he speaks of "troubadours" at the court.[39]

The reasons that the staff is such an essential accessory for the singer have still to be determined. But its importance is brought out equally well in Skertchly's and in Burton's writings. The latter mentions it three times in the space of three pages.[40] Speaking of King Glélé, who was a great music enthusiast, Burton describes how the king sang in public during the Annual Customs, holding in his left hand "a kpo-ge, or singer's staff—a silver-headed and ferruled stick, two feet long." On the following page, he shows the king leaning his elbow on his singer's staff while he is singing. A little further on, he writes that "decorations were distributed—a pair of singer's staves to a male who received them with cries of 'Tamule.' "

As I said earlier (see n. 24), the singer of long songs in public is called a *hãsinɔ* (hansinon) at Porto-Novo as well as at Abomey. At Porto-Novo, these singers usually appear either during the ceremonies following the funeral of an important person whose praises and great deeds they sing or else during a festival organized by one or another of the town quarters. During this festival they sing the praises or the histories of the different clans and lineages living there. Burton speaks of "fearfully lengthy songs." [41] In 1964, at the festival of the Sôkomè (*Sokɔmɛ*) quarter of Porto-Novo, on the main square, flooded with the people of the quarter, I saw two of these singers perform for the best part of a morning without a break, and the same again in the afternoon. These were really "long songs"! Side by side, leaning on their canes, they stood facing a group of important people comfortably installed on seats which had been brought beforehand; they sang a long series of stanzas dealing with this clan or that lineage. The song being over, after a short and rapid tune taken up in

39. Forbes, *Dahomey and the Dahomans*, II, 12–13.
40. Burton, *A Mission to Gelele*, I, 241–43.
41. *Ibid.*, II, 152.

chorus by everybody, they moved over a few steps and began to sing again.

I am unable to give precise details about the texts of these songs, as I have not made any recordings of them, but they had been carefully memorized. However, I later recorded several hansinon songs of this type at Porto-Novo. They are narratives connected with recent events, difficult to understand without gloss, and intermixed with proverbs. Regarding their literary form, they are comparable to the ajogan song mentioned above, which relates certain events that occurred at Porto-Novo Palace.

The two singers in question, then, sang in the square of the town quarter. In the middle of this square, a few men formed a compact group watching over a fire that was heating a cooking pot full of magical preparations. This was done in order to prevent the enemies of the town quarter from spoiling the feast by causing rain or making the singers' voices break. Thirty years ago, the town quarters (or before that, the villagers) would challenge each other and organize contests. One quarter would invite another to send its singers. Just like the ajogan, their songs were a mixture of praises for their own quarter and veiled insults directed at those who had invited them. These songs of defiance had different names, notably *avohǔ* at Porto-Novo, and *avogã* at Abomey,[42] designating the group formed by the singers, their assistants and drummers.

A. Adandé and P. Verger have described a presentation of this sort which also took place at Sôkomè.[43] The texts are comparable with those of ajogan, to which allusion is sometimes made.[44] The singers carry fly-whisks instead of staves. Without being in a position to make a categorical affirmation, I would be tempted to say that at Porto-Novo the repertoire of the singers with staves is chiefly made up of praises and that of

42. Melville J. Herskovits, "Freudian Mechanisms in Primitive Negro Psychology," in *Essays Presented to C. G. Seligman* (London, 1934), p. 77; and Melville J. and Frances S. Herskovits, *Dahomean Narrative: A Cross-cultural Analysis* (Evanston, Ill.: Northwestern University Press, 1958), p. 61.

43. Alexandre Adandé and Pierre Verger, "Tam-tam Avohu," *Notes Africaines*, no. 59 (Dakar: Institut Français d'Afrique Noire, 1953), pp. 72–76.

44. *Ibid.*, p. 76.

the singers with fly-whisks chiefly of insults. They all make abundant use of anecdotes, proverbs, and references to ancient times.

As the texts quoted above show, singers with canes and fly-whisks were present in large numbers at Abomey during the Annual Customs. Forbes, Burton, and Skertchly called them "bards," "chroniclers," and "troubadours." But when they spoke of the contents of the songs in a concrete manner, sometimes giving translations, it was to illustrate how the singers proclaimed the great deeds of the reigning king and his ancestors, particularly his immediate predecessor.

In his *Contribution à l'histoire du Moyen-Dahomey* (1957–58), Dunglas published around 20 songs,[45] certain of which are said to have been improvised by the king himself, others having been composed or improvised by the "singers of the Court," whose repertoire constituted "genuine sung annals."[46] Accounts of battle, always given in an allusive form, praises of the king, living or dead, recitation of "his strong names," insults directed at his enemies—such is the substance of these songs. None of them offers any consecutive account of historical facts. Apart from dealing with battles and kings, these songs essentially belong to the same category as those of the singers of long songs of Porto-Novo we have just been considering.

In his chapter devoted to Fon literature, M. Quenum mentions the existence of historical songs and writes that "thanks to the historical songs, we have a few precise, authentic facts about the most distant past of the country; the songs are long-winded, and go into the minutest details."[47]

Yet Quenum does not give a single example of this type of song. In what has just been quoted, there is nothing to indicate that these "historical songs" may be distinguished from those sung by the singers we are speaking of.

45. Most of them are in Vol. XX of Etudes Dahoméennes; see pp. 48, 58, 59, 60, 62, 67, 78, 100, 101, 113, 114, 118, 135, 144, 146, 147. From the linguistic point of view, Dunglas' texts and translations are wide open to criticism. However, thanks to the line-by-line translation, the material is quite useful.
46. *Ibid.*, pp. 60, 61.
47. Quenum, *Au pays des Fon*, p. 53.

According to Herskovits, real attempts to assemble a general history of the kingdom must have been made on two occasions by the kings:

First in the reign of Agadja (1708–1729), and again in the reign of Glele (1858–1889), the king . . . "invited" all the clans to send to Abomey the clan elders of each who were the responsible repositories of the family "history". . . . The king addressed these men . . . telling them that since the memory of man was faulty, he had assembled the best singers of the land to put their "histories" into song, so that their past would continue to be known by their descendants. Each was asked to recite the clan "history" to a singer who, with the help of the officials of the king, put it into words to be sung.[48]

Did this really concern all the clans in the kingdom? Or did it only concern the different lineages of the royal clan, which is the hypothesis I make (see p. 29), based on a remark of Le Herissé? There is nothing that enables us to decide. In any case, none of these sung histories has ever been published. Thus, one cannot say anything about either their historical substance or the form in which they relate the history.

On the other hand, we know for certain that the repertoire of the singers of long songs is rich in the extreme and that one finds in it a very great number of references to past events. If we consider it from the point of view of history in the Western sense of the word, of what value is it? In making a judgment, I will restrict myself to what has been published and to the documents that I personally have collected at Porto-Novo and Abomey. On this basis, we find that there are numerous examples of long songs giving accounts of historical events, but that most of the time they are allusive, and that we know of no example where such an account exceeds the dimensions of anecdote. In the present state of knowledge, there is no reason to think that songs or sequences of songs are sung in Dahomey for the purpose of retracing, in a consecutive account, the events of a whole historical period. Songs in Dahomey had been so expressly given as "prime carriers of history," as "historical archives of the kingdom," as "real annals," and singers as "keepers of the records," as "troubadours," "bards,

48. Herskovits, *Dahomean Narrative*, p. 20.

preserving all history," or "chroniclers" singing the "romance
of the kingdom," that one had the right to presume that Dahomey possessed *chansons de gestes* or epics comparable to the
"dynastic poems" of Ruanda, to the Cameroon or Gabon Fangs'
famous epics known under the name *mvet* (the chanting and
singing of which lasts a whole night) or even to the *Iliad*.[49]
Unless new discoveries are made, we must consider that such
is not the case.

The reader will certainly wonder whether the survey of the
few musical genres which has been made here so far (jenglen,
ajogan, and zenli; tokhosu and hansinon songs) covers the
whole repertoire of Fon and Gun music. This is indeed far
from being the case. There exist at the courts of Porto-Novo
and Abomey a great number of other musical genres. Clément
da Cruz's inventory gives, under the headings of "Royal orchestras" and "orchestras at the service of the Abomey King
for agrarian rites and the purification of markets and public
places," some thirty-eight different ensembles.[50] A comparable
list could be made for Porto-Novo. An inventory of the texts
used in these ensembles has still to be made, but I doubt
whether it would make any difference to the above statement
about the absence of sung epics in Fon and Gun music. However, new facts might well come to light.

Two of these ensembles employ texts that are particularly
rich in historical references. Both are the special preserves of
princes and princesses. One is called *hāye* and is performed
mostly by women.[51] According to Segurola, this name comes
from *hɛ̃ ayi*, "keep on [your] guard," "be careful." [52] Psy-

49. See notably "The way of enthronement," in M. d'Hertefelt and A.
Coupez, *La Royauté sacrée de l'ancien Rwanda* (Tervueren, 1964). This
dynastic poem runs to 1,249 lines. I analyzed it very briefly from the
point of view which interests us here in "African Traditional Non-Prose
Forms: Reciting, Declaiming, Singing and Strophic Structures," Proceedings of a Conference on African Languages and Literatures held at
Northwestern University, 1966 (mimeographed), p. 50. A text of a
Mvet epic recorded by Herbert Pepper in Gabon is scheduled to be published in the *Classiques Africains* collection.
50. Da Cruz, *Les Instruments de musique*, pp. 38–46.
51. One *hāye* has been published in a record by Charles Duvelle, *Musique dahoméenne*, OCR 17, 12", OCORA, 1963, side A, band 3.
52. Rev. Père B. Segurola, "Dictionnaire Fon-Français," 2 vols.
(Cotonou: Procure de L'Archidiocèse, 1963). Mimeographed.

chologically, its role would thus be comparable to that of ajogan. The other one, performed at night by men, is called by the general name zădrɔ́ (night—to keep awake) "wake." The singer of zădrɔ́ has the same sort of staff as the one described above for the singers of long songs of Porto-Novo.[53]

Lastly let us add that mottoes (mlămlă and ɲikɔ́ siɲɛsiɲɛ) are very often drummed among the Fon and Gun,[54] just as are oríki among the Yoruba. However, these drummed mottoes are not used to compose a *suite* comparable to the one Rattray has described among the Ashanti.[55]

HISTORICAL CHANTS AND RECITATIONS

We now come to a chant peculiar to Abomey and entirely different from the songs dealt with so far, after which I will turn to a chant made at Ketu, capital of a neighboring Yoruba kingdom. This latter piece can be compared in some ways with the former one and it will lead to a reexamination of the nature of Abomey chant. I will then deal with a declamation and a recitation made at Porto-Novo Palace, both of which can be related to the foregoing chant and recitation.

At Abomey, in the days of the ancient kings, a herald was charged with going round the precincts of the royal palace three times a day—before daybreak, toward midday, and at night—and calling out a text, of which Skertchly, the first to report it, writes: "All the strong names and exploits of the various monarchs are given out in detail, in a long drawling voice, similar to that in which the *Ezann* is droned out in Mohammedan countries." [56] This took place during the turns of guard duty organized night and day around the palace. Burton gives a résumé of the ritual and notes that the "heralds recapitulating the titles and exploits of all the Dahomean

53. Personal communication from M. Glélé.
54. For the "drum language" technique of the Gun people, see G. Rouget, "Tons de la langue en Gun (Dahomey) et tons du tambour," *Revue de Musicologie*, L (Paris: Heugel, 1964), 3–29.
55. R. S. Rattray, *Ashanti* (London: Oxford University Press, 1923), pp. 226–86. The drummed history of the *Mampon* consists, in fact, of a chronological list of the kings, proclaimed in hyperbolic form.
56. Skertchly, *Dahomey As It Is*, p. 172.

dynasty" were called *"panigan"* after the name of the bell they carry.[57] All the time he is performing, the kpanlingan (to use the modern spelling) sounds his bell. He is accompanied by an assistant who carries a double bell.

Burton states that the recitation from "11 A.M. till noon" was instituted by King Glélé.[58] I have it from Maurice A. Glélé, one of his descendants, that this was done in memory of a battle that the king had won at midday.[59]

Describing the morning rising of the king, Quenum writes:

The different musical instruments succeeding one another for this occasion were:
1) the kpanlingan, the two notes of which alternated to the beats made by the historian whose duty it was each morning to narrate the exploits of all the kings since the founder, in exact chronological order, under pain of beheading. When he came to the reigning king several gunshots were fired.[60]

Maurice A. Glélé indicates that the kpanlingan "recites the history of the kingdom and sings praises starting with Hwegbadja, who is considered to be the founder of the dynasty of the kings of Dahomey."

According to M. A. Glélé, the recitation of the kpanlingan took place three times a day during the Annual Customs.[61] The rest of the year, it took place only in the morning. Nowadays it is still done, but only on great ceremonial occasions. Herskovits speaks of the kpanlingan in the section of his introduction to *Dahomean Narrative* where he shows the im-

57. Burton, *A Mission to Gelele*, II, 61 n. 1. Actually, the word is *kpáligã*, in which one can probably make out the verb *kpã-*, which means "tie on the back," and *-gã*, designating the bell and stemming from the word *ogã*, "iron"; *-li-* remains for me an enigma. One can also say *gãvíkpã* (bell—little—tie to the back). The word signifies a double bell, i.e., two bells of very unequal size joined together at the handle. When played, the smaller bell faces upwards. This bell is used for all vodun ceremonies, as has been noted above. Skertchly calls the herald *panigan*, or *kpanigan hunto* (*kpáligã hutɔ*), "the kpanlingan beater," or *panigan afwan* (*kpáligã ná fɔ*), "kpanlingan will rise up," when it concerns the morning declamation.

58. *Ibid.*

59. Maurice A. Glélé is the author of a study, soon to appear, entitled *Les Institutions politiques du Dan Homé*. It contains a photograph of the kpanlingan and his assistant.

60. Quenum, *Au pays des Fon*, p. 18.

61. Personal communication from M. Glélé.

portance of song in the conservation of historical traditions. But he is mistaken in giving the singer the name of *ahanjito* (see above p. 39). His text undeniably concerns the kpanlingan. Of the "King's professional minstrel-rhapsodist," whose title was *ahanjito*, he writes:

It was his daily task to chant the names and praise-names of the king's predecessors, before the king's awakening. His rendition had to be letter-perfect, since an omission or an error would have cost him his life.[62]

The kpanlingan's declamation is without doubt of great interest for the history of the kings. Unfortunately, its text has never been published. M. A. Glélé, who made a complete recording of it during the Annual Customs at Abomey in 1964 but has not yet transcribed it, writes that "the kpanlingan risks the death-penalty if he makes a mistake. In this we do have a litany which is quite faithful, but it does not teach us very much and the kpanlingan himself is unable to explain it or comment upon it." [63]

The list of kings from Hwegbadja to the present day is actually neither long nor confidential. It contains only ten names and is known by everyone. All the interest in the text recited by the kpanlingan thus lies in the wording of the "strong names" and great deeds attributed to each of the kings. As is well known, the "strong names" (*ñikɔ siñɛsiñɛ*) and mottoes are eminently allusive formulas. From a conversation I had with Maurice Glélé on this subject, it would seem that the parts of this declamation connected with the great deeds are also worded in a very elliptic form and are full of allusions, which means that it can only be understood by those who already know the events to which it refers. Despite its undeniable interest, this chant furnishes the historian with information which in the final result is rather poor and requires long commentaries.

At Ketu, the capital of the Yoruba kingdom that borders on Abomey and was vanquished by King Glélé in 1887, the enthronement of the sovereign is the object of a long ritual

62. Herskovits, *Dahomean Narrative*, p. 21.
63. Glélé, *Les Institutions politiques*.

in which one episode is the solemn enumeration of all the
kings to have succeeded to the throne. According to Dunglas,
this recitation is made while the king, during his enthronement, resides in a hut called Ilé-era, the "charm-hut."

Dunglas describes this recitation in the following terms:

> The griot, official herald to the King, belonging to the Oyédé
> family and popularly called "Baba Elegun," advances.[64] Hav-
> ing saluted the King, he announces to the attentive assembly
> who the King's predecessors were. In an assured voice he re-
> cites in one go and without hesitation the entire list of kings
> of Ketu, beginning with the legendary ancestor Itcha-Ik-
> patchan, leader of the original migration, issue of the royal
> family of Ilè-Ifè and founder of the Ketu dynasty. One thing
> which complicates the task of Baba-Elegun is that he includes
> the filiation of each king.[65]

In 1949, at the enthronement of the king of Ketu (who died
only a few years ago), P. Verger witnessed this recitation,
which took place in the palace. I am grateful to him for two
particularly significant observations. Baba-Elegun means
"Old man of the Egun" and stands for a character who plays
an important role in the Egun (Yoruba *égún*) society, which
is connected with the cult of the dead since its members represent dead persons. In Dahomey, the word *égún* is translated
into French as "revenant." The Fon and Gun equivalent of the
Yoruba *égún* is *kúvitɔ́* (death—to calm—he who does), "he
who calms death." During the recitation, Baba-Elegun sits on
a rush-mat with forty-nine cowries in front of him. Each time
he finishes all there is to say about an ancient king, he puts one
of these cowries down by his side, in such a way that when he
has finished the series all the kings can be seen to have been
named. This shows how important it is considered that no
omission be made.

According to P. Verger, the name of each of the ancient
kings was accompanied by a formula of salutation. Since Baba
Elegun is connected with the cult of the dead, there is every
reason to believe that he is addressing the kings as dead per-

64. From all Dunglas writes about him, it is clear that Baba Elegun
is not what is commonly known as a "griot."
65. Dunglas, *Contribution à l'histoire*, I, 34, 41, and esp. 53–54.

sons, with the idea of disposing them favorably toward the newly elected king. It is well known how the dead are revered and feared in Dahomey, among the Fon, Gun, and Yoruba, and how important it is to keep on the right side of them. The recitation of Baba Elegun would therefore be above all a propitiatory rite. If one is afraid of forgetting to name an ancient king, it is no doubt not so much from a desire to be faithful to history as from fear of arousing his wrath.

Taking into account the differences between the two rituals, we have the right to assume that at Abomey the declamation of the kpanlingan fulfilled a comparable role. Essentially, the Annual Customs were intended to celebrate the dead kings with the aim of securing their protection for their successor and thus for all of the kingdom. During these ceremonies, the declamation of the kpanlingan was of great importance.[66] Any error on the part of the kpanlingan was punishable, as has been said, by death. To make a mistake, to forget part of the declamation, would mean to lack respect toward one or another of the dead kings, thereby offending him and provoking his wrath. We have every reason to believe that an error would have been so interpreted—hence the gravity of the sanction.

If our interpretation is correct, the kpanlingan does not call out the names of the ancient kings, their mottoes, and their great deeds with the idea of keeping their memory alive among the living; his discourse is addressed to the deceased kings with the idea of making them favor their descendant and successor, the present king. It is essentially an act of propitiation and consequently the tone of voice is one of incantation. We have already seen what great care Skertchly takes to indicate that these texts are delivered in a "long drawling voice."

I cannot describe this voice myself since I have unfortu-

66. The kpanlingan's round of the palace precincts was made in several stages. One part of his declamation corresponded to each of these stages. It is well known that the Palace of Abomey consists of a collection of buildings constructed at certain distances from one another, which were built by the different kings succeeding to the throne. One would imagine that the kpanlingan recites his lines for a particular king at the very moment he finds himself in front of that king's building. However, this has still not been established for certain.

nately never heard it. What Skertchly writes about it makes one think that it was nearer to singing than speaking but that it was not singing in a full voice.

In describing the ritual for the enthronement of the King at Porto-Novo, Akindélé and Aguessy devote a whole paragraph to Adjagan, "Chief of the Aja," one of the principal ministers in the kingdom:

His principal role was that of a eulogist. In fact he was waking the court with his voice as he announced the awakening of his Majesty, calling out in turn each of the kings to have succeeded to the throne since the origins of Porto-Novo. This function, in a country where instruction was unknown, demanded an excellent memory, along with good intonation, in order to make oneself heard by all the court.[67]

This declamation, made at the moment of the king's awakening, can be compared with "the kpanlingan will rise up," quoted above, of which Skertchly speaks. Like the recitation of Baba Elegun, it is made during the enthronement ritual. Ultimately, like the other two, it consists of calling out the filiation of the kings. At least this is what the text we have just quoted says. In reality, the facts are a little different, as we shall now see.

In 1966, King Gbèfa was willing to ask Adjagan to record this declamation for me. It was agreed that he would take care to repeat the same words he had pronounced for the enthronement, eighteen years before. The recording was made in one of the palace courts, in the presence and with the participation of the king. The long-awaited declamation revealed itself to be nothing but one part of a ritual called *aja hũ ná kpɔ tɔ́* (cage—to open—in order that—leopard—to come out) "the cage opens to let the leopard [the King] out." This ritual has two parts. The second part includes a sacrifice and a harangue to the ancestors. As it was impossible to pronounce a text of this kind "for nothing" (*tata*), the sacrifice was actually made. Consequently, I have good reasons to believe that the texts recorded on this occasion give a faithful image of what was pronounced during the actual enthronement.

67. Akindélé and Aguessy, *Contribution à l'étude*, p. 49.

The ritual called "the cage opens to let the leopard out" is performed each day during the whole period that the king, newly entered into the palace, sleeps in one of the interior courts where a hut has been especially built for the purpose. Each morning Adjagan comes to the palace to awaken the king. Presenting himself before the first door, he asks permission to pass through it by calling out in a loud voice the following formula:

> *hawe!*
> *kpɔ dɔ́ kpɔ fɔ́!*
> *alā dɔ́ alā fɔ́!*
> *dídɔ́ káká wɛ to ayíhɔ̃mɛ!*

> Hello there!
> [If] the leopard sleeps, [may] the leopard rise!
> [If] the animal sleeps, [may] the animal rise!
> May he be long in this world!

The formula being chanted three times, the door is opened. Adjagan enters into the court and goes toward a second door, in front of which he calls out the same formula. Here he recites it three times more, but each time the blessings become more numerous. The door being opened to him, he goes into the court where the king's hut is located and finds the king awake. Adjagan addresses him with the greetings one must make in all circumstances, whenever one presents oneself before the king; these greetings are completely different from the preceding declamation. Here ends the first part of the ritual.

The second part involves the offering of a sacrifice and a libation to the king's ancestors, as well as addressing a harangue (*odɛ*) to them. This ritual is in every way similar in form to the rituals one observes in all Gun families surrounding every ceremony connected with the ancestors and the vodun. The words of this harangue, for the most part, always consist of a series of stereotyped formulas recited by heart. Adjagan's words conformed to this model. The greater part of his recitation consisted in calling down all kinds of blessings upon the head of the king and in banishing misfortune. Names of persons, vodun, and specific places were pronounced. Four names were connected with the history of the kings of Porto-Novo. In order of naming these were: Adjahuto (*Ajáhutɔ̃*), who left Tado and later on founded the kingdom of Alada: Tè Agbanlin, who left Alada and later on founded the kingdom of Porto-Novo (but did not himself bear the title of king); Dé Lokpon, second king of Porto-Novo (1739–46) and, according to Akindélé and Aguessy, founder of the line from which the present King Gbèfa is descended; and, finally, Dé Khakpon, first king of Porto-Novo (1729–39), again according to Akindélé and Aguessy.

As we can see, the historical documents furnished by this ritual declamation are slender in the extreme.

Whenever Burton and Skertchly refer to singers, bards, chroniclers, or troubadours, they make use (and we have given examples above) of the word which we have transcribed *hwenuxódɔtɔ́*, which signifies "story-teller." The word *hwenuxó*, "word of ancient times," designates a narration connected with facts held to have really taken place in the past, as opposed to a "tale," as both Herskovits and Glélé indicate, the former in his classification of the different literary genres in Dahomey, the latter in his work yet to appear.[68] Nothing in this term specifies whether the narrative is sung or spoken. If it is sung, it corresponds to the "verse-sequences" that Herskovits speaks of, indicating quite rightly that they are "composed mainly by professional verse-makers." [69] If it is spoken, it corresponds to stories told in the tone of voice normally adopted for telling a story and presents none of the formal characteristics that denote a poetical genre.

Thus, the two story-forms of *hwenuxó*, the sung and the spoken, coexist and complement each other. But the greatest part of history is actually transmitted in the spoken *hwenuxó*.

68. Herskovits, *Dahomean Narrative*, p. 15. However, after having given *hwenuxó* the meaning just indicated, Segurola ("Dictionnaire, p. 243) mentions that the word can be used equally well for the stereotyped formula that precedes the telling of a tale. The distinction thus does not appear to be as clear as the above statement suggests.

69. Herskovits, *Dahomean Narrative*, p. 17. It is clear, however, that the verse-sequences sung by the minstrels Herskovits speaks of (p. 21), who are the hansinon already mentioned above, are not of the same type as those sung by the kpanlingan.

It was by collecting oral information from old or particularly well-informed people that the historians of Dahomey (Le Herissé, Herskovits, Akindélé and Aguessy, Dunglas) composed their works. In order to jog his memory, or to add a concrete detail, to get a filiation right, or to recall the name of a character or a specific place, the narrator might memorize a song, following a process whose importance has been rightly stressed by Herskovits.[70] It is nonetheless true that the essentials of the information are communicated in spoken form. Ultimately it would seem that history, as it exists for Dahomeans themselves, ought to be seen as a patchwork of spoken narrations concerning the past and commentaries that either make some obscure aspect explicit or expand on a stereotyped formula—especially the mottoes constantly employed in these songs. Against this background are set songs dealing with the past which form, here and there, sparse patches of color that vary in hue according to the poetical genre to which they belong.

VOCAL DELIVERY, TYPOLOGY, AND CREDIBILITY

Speaking and singing, two fundamentally different ways of delivering speech, are linked by an uninterrupted chain of intermediate degrees. Speech may be purely spoken or purely sung, and between these two "pure states," so to speak, it may be intoned in a manner closer to song or closer to speech. *Sprechgesang* is a universal of vocal music and has a countless variety of forms.[71] None of these vocal behaviors is used indiscriminately with any kind of musical form, and musical forms are themselves not indiscriminately used with any kind of speech. In fact, in the realm of unwritten "literature," a text cannot be dissociated from its manner of delivery.

Poetry is to be considered, essentially, as a message focused

70. *Ibid.*, p. 60.
71. I have tried to show what kind of criteria could be used for a typology of *Sprechgesang*, in collaboration with J. Schwarz in "Chant fuégien, consonance et mélodie de voyelles," *Beiträge zur Musikethnologie; Marius Schneider zum 65. Geburtstag*, (in press).

mainly on itself—let us say, a message for its own sake—poetical features being the different kinds of "figures of sound"
that such a message uses.[72] Since there apparently exist no
plainly spoken poetical texts in oral literature, or, to put it
another way, since oral poetry is always delivered with a
special intonation [73] (different from ordinary speech and most
of the time in a more or less singing voice), the vocal delivery
—singing, chanting, sing-song voicing, declaiming, etc.—
should be considered as a poetical feature among others. This
means that a text, whose nature it is to be sung, chanted, or
declaimed, must for that very reason be considered as a poetical text, even if it does not offer, at the level of the words, "the
same figure of sound." Vocal delivery, inherent in the melodic
and rhythmic form of the song—or chant, psalmody, etc.—
gives, or contributes toward giving, a text its poetical character. Dealing with the texts that interest us here, it will be
simpler to speak from now on of poems, thus indicating that
the texts concerned are, in one way or another, sung, half-sung,
declaimed, recited, and so on.

The songs, chants, and recitations which have been dealt
with here are poems of different kinds. Would a typology of
these poems be of any help in evaluating their interest for
history, both in the traditional and in the modern sense of the
word? Since the more we know about the nature of any evidence the better we can evaluate it, the answer must evidently
be yes.

The typology of a poem is the typology of its poetical structure, which is itself constituted by the relations between form,
content, and function. As has just been seen, the musical aspect of a poem is to be regarded as an inherent feature of its
poetical form. Will the musical features of these poems therefore be of interest for history and for historians? A priori,
the answer is again yes. We ought therefore to examine our
poems from this point of view. But the problem is complex

---

72. Roman Jacobson, "Closing Statement: Linguistics and Poetics,"
in *Style in Language,* ed. T. A. Sebeok (Cambridge, Mass.: M.I.T. Press,
1960), p. 356.

73. I have dealt with the African aspect of this question in "African
Traditional Non-Prose Forms," pp. 45–58.

and goes beyond the scope of this paper. We will limit our-
selves to a sketchy picture of the ways the problem could apparently be handled.

These poems make use of six different types of vocal delivery:

1. Singing with a normal singing voice—*normal* being understood, obviously, in a Dahomean perspective. Example:
jenglen and certain ajogan songs.

2. Singing with a special intonation. Example: the song
about the secret of the vodun in the ceremony for the "kings-
of-water."

3. Singing in what Skertchly has described as a "plaintive
way." No example of this sort of singing has been published.
As far as my Porto-Novian experience is concerned, certain
ajogan songs, different from those fitting the definition of
category 1, should be classified here.

4. Chanting. The kpanlingan's text is an example par excellence of this type. Presumably, Baba Elegun's text as well.

5. Declaiming. Example: Adjagan's text for the first part
of the ritual described.

6. Reciting. Example: Adjagan's text for the second part.

The different types of vocal delivery would apparently be
connected with the differing relationships between the singers
and what they sing.

Taking up K. Bühler's ideas and developing them, R. Jacobson shows that the different poetic genres could be characterized in terms of the three main functions of language—
emotive, conative, and referential—and of the person, in the
grammatical sense of the word, who is mainly concerned in
the poem.

Epic poetry, focused on the third person, strongly involves the
referential function of language; the lyric, oriented toward the
first person, is intimately linked with the emotive function;
poetry of the second person is imbued with the conative function and is either supplicatory or exhortative, depending on
whether the first person is subordinated to the second or the
second to the first.[74]

74. Jacobson, "Closing Statement," p. 357; see also pp. 355–61.

With this in mind, let us go back to the six different types of vocal delivery just mentioned.

1) The jenglen song whose text has been given above (page 34) evidently belongs in the lyric genre. In their song, the queens address themselves to the king and beg him to take them to his bed. What better example could there be of first-person implication in a poem?

Certain ajogan songs also belong in the lyric category, although their content does not concern the first person so directly, since their object is to praise the king and defy or slander his enemies. In singing these songs, however, the queens largely identify with their husband and are thus deeply involved in what they say: praising the king, they indirectly praise themselves; defying his enemies, they are themselves defiant.

Nonetheless these ajogan songs are less purely lyric than the jenglen ones. The references to history and the fact that the first person is implicated only at a remove relate ajogan songs, in some ways, to the epic genre.

2) The song about the secret of the vodun (see p. 42), also sung in a full voice but making use of special intonation, can be compared with the ajogan songs just mentioned, since the vodun's message is essentially defiant and the singers, themselves the keepers of the secret, are, here again, involved. Thus this song, too, belongs in the lyric genre.

3) Certain ajogan songs from Porto-Novo are sung in a way that probably corresponds to what Skertchly had in mind when he wrote that the historical chants of Abomey were sung in a "plaintive" way.[75] These songs differ from the ajogan songs just spoken of in that they are, so to speak, less polemic (polemic covering praise and defiance) than simply narrative. Such is notably the case with the ajogan song spoken of at the beginning of this paper, relating the sack of the palace. This song is mainly narrative, its function is mainly

---

75. "Several *Whenukhodotoh*, or singers, then chanted a plaintive ditty, praising the King for his kindness to his friends, extolling his greatness and ending in a kind of rhapsody in which the most extravagant speeches were made and the most plaintive tunes yelled out" (Skertchly, *Dahomey, As It Is*, p. 170).

referential, and its references are mainly to the third person. But, at the same time, it praises the king, who has vanquished his enemies, and it insults the defeated. Since the singers identify themselves, at least partially, with the king, the function of the song is also partially emotive and the referent is also the first person. Consequently this ajogan would be classified as epic-lyric. It is sung, but not like the ajogan song mentioned above and classified as lyric. The decisive difference lies in the fact that it is not sung in a full voice. Such, I think, is the way in which "plaintive" should be understood. It is nearer the arioso than the aria.

Similar remarks, equally tinged with impressionism, could be made about the long songs which I heard at Porto-Novo during the Sôkomè feast mentioned above. The long songs should probably be classified as epic-lyric as well.

4) Let us remember that Skertchly described the kpanlingan's song as "given out . . . in a long drawling voice." According to our hypothesis, this chant would not enumerate the deceased kings for the sake of remembering them, but it would evoke them in order to propitiate them. Thus, the kpanlingan's song is essentially an incantation, corresponding to that "magic function" of speech which is characterized, in poetry, by the use of the second person: [76] that person to whom the singer addresses himself. Here, the second person referred to is the line of deceased kings. The one who sings is thus subordinated to the one to whom he sings. Borrowing R. Jacobson's term again, we would say that the function of the singer's speech is "supplicatory."

5) The text declaimed by Adjagan, during the *first* part of the ritual, in front of the palace door when he comes to awaken the king, is obviously an incantation. "If the leopard sleeps, may the leopard rise! May he be long in this world!" he declaims. This is an example of the message with a magic function, spoken of by R. Jacobson, which "is chiefly some kind of conversion of an absent or inanimate 'third person' into the addressee of a conative message." [77] The vocal delivery

76. Jacobson, "Closing Statement," p. 355.
77. *Ibid.*

used in this declamation is a sort of speech-song. It is not possible to compare it, from that point of view, with the kpanlingan's chant. However, if Skertchly's description is good, the kpanlingan's text is more sung than is Adjagan's, so it might be called song-speech.

6) The text that Adjagan recites during the *second* half of "The cage opens to let the leopard out" ritual consists, as has been said, of a sequence of propitiatory formulas addressed to the ancestors of the king. Here again we are dealing with poetry in the second person. It is, however, less clearly conative than Adjagan's declamation during the first half of the ritual, mentioned in the previous paragraph. Adjagan's prayer during the second half, which takes a very common form, is more a dialogue than a supplication. One talks to the dead with a view to propitiating them, but the object of the talk is also to tell them what is going on in the world of the living. So the message is referential as well as conative. Besides, it is hardly "focused on itself" or conceived "for its own sake."

Adjagan's text is rendered in that particular tone which precisely characterizes recitation. Most of it is uttered in a sing-song voice. It constantly makes use of a prosodic device which has rightly been called *respiratory group* (i.e., a unit of text that relies on the length of the reciter's breath rather than on what is traditionally called a line), whose importance in oral poetry I have underlined elsewhere.[78] Briefly characterized, the vocal emission is certainly much more spoken than sung.

Any music can be looked at from two different points of view, according to whether we are considering the creator or the performer. These may well be one and the same person, but in oral as well as in written tradition this is certainly not always the case; far from it. The correlations that have just been made have to do with the relationship between the singer and what he is singing. The connections that exist between the creator of a song or a chant and the song or the chant created ought equally to be considered. The distinction between poems with which the poet is connected, by some degree

78. Rouget, "African Traditional Non-Prose Forms," p. 47.

of inclusion (i.e., poems dealing with himself in one way or another), and poems from which, on the contrary, the poet is disconnected, by some degree of exclusion, would supply criteria of correlation which would cross usefully with the preceding ones.

As we have seen many times in the foregoing pages, the poems dealt with have been either improvised or composed. This is yet another distinction—a fundamental one since it concerns the very process of creation—which could contribute to make the typology more precise.

In any case, the musical analysis that deals with the different elements of melody, rhythm, and form, and aims at uncovering the system governing their interconnections,[79] naturally remains the basis for the identification of a song or a chant as a musical piece. The study of a Yoruba ritual chant has shown that a definite correlation exists between its musical features and its words, seen from the angle of the degree of inclusion just mentioned.[80] To arrive at a precise typology and a rigorous identification of the songs and chants dealt with here, all these correlations must be treated as a whole. We are a long way from this.

Let us imagine, however, that our songs, chants, and historical recitations have been fully identified; what profit will the historian gain from it? Will he or will he not be better informed as to their value as historical documents (historical being understood, this time, in its Western meaning)? As has already been said, a priori the better a piece of historical evidence is identified, the more valuable it is. But there is still something more. It would seem that, as it has just been described, the identification of a poem, i.e., its definitive placing in the poetical system of a given culture, could well contribute toward making its degree of credibility more precise.

79. I have tried to bring out the main lines of such an analysis in "Transcrire ou décrire? Chant soudanais et chant fuégien," in *Echanges et communications. Mélanges offerts à Claude Lévi-Strauss à l'occasion de son 60e anniversaire*, collected by Jean Pouillon and Pierre Maranda (Paris, The Hague: Mouton, 1970), I, 677–706.

80. See G. Rouget, "Notes et documents pour servir à l'étude de la musique yoruba," *Journal de la Société des Africanistes*, XXXV, fasc. 1, (1965), 103–7, 135.

On the level of the text, the critique of the evidence given by oral tradition has been studied by J. Vansina. About "songs and historical poems," he writes notably that "their aim is to raise enthusiasm, turn in derision, arouse pity or provoke hatred and that, on the other hand, their content is full of allusions to facts that are sure to be forgotten." [81]

These remarks fit the ajogan songs spoken of at the beginning of this chapter so well that one would think they had been written with them in mind: their credibility gives rise to much doubt and their utilization by the historian causes many difficulties.

On the musical level, if one were to schematize what has been said above about vocal delivery, one might say that the more a poem is chanted (*aria*), the more it will include the first person, the more emotive its function will be, and the greater its subjectivity. Conversely, the more a poem is spoken, the more it will exclude the first person, the more referential its function will be, and the greater its objectivity. The degree of credibility given to poems "of the second person," which lie in an intermediate position between song and talk, cannot be evaluated without taking into account, even more than for the others, the connection that exists between the *addresser* and the *addressee*.[82] The more conative its function and the more subordinate the addresser to the addressee, the greater its probable veracity will be.

Thus, such correlations would contribute to the constitution of a system. If this system proved able to characterize Fon and Gun "historical" music and poetry, it would be useful for the historian, in supplying him, to a certain extent, with criteria of credibility. But it cannot claim the status of a system until further research reveals the existence of other systems, comparable and at the same time different, outside Gun and Fon cultures.

Songs, chants, psalmodies, and historical recitations indeed provide the historian of Dahomey with many useful pieces of information. One is tempted to say, however, that in the actual state of things they create more problems than they solve.

81. Vansina, *De la tradition orale*, p. 124.
82. Jacobson, "Closing Statement," p. 353.

3.

Musical Instruments on Benin Plaques

PHILIP J. C. DARK and MATTHEW HILL

Editor's Note: Mr. William Fagg originally suggested to Professor Dark that he compile the information contained in this paper from the great archive of Benin antiquities which Dark has formed during the past ten years, since it would be useful for both ethnomusicologists and historians to know what musical instruments were in use at Benin, in western Nigeria, during the period when the well-known rectangular bronze plaques were made. As Professor Dark shows in the section on dating, there are reasonable grounds for supposing that all or almost all of these plaques were cast in the period from ca. 1550 to ca. 1650.

SEVENTEEN TYPES OF MUSICAL INSTRUMENTS are represented on the rectangular bronze plaques which the artists of Benin have left us as a record of the history of the Edo-speaking peoples. The seventeen types, together with a number of sub-types, were distinguished as the result of an examination of approximately 895 plaques;[1] 295 were found to have representations of musical instruments on them. The presence on a few other plaques of such instruments must remain dubious.

DATING

The period during which the Edo artist turned his hand to the production of the unique form of art, the plaque cast in bronze by the lost-wax process, must remain problematical. Evidence concerning the time at which the plaques were first made and the duration of their production can only be summarized here and briefly commented on.

Direct evidence is meager. In all the chronicles there is only one mention of a traveler having seen the bronze plaques decorating the pillars of a palace building, and that is in Dapper's account, published in 1668 but referring to the 1640s.[2] No other mention of plaques is known until their discovery in 1897. All the bronze plaques might have been made prior to Dapper's observations, or their production could have continued subsequently. Precisely when the Edo ceased to make this type of bronze work must remain highly speculative.

It would be highly speculative, too, to infer from the tra-

1. A count of the number of plaques for which records are on file in the Benin Scheme's files of Benin art yielded the figure 895, together with 78 fragments. Allowance should be made for as yet undiscovered duplicate records. The count, based on as complete a coverage as has been possible but which must be considered tentative, was 776 in European collections, 66 in Nigerian collections, and 53 in collections in the United States; not all of these last were examined for musical instruments. The authors wish to give thanks to Dr. K. O. Dike for access to materials gathered for the Benin History Scheme of the University of Ibadan (which Professor Dike directed), to museum directors and curators and private collectors for their kindness in permitting data on Benin art objects to be collected, and to the British Museum and the Pitt-Rivers Museum, Farnham, Dorset, for permission to use photographs of plaques in their collections.

2. Otto Dapper, *Nauwkeurige Beschrijvinge der Afrikaansche Gewesten* (Amsterdam, 1668; 2d ed., 1676). See also H. Ling Roth, *Great Benin, Its Customs, Art, and Horrors* (Halifax: F. King and Sons, Ltd., 1903), p. 160. A. F. C. Ryder mentions that the information was gathered in the 1640s; see "The Benin Mission," *Journal of the Historical Society of Nigeria*, II, no. 1 (1961), 231–59.

dition, which Egharevba records, "that the long-stored treasures of the former kings were wasted," [3] that the reign of Ahenzae saw the cessation of the production of plaques, though it could be inferred that Ahenzae's dissipation of his wealth through gambling and the opportunism of his courtiers [4] led to a low level of art production. According to Egharevba, Ahenzae reigned in the 1640s and 1650s.

At the end of the seventeenth century, there was a civil war, the results of which were observed by Nyendael in 1704.[5] But Nyendael does not refer to the bronze plaques in his account, though he does refer to other features of the palace, mentioning a turret that is also referred to by Dapper and, in addition, a copper snake.[6]

Inferences as to stylistic resemblances between the plaques and other objects of Benin art tend to be highly subjective, but, nevertheless, these must be the key to a chronology, however relative it may be. Refinement of that chronology will gradually come from detailed analysis. The broad schemes of the stylistic development of Benin art which have been advanced must be the starting point for testing and refinement. One thinks particularly of the work of William Fagg [7] and of Murray's considerations.[8] As investigations of Benin styles and their development currently stand, and with historical evidence either negative or a matter for speculation, one can only hypothesize that production of the plaques ceased

3. J. Egharevba, *A Short History of Benin*, 3d ed. (Ibadan: Ibadan University Press, 1960), p. 35.

4. See Ryder, "The Benin Mission," p. 247.

5. D. van Nyendael, in *Nauwkeurige Beschrijvinge van de Guinese*, by William Bosman (Utrecht, 1704). For a discussion of this period, see R. E. Bradbury, "Chronological Problems in the Study of Benin History," *Journal of the Historical Society of Nigeria*, I, no. 4 (1959), 272–74; and Ryder "The Benin Mission," pp. 249–57.

6. See Roth, *Great Benin*, p. 162, who quotes from Nyendael.

7. See Eliot Elisofon and William Fagg, *The Sculpture of Africa* (London: Thames and Hudson; New York: Praeger, 1958).

8. K. C. Murray, "Benin Art," *Nigeria Magazine*, no. 71 (December, 1961), pp. 370–78. But it should be noted that, presumably through an editorial error, the dates given in the captions to some of the illustrations have been confused and do not appear to represent Murray's views. The debt that Benin scholarship owes to F. von Luschan, *Die Altertümer von Benin* (Berlin and Leipzig, 1919), and to B. Struck, "Chronologie der Benin Altertümer," *Zeitschrift für Ethnologie*, LV (1923), 113–66, with respect to chronology and other aspects should not be forgotten.

some time toward the end of the seventeenth century. The exact time, if before the 1690s and after the 1640s, must remain speculative. If it is accepted that the reign of Eresonye, from 1735 on, was a time of "an abundance of brass"[9] and resulted in the production of a complex of objects with a distinct configuration of stylistic features,[10] then one's impression is that such a configuration is different from the rich and varied iconography of the plaques. Such an impression leads to a separation of styles according to time period, and the dating of the plaques must then be prior to the Eresonye period.

As regards the time at which the artists of Benin first began to make plaques, only indirect evidence is available for speculation. One can only surmise, too, that the form of the plaque derived from impressions obtained by the Edo artists of objects in the baggage of the Portuguese. In summary, the following points provide a basis for such speculation:[11]

1. Read and Dalton identified the costume and dagger worn by the European on plaque 98.1–15.11 in the British Museum as "not later than the middle of the sixteenth century."[12] This is, however, not conclusive evidence of manufacture before that date, since Benin artists have often copied earlier designs.

2. Of 788 plaques examined, 71 figured Europeans.[13] Of this number only 13 plaques show a European with a musket. In addition, one plaque, formerly in the Cranmore Ethnographical Museum, depicts a chief with six African retainers and a European carrying a matchlock.[14] This plaque represents

9. Egharevba, *Short History of Benin*, p. 42.
10. See W. and B. Forman and Philip Dark, *Benin Art* (London: Batchworth Press, 1960).
11. The selection made can only influence the inferences advanced.
12. The plaque is illustrated in Charles H. Read and O. M. Dalton, *Antiquities from the City of Benin and from Other Parts of West Africa in the British Museum* (London: British Museum, 1899), p. 18, pl. 13/5.
13. The small-torso, medallionlike representations of Europeans that occur relatively infrequently on the plaques were not considered.
14. The plaque in the Pitt-Rivers Museum, Farnham, Dorset (see Lt. Gen. Pitt-Rivers, "Antique Works of Art from Benin" [1900], pl. 47,

FIGURE 2. "Bird-and-human" percussion instrument. British Museum, no. 98.1–15.117

FIGURE 1. Slit-drum. British Museum, catalog no. 98.1–15.77

FIGURE 4. Two single bells joined. British Museum, no. 99.1–15.51

FIGURE 3. Single percussion bell. British Museum, no. 98.1–15.115

FIGURE 5. Double percussion bell. British Museum, no. 98.1–15.68

FIGURE 6b: Modern bell of this type from Benin City

FIGURE 6a: Pyramidal clapper bell. Formerly British Museum, no. 98.1–15.138; now Nigerian Museum (Lagos), no. 51.18.7

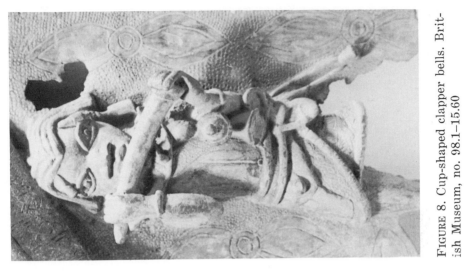

FIGURE 8. Cup-shaped clapper bells. British Museum, no. 98.1–15.60

FIGURE 7. Cup-shaped clapper bells. Pitt-Rivers Museum (Farnham, Dorset), no. 0/3

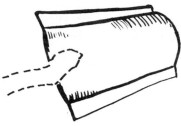

FIGURE 10. Trapezoidal welded clapper bell

FIGURE 11. Long-narrow bell. British Museum, no. 98.1–15.16

FIGURE 9. Cup-shaped clapper bells. British Museum, no. 98.1–15.16

FIGURE 13. Rattling staff *uxurhe*. British Museum, no. 98.1–
15.134

FIGURE 12. Calabash rattle. Formerly British Museum,
no. 98.1–15.148; now in the collection of H. Rome

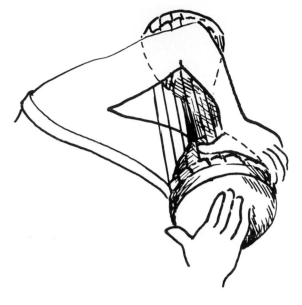

FIGURE 15. Hourglass drum. British Museum, no. 98.1–15.129

FIGURE 14. Pellet-bell. British Museum, no. 98.1–15.122

FIGURE 17. Single-skin drum with cord-and-peg bracing. Pitt-Rivers Museum (Farnham, Dorset), no. 1/18

FIGURE 16. Single-skin drums with cord-and-peg bracing. British Museum, no. 98.1–15.128

FIGURE 19. End-blown whistle or cone flute; also side-blown trumpet. Pitt-Rivers Museum (Farnham, Dorset), no. 0/5

FIGURE 18. Bow-lute. British Museum, no. 98.1–15.72

FIGURE 20. Side-blown trumpet. The insertion of the right hand into the position is much used today for altering the pitch of the sound. The position of the thumb over the tip, as in this example, may indicate the presence of a hole that can be used to change the pitch of the trumpet. British Museum, no. 98.1–15.21

FIGURE 22. Angels with drumsticks, from Ethiopian MS Or. 533, by courtesy of the Trustees of the British Museum

FIGURE 23. Lyre players, from Ethiopian MS Or. 533, by courtesy of the Trustees of the British Museum

a type of bearded warrior common to a small number of the plaques.[15] Are these the Edo warriors who fought in the wars of 1514–16? Other wars occurred in the sixteenth and seventeenth centuries and could have provided the subject matter for these plaques.

3. Ryder recounts that the Portuguese were careful to see that "no arms should fall into the hands of the Bini" until their conversion to Christianity. Between 1515 and 1516, some Portuguese from a mission to the Oba were present on a campaign against Idah with him. Conversion of the Oba came on his return to Benin City from the war. Whether this led to arms being supplied by the Portuguese to the Edo must remain conjectural. In any event, the mission appears to have failed, as did one which followed the next year in 1517. Ryder says:

Because the mission had failed, the Portuguese supplied no firearms to Benin. On the contrary, they took stringent precautions to prevent arms smuggling from the islands and the seizure of weapons from vessels trading in the rivers. These measures were generally successful, so that even by the end of the sixteenth century Benin armies possessed only the stray firearms.[16]

4. Bradbury, postulating a later date for the Idah war, suggests, very tentatively, that Oba Esigie came to the throne in 1517. He writes that the Iwoki, who look after the oba's

---

figs. 369–71), shows the oba's butcher, Uhondo, with his assistants and a small medallion of a European, who may be holding a gun. Two closely similar plaques, one in the British Museum (98.1–15.105) and the other in the Schnell Collection, each show an African soldier shouldering an object made up of three stafflike forms bound together. This object may represent a gun but probably does not; compare this with a plaque in the Reiss Museum, Mannheim, showing a soldier with a shield and spears.

15. See Forman and Dark, *Benin Art*, p. 42. For examples of plaques of this type, see Read and Dalton, *Antiquities*, pls. 19/4–6; Luschan, *Die Altertümer*, pl. A382–83; Pitts-Rivers, "Antique Works of Art," pl. 2, figs. 5–6. The only three plaques on which lutes are depicted are those which show bearded warriors; see note 47 below.

16. Ryder, "The Benin Mission," pp. 233–37.

guns and cannon, claim their origin from Esigie's reign, "and some claim to be descended from Europeans." [17]

Considering the above, along with Ryder's aforementioned observation, an outstanding feature of culture contact between the Portuguese and the Edo is likely to have been not only the Portuguese themselves but also the firearms which they had and which could have been of use to the Edo in their wars. But the supply of firearms was restricted and could not have been plentiful. Given the necessary cultural conditions and impetus to art production, both the Portuguese and firearms would be prominent themes for depiction by an artist.

5. Work in bronze requires supplies of metal. The advent of the Portuguese has always been coupled with an increase in the supply of metal available to the Edo brass-smith. Increases in supplies of metal were, in fact, available shortly after first contacts, and they increased in quantity very rapidly, as Ryder's researches attest. Ryder also notes that "Pereira remarked that the Binis preferred copper to brass manillas." [18]

6. Evidence for an increase in bronze casting in the first half of the sixteenth century at Benin is traditional. Egharevba notes that "Esigie encouraged and improved the brass work which had been introduced to Benin by Oba Oguola." Egharevba also notes that "in 1540, Esigie made a crucifix in brass and sent it to the king of Portugal as a present. Valuable presents were sent to the Oba in return." [19] Though the art of casting in bronze by the lost-wax technique is considered to have been learned from Ife in the time of Oguola, before the advent of the Portuguese, the brass-smiths may not have been formally organized until the time of Esigie.

17. Bradbury, "Chronological Problems in Benin History," pp. 279–80, states that the descent was claimed from two Europeans who stood on either side of the oba to protect him. Bradbury further states that "up to the present day, on ceremonial occasions, the Oba is flanked by two Iwoki with guns."

18. A. F. C. Ryder, "An Early Portuguese Trading Voyage to the Forcados River," *Journal of the Historical Society of Nigeria*, I, no. 4 (1959), 316, n. 2, 302, n. 1.

19. Egharevba, *Short History of Benin*, pp. 29, 30.

And if this were the case, then an increase in the supply of metal and an impetus to production, through contact with the Portuguese, may have led to their organization into a ward-guild, with their own location in the city, during Esigie's reign.[20]

In view of the above points it is tempting to speculate that the production of bronze plaques may have started in the second quarter of the sixteenth century. It can only be hoped that, gradually, further work may allow us to be more certain as to when, in fact, the bronze plaque was first introduced into the artistic traditions of the Edo, and, also, when its production ceased.

THE INSTRUMENTS

The musical instruments represented in the plaques are of the following kinds (classification and terminolgoy follow as far as possible the Hornbostel-Sachs system).

I. Idiophones

A. *Slit-drum.* Two examples of the slit-drum are represented on one plaque in the British Museum. Each has the form of a cylinder, representing a log of wood, with a longitudinal slit (Figure 1).[21]

B. *"Bird-and-human" percussion instrument.* Two types of these percussion instruments, which in Benin studies are usually referred to as idiophones, are distinguished

20. Chief Ine, chief of the brass-smiths today in Benin City, stated that his title originates from the time of Oba Oguola. Two other informants disagreed with this and stated that it originated in the time of Esigie. All agreed, however, that the title of *Olague* was awarded to the brass-smiths by Oba Orhogbua, who succeeded Esigie. Chief Ine's opinion was that the brassworkers were organized at the time of the arrival of Iguehae, who came to Benin City in the reign of Oguola to teach the Edo how to cast bronze. But other opinions differ and name the reign of Esigie as the time at which the brassworkers were formally organized. This information was gathered while working in Benin with Bradbury, who writes: "Some informants have it that the organization of the bronze casters into a ward-like guild dates from his [Esigie's] reign" ("Chronological Problems in Benin History," p. 279).

21. See Forman and Dark, *Benin Art*, pl. 27.

by their form. Five examples of this instrument in the form of a bird, representing an ibis, appear in the corpus of plaques (Figure 2).[22] Such objects in bronze are relatively common in the round. Three examples of this instrument in the form of a human, representing an oba, appear among the plaques.[23] In the round, examples in ivory are known which may represent obas on horseback, queen mothers, or their attendants. Egharevba, the Benin historian, says that the bird forms are not musical instruments but rather symbols of castigation of the bird. The qualification may also apply to human figures.

C. Bells

1. Percussion bells

(a) *Single bell.* Examples of single bells occur on twelve of the plaques (Figure 3).[24]

(b) *Two single bells joined.* Where a player holds a bell in each hand, a chain joining the two bells is usually shown (Figure 4).[25] It is possible that such single bells, in the round, contained clappers and should therefore be included under clapper bells.

(c) *Double bell.* This type consists essentially of two single bells, a smaller one alongside a larger one, fused together (Figure 5). There are four examples of this type represented on the plaques. Three are without decoration,[26] but the fourth is elaborately decorated with low-relief forms and imitation crotals,[27] recalling the few

22. See Pitt-Rivers, "Antique Works of Art," pl. 37, pp. 286–88; Read and Dalton, *Antiquities*, pl. 29/3.
23. For example, see Luschan, *Die Altertümer*, pl. T38/d; Read and Dalton, *Antiquities*, pl. 29/3.
24. For example, see Philip Dark, *The Art of Benin* (Chicago: Chicago Natural History Museum, 1962), pl. 15. Luschan, *Die Altertümer*, pl. T49/h, shows a plaque of a gong.
25. For example, see Read and Dalton, *Antiquities*, pls. 22/3, 22/5.
26. See Annemarie Hefel [Schweeger-Hefel], *Afrikanische Bronzen* (Vienna: Kuntsverlag Wolfrum, 1948), pl. T36; Pitt-Rivers, "Antique Works of Art," pl. 27, p. 181; Read and Dalton, *Antiquities*, pl. 29/3.
27. See Read and Dalton, *Antiquities*, pl. 25/1.

splendid examples of this object in the round, which are representative of one of the high points of the Edo carver's skill in working ivory and of the brass-smith's control in casting bronze.

2. Clapper bells

(a) *Pyramidal bell.* Bells in the form of a truncated pyramid of four either straight or gently concave sides, usually with an almost square base and a handle at the head and with a clapper suspended in the interior, are common products of the brass-smith's art and are widely used as part of altar furniture. They vary considerably in size and decoration. Some are beautifully chased with floral or geometric patterns; others are decorated with low-relief motifs, such as animals or human heads; still others have panels of pierced designs, with some form of lattice being common. Where low-relief decoration is added to the panels of bells, the emphasis is on the front panel with a central motif, such as a human head. The pyramidal form of bell is always shown on plaques as being worn suspended on the chest.[28] The method of suspension is not always easy to determine. In a number of cases it is depicted as suspended from a collar of teeth.[29] The pyramidal bell occurs on 132 plaques (Figure 6).

(b) *Cup-shaped bell.* The term "cup-shaped" is used to include forms of bells in which the body widens at the lip and narrows at the head, where an eyelet is left for the attachment of the bell. A Western person's general concept of a church bell would approximate the form of the bell considered here. This form, however, varies as

28. *Ibid.*, pl. 18/6.
29. The method of attachment is illustrated in Read and Dalton, *Antiquities*, pl. 32/3.

to both size and method of modeling. The size of this type of bell, in proportion to the rest of the plaque, varies considerably. The three different ways of modeling this bell in the wax are suggested by the fact that some are striated vertically, some are striated horizontally, and other are plain.

Cup-shaped bells are found attached to various types of tassels attached to different parts of costumes. Most commonly, tassels are attached to a breastplate or to an elaborately tied costume decoration above the left hip (Figures 7–9). Because of the impressionistic representation of small decorative elements, referred to above, it is not always easy to differentiate a small bell at the end of a tassel (or attached to a breastplate) from a crotal or from what may be nothing more than a tassel of some other material. This is especially true for tassel-like appendages to the large costume protrusion that rises vertically from the left hip beside the body, sometimes reaching the level of the head.[30] A bell of this type is always found attached to the sleeves and hem of certain types of costumed figures.[31] It also occurs suspended from the hilt of a sword. The cup-shaped bell occurs on 205 plaques; the plain form is the most common, appearing on 150 plaques; the vertically striated form occurs on 25 plaques; and the horizontally striated type is found on 30 of the plaques.

(c) *Trapezoidal welded bell.* This type of bell is trapezoidal in form, with an ellipitcal or circular mouth (Figure 10). It is found attached to breastplates, harness bands, or straps.[32]

30. For example, see *ibid.*, pls. 15/1, 20/1, 21/2.
31. For example, see *ibid.*, pl. 21/2.
32. For example, see Luschan, *Die Altertümer*, pls. T8/c, T12, T28/b.

(d) *Long-narrow "bell."* This bell-like object is long and narrow and has the appearance of a pendant.[33] It may, in fact, not be a clapper bell at all. It is always attached to the hilt of a sword (Figure 11). There are 19 examples of this type, but the body of one is striated spirally.[34] This type should be distinguished from a similar long and narrow pendant form that ends in a crotal (see below, I.D.3.[c]).

D. Vessel rattles

1. Calabash rattle. A number of plaques picture people holding in their hands a small spherical calabash without a handle, covered by a net with rattling beads at the intersections of the netting (Figure 12). This form of rattle is sometimes depicted held in both hands [35] and sometimes only in one.[36] The calabash rattle is depicted on 25 plaques and possibly on 6 others. A remarkable feature in some of these representations is the method of holding the rattle by inserting a finger into a hole in the calabash (central figure, Figure 3).

2. Rattling staff uxurhe. The *uxurhe* is usually carved from wood, though some were cast in brass. Near the top of the staff a small chamber is hollowed out, and two slits are left open to the outside. Inside the chamber is a wooden rattling object in the form of a stick. One or two examples of *uxurhe* appear on plaques (Figure 13).[37]

3. Pellet-bell, or crotal. Three principal types of crotals are represented on the plaques.

(a) The first type is small and occurs attached to ornamental masks depicting a leopard, a per-

---

33. For example, see Read and Dalton, *Antiquities*, pls. 15/3, 26/6.
34. Luschan, *Die Altertümer*, pl. T28/d.
35. For example, see Read and Dalton, *Antiquities*, pls. 14/3, 30/5.
36. For example, see Luschan, *Die Altertümer*, pl. T39/a.
37. For example, see Read and Dalton, *Antiquities*, pl. 25/6.

son, or a crocodile.[38] Representations of crocodile masks *only appear* as pendants from a waist belt. Leopard masks are *only worn* above the left hip, except in one instance.[39] Masks of human beings, if an African face is represented, *only occur* as waist pendants. The first type of crotal also occurs attached to anklets (Figure 14).[40]

(*b*) The second type of crotal is found as a combination of several crotal forms to make an anklet (see in Figure 12).[41] A number of such anklets are known in the round.

(*c*) The third type of crotal is a long, narrow pendant ending in a typical crotal form. There are, however, only two or three examples of this form shown on plaques (see in Figure 6).[42]

II. Membranophones. Two principal types of membranophones are represented on the plaques: the hourglass drum, and the single-skin drum with cord-and-peg bracing.[43]

A. Hourglass drum. There is only one example on the plaques of this form of drum, which is probably not native to the Edo (though it is widespread in West Africa).[44] The shape of the body is that of an hourglass. Thongs tension the membranous heads, and the tone is regulated by the pressure of the arm on the thongs (the drum is held under an arm suspended from a strap passing over the player's shoulder). On this unique plaque the drum-

38. For example, see *ibid.*, pls. 19/1, 16/4, and Luschan, *Die Altertümer*, pl. T43/a, respectively.
39. Read and Dalton, *Antiquities*, pl. 17/5.
40. For example, see *ibid.*, pls. 21/4, 21/5.
41. For example, see *ibid.*, pl. 22/3.
42. For example, see plaque 98.1–15.132 in the British Museum.
43. It has been suggested that the rectangular form held up by women, who are always queen mothers and who appear on some pendant plaques (e.g., Read and Dalton, *Antiquities*, pl. 11/5), is a frame-drum, a membranophone, though there is no evidence that such a form represents any type of drum. See also André Schaeffner, "Le Tambour-sur-cadre quadrangulaire," Les Congrès et Colloques de l'Université de Liege, 29, Ethnomusicologie III.
44. See Read and Dalton, *Antiquities*, pl. 29/2.

mer strikes the membrane with the fingers of his right hand (Figure 15), but in modern times a drum of this type is more commonly struck with the tip of a curved stick.

B. *Single-skin drum.* As depicted on the plaques, this type of drum varies in size and shape. The essential feature, however, is that the membranous head is tensioned by adjustable pegs, driven into the side of the body, to which thongs from the head are tied. Two types can be distinguished: a small one is carried under the arm, on the hip; the other type, which is larger, is played standing. There are 6 plaques on which the small drum is represented;[45] three varieties of the larger, standing drums are shown on 2 plaques (Figures 16–17).[46]

III. Chordophones. Only one type of chordophone is represented on Benin plaques. This is the *bow-lute,* or *pluriarc,* which is found mainly in West Africa east of the Ivory Coast. It also occurs as far away as the region of the Bushmen to the south, including the Congo, but not in East Africa. Only three examples are represented among all the plaques (Figure 18).[47]

IV. Aerophones. Two main types of aerophones were made by the Edo. They can be distinguished by the method required to blow them. In the first type, the hole was at the top and the instrument was held vertically. In the second type, the instrument was blown through a hole in its side; the instrument was held horizontally, extending to the side of the player. The two types can be called the end-blown flute and the side-blown trumpet.

A. *End-blown flute.* A plaque in the Pitt-Rivers Museum, Farnham, Dorset, pictures a diminutive attendant who appears to be blowing a whistle (Figure 19).[48] A plaque in the Portheim-Stiftung Museum, Heidelberg, shows

45. For example, see *ibid.*, pl. 19/6.
46. See *ibid.*, pl. 29/1; Luschan, *Die Altertümer,* pl. T10/c.
47. See Read and Dalton, *Antiquities,* pls. 23/4, 30/6.
48. See Pitt-Rivers, "Antique Works of Art," 2/5, 2/6.

two torso medallions of Europeans, one of whom appears to be blowing into a long tube which ends in a round form. The object is like a flask with a long neck; it has suggested to observers either a whistle or a bagpipe.

B. Side-blown trumpet. Two subtypes of this instrument, distinguished on the basis of form (plain and spiral), occur on the plaques. In the round, side-blown trumpets range from large, plain forms, some three feet in length and made from horn or ivory, to smaller trumpets, some six inches or more in length and made from bronze, ivory, or horn. Plain, undecorated trumpets are shown on 35 plaques; [49] 17 plaques show instruments which are spiral in form (Figure 20). [50]

49. For example, see Read and Dalton, *Antiquities*, pls. 19/4, 19/6.
50. *Ibid.*, pls. 16/3, 18/6; Luschan, *Die Altertümer*, pl. T49/g depicts a plaque of two side-blown trumpets of unusual form and perhaps foreign origin.

East Africa

4.

Africa and Indonesia:
An Ancient
Colonial Era?

A. M. JONES

HISTORIANS STUDYING THE PAST hope to find documentary evidence, or at least monuments and inscriptions, to provide a firm framework for their study. Thus Kunst is able to verify musical practice in Java back to about the eighth century A.D. from bas-reliefs on ancient temples.[1] In Africa we have had, so far, no such good fortune; all we have is a rather confused musical scene. While in some cases Egyptian influence seems likely, and in others Islamic influence is obvious, are we to say that the rest is truly indigenous, or can we claim outside origins for at least some of the musical phenomena?

The thesis set forth here is that a critical, as distinct from a superficial, examination of African musical practice reveals

1. J. Kunst, *Music in Java* (The Hague: Martinus Nijhoff, 1949), Vol. II, figs. 6–60.

a rather startling historic past: At some time before Europeans arrived, Africa was the scene of colonization by Indonesians and people of Southeast Asia, who settled on the coast of the Gulf of Guinea, in the Niger basin, in the Congo Basin, and near the East African coast opposite Madagascar. I would be the first to scoff at this idea if it were possible, but the more I study the evidence the more it seems inevitable that this colonization must have taken place.

It is unfortunately impossible in this short chapter to demonstrate this proposition with the fullness which is necessary to carry conviction. All that can be done is to indicate briefly the lines of inquiry which have led to this conclusion and to discuss one or two points in more detail. The evidence is by no means only musical, but the whole concept arose from musical research, and thus the discussion will be limited to this field.

Let us first consider African chorus-singing. While in some areas this is all unisonal (which is always the case where Islam is predominant), there are in sub-Saharan Africa two forms of simple "harmony," or, as I prefer to call it, "diody." The chorus sings either in organum (in parallel fourths or fifths) or in parallel thirds. I shall call these the 8–5–4 tradition and the thirds tradition, respectively. For many years I taught boys from both traditions. The 8–5–4 boys could not sing thirds, and vice versa unless deliberately taught. I know of no evidence to suggest that 8–5–4 singing is kept for certain occasions and singing in thirds for others. The evidence indicates that the systems are mutually exclusive.

Now if the thirds areas are plotted on a map we find that they occur in specific areas: (1) around the coast of the Gulf of Guinea, penetrating eastward below the Sahara as far as the northeastern Congo; (2) in a large part of the Congo Basin; and (3) on the East African coast near the mouth of the Zambezi. It looks as if the thirds tradition has impinged from the coast onto the 8–5–4 tradition.

Singing in parallel thirds is highly characteristic of Madagascar (e.g., among the Sakalava, Tankara, and Tsimiheti), whose inhabitants are of the same stock as the Indonesians. In Indonesia itself, if we penetrate below Hindu and Muslim influences, we find the same thirds choruses—for instance in parts of Sumatra. The feature is also characteristic of the Philippines.

Turning now to musical instruments, we consider first a special form of bar-zither called by ethnomusicologists the *zeze* (sometimes spelled *sese*). It is a rectangular bar of wood, under one end of which is an inverted half-calabash resonator, with a string along the top and sometimes another at the side. Its characteristic features are the presence of a collar of calabash between the bar and the resonator and also three rectangular knobs of wood protruding on the upper and often on the lower edge of the bar at its head. No one has satisfactorily explained the lower knobs—they appear to have no function. Ankermann,[2] De Hen,[3] and others show that the *zeze* occurs along the east coast of Africa between latitudes 2° and 11° south and all over the Congo Basin down into Zambia.

But the *zeze* is a characteristic instrument, identical in form, in Madagascar [4] and is plentiful in Celebes.[5] It is difficult to believe that this particular form of bar-zither could have been invented separately on both sides of the Indian Ocean.

Next we consider African clapperless bells. The Ewe in Ghana (i.e., near the coast of the Gulf of Guinea) use two main types of bells, one of which is called *atoke*. This strange object certainly does not look like a bell. It is made of iron and is like a leaf complete with stalk, the sides of the leaf being curled upward till they nearly meet. It is played by laying it loosely along the palm of the hand and striking it near the slit between the edges with a short metal rod. This *atoke* is used by the Pangwe as well—who also live along the Gulf of Guinea.

2. B. Ankermann, "Die Afrikanischen Musikinstrumente," *Ethnologisches Notizblatt*, Vol. III (1901), bk. 1, map 1.

3. F. J. De Hen, *Beitrag zur Kenntnis der Musikinstrumente aus Belgisch Kongo und Ruanda-Urundi* (Tervuren: Musée Royale de l'Afrique Centrale, 1960), map 2.

4. Curt Sachs, *Les Instruments de musique de Madagascar* (Paris: Institut d'Ethnologie, 1938), pp. 47 ff.

5. W. Kaudern, *Musical Instruments in Celebes* (Göteborg, 1927), pp. 148 ff.

This special bell is a traditional instrument in Java, where it is called the *kemanak*. There it has the same shape and is held and played in the same way, the only differences being that the playing stick is made of wood instead of metal and the stem is a little longer.

In his *Music in Java,* Kunst shows a picture of some ancient *kemanaks* which were dug up in Java.[6] Among them were two metal objects of a very different shape yet still apparently clapperless bells. They have a handle to which is fixed a sort of short metal tube open at both ends and having a slit running down from top to bottom. He concluded that it was an obsolete and alternative form of *kemanak*.

In the Gulf of Guinea area, down the west coast in Angola, and throughout the Congo Basin, there occurs a clapperless bell which is quite unlike the *atoke*. It is usually conical, sometimes single, sometimes in pairs, and is played by beating the side with a stick. Often it has flanged and welded sides. But among the Yoruba and the Ewe, to mention only two tribes, old forms have a slit running down the side; so have the Akan models in Ghana. This particular bell, an Ewe master drummer told me, is exactly the same in essential shape as the old *kemanak* referred to, the only difference being that the sides are slightly conical in shape. We are thus presented with the fact that two very characteristic and unusual bell-forms from Java also occur in the Gulf of Guinea area.

There is another instrument, the drum-xylophone,[7] which consists of a hollow cylinder blocked at each end and having on its upper surface a number of slits of varying lengths, thus isolating parallel strips of the surface. Wedges are inserted in the slits near their ends so as to tune these strips, which are played as in a xylophone. There may be from one to four strips, or keys. The drum-xylophone is found in Guinea, Liberia, Portuguese Guinea, and Sierra Leone—that is, around the coastal areas beyond the northwest edge of the Gulf of

6. Vol. II, fig. 57.
7. The "percussion tube" in Erich M. von Hornbostel and Curt Sachs, "Classification of Musical Instruments," trans. Anthony Baines and Klaus P. Wachsmann, *The Galpin Society Journal*, XIV (1961), 15.

Guinea. It is made either of wood or of an internodal section of bamboo (as in the case of the Kono tribe).

The drum-xylophone is found also in Java, and Kunst regards it as being of ancient lineage.[8] As in Africa, it may be either of wood or of bamboo. In either case the lengths of the instrument are about the same in both countries—for wood, between one and two yards long; for bamboo, a single internodal section. The modern Javanese form has only one strip, which is played with a beater as in Africa.

While it might be conceived that in spite of these details the instruments are of independent invention, one has to remember that the Mano in West Africa call the drum-xylophone *kuo-kele,* and the Kissi call the slit-drum, which is also made of either wood or bamboo, *kelende* (the last syllable, *-nde,* being a suffix). In old Javanese, the name for an internodal section of bamboo was *kele.*

Yet another instrument relevant to this discussion is the leg-xylophone. This consists of from two to four roughly shaped tuned wooden keys placed across the outstretched legs of a seated person and played by someone else. It has been reported from Guinea, central Dahomey, northern Togo, and Zambia, the three former being in the Gulf of Guinea area and the latter just south of the Congo Basin (yet still influenced thereby).

Now, the leg-xylophone is characteristic of Celebes, and it occurs also in Nias and farther west in the Pacific; in these places it has three or four notes. Furthermore, it is the one type of xylophone found in Madagascar, where it is widespread and, according to Curt Sachs, may have from six to twelve notes.[9]

This rather primitive form of instrument is nonetheless somewhat specialized in that it uses the human body as part of the instrument. It may be a separate invention in each case; yet in view of the other cases of similarity which we have noted, which also occur in the same area in Africa, it

8. Kunst, *Music in Java,* Vol. II, fig. 153; I, 192 ff.
9. *Les Instruments de Madagascar,* p. 62.

would seem to be rather rash merely to dismiss it as such.

The instruments thus far dealt with are all simply constructed and have only a limited range of performance. When we turn to the fully developed xylophone, however, we are presented with an instrument having a considerable complexity of construction and often a wide range of notes, which together with other features of organization and performance provide us with a large corpus of integrated evidence for critical evaluation, ranging from the construction, tuning, and pitch, to the music played and the matter of terminology.

Let us look first at Southeast Asia and Indonesia. In Thailand and Cambodia the xylophones are tuned to a scale which has seven notes to the octave, as do our Western scales, but which contains no semitones. It is divided into seven equal intervals and is therefore called an equitonal heptatonic scale. In Java one finds two distinct families of orchestras, those tuned to the *pelog* scale, and those tuned to the *slendro* scale. The *pelog* scale has seven notes to the octave but the intervals are not all equal, there being two small ones of about a semitone, two big ones of more than a whole tone, with the remainder being about the size of the Cambodian or Thai intervals. The *slendro* scale is pentatonic, its five intervals being nearly equal in size. It is a matter of debate whether the observed inequalities are inherent in the scale or arise by lack of precision. In Southeast Asia and Indonesia, then, we are confronted with three distinct scales.

In Africa, the majority of xylophones so far tested are tuned to a very fair approximation of the equitonal heptatonic scale, that is, to the scale of Thailand and Cambodia. The tribes who tune most closely to this scale are the Chopi, near the coast in southeast Africa, and the Malinke, near the coast in Sierra Leone. It is significant that the further one goes inland from the coast, the rougher the tuning becomes; the scale is still recognizably the same, with the inaccuracies being capricious in their occurrence even in different instruments belonging to the same tribe. There are also xylophones, particularly in the Congo, tuned to the *pelog* scale. Furthermore, both in West Africa and in the northern Congo one finds xylophones tuned to the quite different equitonal pentatonic *slendro* scale. If it were a question of only one scale, convergence might be held to explain the similarity. To ask us to believe that all three scales are due to convergence, however, is neither reasonable nor credible.

It may be alleged that xylophones are untrustworthy witnesses to the tuning intended by the makers, since the keys may become worn by use or shrunk and distorted by age and storage in museums; again, the accuracy of the assessment of pitch by the researcher may be impugned. Yet a number of scholars have measured these instruments, and they give similar results. Furthermore, the African *sansa*, or "Kaffir piano," whose keys are often made of iron, also reveals the same scales; thus a refutation of tuning similarities would have to maintain that the iron had shrunk in the same proportion as the wood of the xylophone keys!

In more than half the African heptatonic xylophones tested, there are gaps here and there in the scale. This results in many cases in an octave which, even though it is tuned to the equitonal heptatonic scale, is actually pentatonic, for two of the expected seven notes are missing. This applies to both the equitonal heptatonic and the *pelog*-type xylophones, but particularly to the latter. Now, a constant characteristic of Indonesian heptatonic xylophone music is that two notes in the octave are always omitted in playing. This applies both to the mainland (e.g., the *piphat* band) and to the *pelog* orchestras in Java. Thus the fact that all the notes of the scale are present on the instruments hides the presence of this standard pentatonic performance-technique. The complete set of notes is necessary, for in both Cambodia and Java a "modal" or "transposing" system operates so that it is not always the same two notes which need to be omitted. Yet the principle of playing pentatonic scales on a heptatonic instrument is exhibited in both Indonesia and Africa.

A still more striking parallel is found if one examines the actual pitch of the xylophone notes. One might imagine that African xylophones, even if tuned to the same set of scales, would, in different tribes and even from maker to maker, differ in the actual pitch on which the scale is laid. It can be shown that this is not so. In equitonal heptatonic scales, each interval is approximately 172 cents in size. Suppose we think of the scale as a ladder whose rungs are half this "distance" (i.e., 86 cents) apart and are numbered consecutively. It is now possible to have two distinct equitonal heptatonic tunings —one whose notes fall on the odd-numbered rungs, and one whose notes fall on the even-numbered rungs. In other words, the scale depends on the exact pitch, that is, the frequency, of the note we start from. If the African scales are pitched at random, about 50 per cent of the tunings will fall on the odd rungs and 50 per cent on the even rungs. In actual fact, nearly 80 per cent of the xylophones whose tunings we have fall on the odd rungs. In other words, the African craftsman is aiming for a definite pitch. One of the African notes is pitched around 182 v.p.s. The average pitch for the corresponding note on the Cambodian xylophones is 184.6 v.p.s. Thus, so far as we have tested them, the African equitonal heptatonic xylophones have not only the same scale but also the same pitch as those of Cambodia.

In Cambodia, a xylophone orchestra contains instruments of two different ranges of pitch—a low xylophone, *ranad thume,* with a range of just over two octaves, and the *ranad ek,* which starts higher and reaches to at least an octave above the top note of the low xylophone. The Chopi in East Africa have a similar disposition of instruments, the *dole* being similar to the low Cambodian xylophone and the *sange* and *cilanzane* to the higher one. They also add two lower-pitched xylophones.

In the same way, when we compare Javanese with African practice, we find the Javanese with, on the one hand, multi-octave xylophones of about three-and-a-half and two-and-a-half octaves, and on the other hand the single-octave *sarons* which, together with the single-octave *demung,* are tuned to a gamut comprising the range of the three-octave *gambanggangsa.* If we plot the compass and range of African instruments we find the same categories, both as to range and as to pitch. It is interesting to note that this is so in spite of the fact that in Africa xylophones are usually played as solo instruments or in small bands of two or three together. Thus the occurrence of families of range and pitch in Africa apparently are not due to the distribution of function and range brought about by the demands of large orchestras, as in Java.

Two tribes, however, do possess full orchestras—the Chopi in Mozambique and the Baganda. Comparing the Baganda orchestra with that of Java, we find many similarities: [10]

<table>
<tr><td>JAVA</td><td>BAGANDA</td></tr>
</table>

Melody section

JAVA	BAGANDA
Flute	Flute
2-string bowed lute	1-string fiddle
Zither (obsolete)	
Xylophone—*Sarons, Genders,* and *Gambangs*	Xylophone—*Akadinda* played by 6 men, i.e., full band on one instrument

Rhythm section

JAVA	BAGANDA
4 gongs	2 different kinds of rattle
2 drums:	4 drums:
1 steady beat	1 steady beat
2 steady beat plus variations (small drum)	2 and 3 complicated variations
	4 much improvisation (small drum)

It is clearly the same setup. The Africans, as would be expected, give additional weight to the rhythm section. In the Chopi orchestra the xylophone section is still more like that of Cambodia and Java. It consists of xylophones of five different pitch-ranges, though it lacks the string instrument.

The parallelism is still clearer if we consider the sort of music they play. Indonesian *gamelan* music is based on a "nu-

10. For Java, see Kunst, *Music in Java;* for Buganda, see Gerhard Kubik, "The Structure of Kiganda Xylophone Music," *African Music,* II, no. 3 (1960), 16. Klaus P. Wachsmann has pointed out that the one-stringed bowed lute, *endingidi,* is a modern addition to one particular orchestra and therefore does not count for comparative purposes; see also Chapter 5 in this volume. On the dating of the *endingidi's* invention in Buganda, see Margaret Trowell and Klaus P. Wachsmann, *Tribal Crafts of Uganda* (London and New York: Oxford University Press, 1953), p. 407.

clear theme," or *cantus firmus,* around which the other instruments build elaborations. The same is true of the Baganda. Moreover the Baganda musical themes so far published are similar to Javanese ones.

Though it is difficult to maintain that all these parallels can be fortuitous, the list is by no means ended. One could go on to adduce various technical details of construction—the types of resonators, the methods of key-suspension, the materials used for the heads of the playing sticks, the way tuning is accomplished, and so on. In all these matters there is a striking identity between Africa and Indonesia.

The mention of resonators raises another question. It used to be held that the use of calabashes or dried fruit shells in Africa, rather than box resonators or bamboo tubes as in Indonesia, argues against the diffusion theory. But besides the fact that Kunst cites the use of shells and calabashes in up-country orchestras in Bali,[11] the very use of the calabashes supports our thesis on the basis of terminology. The name for a xylophone slat or key in Java is *wilah.* In Javanese there is a substitutionary form of nouns, which affects the first syllable; this form of the noun is used when referring to a substitute for the proper object. If one cannot find the right material for an instrument's construction, for instance, it is called by the substitutionary name. The substitutionary form of *wilah* is *mbilah.* But *mbila* is one of the widespread names of the xylophone in Africa, and it really means the keys or slats of the instrument. A number of other word parallels can be adduced, though it is recognized that this form of linguistics can do no more than hint, and it is impossible to substantiate in the absence of documentary evidence.

Now, the xylophone does not occur everywhere in Africa. It exists mainly in the area embracing the Gulf of Guinea and the Niger basin and penetrating inland south of the Sahara, down the west coast as far as Angola, in the Congo Basin including Zambia, on the east coast between latitudes 5° and 17° south, and opposite Madagascar. The best xylophones are

11. J. Kunst and C. J. A. Kunst-van Wely, *De Toonkunst van Bali* (Weltervraden, 1925), p. 63.

found in coastal areas, and a map of distribution gives the impression that the xylophone started on the west and the east coasts and spread inland. These areas are precisely those in which all the other musical phenomena we have cited are found to occur, and, as far as we know, to occur exclusively. This corpus of musical practice in these areas thus forms a whole and distinct complex.

If, then, the xylophone was brought to Africa, how and when did it arrive? The suggestion that early Portuguese traders brought it from Indonesia will not stand, for it can be shown that the instrument was known to Arab scholars 300 years earlier. Neither can it be seriously maintained that, granted Indonesian shipping could have reached Africa, the Indonesians took this essentially African instrument back to Indonesia. For one thing, we know of a tuned lithophone found in Cambodia made by a Stone Age technique, which indicates the antiquity of the xylophone in Indonesia; for another, the indications, as I have tried to show, both of instrumental organization and of vocabulary suggest that the opposite is the true view.

This paper has presented a mere conspectus of the musical evidence and has totally ignored data of an extramusical nature. The more deeply one delves into the details of the musical phenomena, the more irresistible seems to be the conclusion that the observed phenomena could have arisen only if the Indonesians had come to Africa in considerable numbers over possibly many centuries; in short, we can conclude that there must have been an Indonesian colonial period in Africa centered on the Gulf of Guinea, the Congo Basin, and the East African coast.

Whether these Indonesians landed on the southeast coast and gradually moved overland to West Africa, or whether some of them rounded the Cape and sailed there directly, is a matter of opinion; I take the latter view, though the question does not affect the main issue.

Finally, there is the time factor. To what date do we assign this colonization? This can at present receive only an incomplete answer. We need more information from Java and Southeast Asia. In both places metal gongs form part of the orchestra, but they are absent in Africa. When did gongs first appear in Indonesia? We know they were already there by about the eighth century A.D., for they figure in the bas-reliefs of Borobudur. Again, the presence of the two-stringed bowed lute in the Javanese orchestra is probably to be assigned ultimately to Persia by means of the Hindu influence in Indonesia. The musical evidence in Africa suggests for the most part an earlier period. Further, the near absence of Sanskrit words in Madagascar suggests that the Indonesians arrived there certainly not later than A.D. 400, and Berg says almost certainly several centuries earlier.[12] The same absence of Sanskrit in the Indonesian word parallels found in Africa also suggests an early date. On the whole—though this is a very tentative conclusion and we await archaeological, anthropological, and historical research—I am inclined to think that the Indonesian colonization I have postulated took place in Africa in the early centuries of the Christian era and was spread over a fairly considerable period of time.

Since this essay was written, the subject has been further developed by me and discussed by the critics.[13]

12. Professor Berg and I met and discussed this.
13. A. M. Jones, *Africa and Indonesia* (Leyden: E. J. Brill, 1964); A. M. Jones, "The Influence of Indonesia: the Musicological Evidence Reconsidered," *Azania*, Vol. IV (1969).
For criticism, see Mantle Hood, "Sléndro and Pélog Redefined," *Selected Reports*, Institute of Ethnomusicology, Los Angeles, no. 1 (1966); and Gilbert Rouget and J. Schwarz, "Sur les xylophones equiheptatoniques des Malinke," *Revue de Musicologie*, LV, no. 1 (1969).

5.

Musical Instruments in Kiganda Tradition and Their Place in the East African Scene

KLAUS P. WACHSMANN

INTRODUCTION

A STRIKING FEATURE of studies in African history today is their dependence on a host of disciplines, ranging from archaeology, linguistics, and mythology to biochemistry, ethnobotany, and radiocarbon physics—to name only a few of the ancillary forces. A comprehensive list would be lengthy indeed, and its very length would make the absence of music and musical scholarship all the more conspicuous.

Why is it, for instance, that the words *music* and *musical scholarship* do not occur anywhere in the 125 pages of a 1961 report on Oriental, Slavonic, East European, and African Studies?[1] What is there that musicians and anthropologists,

---

1. University Grants Committee, "Report of the Sub-Committee on Oriental, Slavonic, East European, and African Studies" (University of London, 1961).

for example, could do to promote the study of a subject in which they have a common interest?

For Africanists the challenge is perhaps even more formidable than it is for students in Asian fields, where documented traditions can often be consulted. For the interior of East Africa, for example, the lack of early sources of information on music is painfully obvious.

MUSIC HISTORY AND MUSIC ETHNOLOGY IN AFRICA

It was as recently as 1849 that the Baganda, whose musical instruments are discussed later in this chapter, received their first visitor from the outside world [2]—a Zanzibari soldier, Isau bin Hussein, who came to stay as the bodyguard of Kabaka Ssuuna II until the Kabaka's death in 1857. Arab traders were invited in 1852. Among the articles of Western or Eastern manufacture they brought to Ssuuna's capital, Kaggwa mentioned four things above all others: cloth, guns, mirrors, and a musical instrument, *ennanga,* that cannot now be identified.[3] In 1862 Speke, the first European traveler to arrive in Buganda, referred in his reports to the musical scenes at the court. Such are the earliest records from which musical history is to be written.

Stylistic evidence of pre-Western material from Africa is even more recent. In 1906 Hornbostel could proudly write in "Phonographierte Tunesische Melodien" that "with this essay the new study of comparative musicology sets foot on African soil for the first time." [4] Indeed, 1906 through 1907 were memorable years. In the spring of 1906 Béla Bartók paid his first visit to Algeria and became passionately interested in Arab music, which he later recorded and described. In the

2. Compare the discussion on early visits to Buganda in Sir John M. Gray, "Ahmed bin Ibrahim—The First Arab to Reach Buganda," *Uganda Journal* (hereafter cited as *UJ*), XI (1947), 80–97.

3. Sir Apolo Kagwa [Kaggwa], *Ekitabo kya Basekabaka Bebuganda* [The Book of the Kings of Buganda] (1901; reprint ed., London: Sheldon Press, 1927), p. 105 (hereafter cited as *Basekabaka*).

4. Erich M. von Hornbostel, "Phonographierte Tunesische Melodien," *Sammelbände für vergleichende Musikwissenschaft,* I (1922), 313.

same year, Witte published his paper on recorded music from the Ewe of Togo, and Czekanowski followed closely on his heels with a collection of recordings from the peoples of Ruanda-Burundi in 1907.[5] It was indeed difficult, if not impossible, to think of music history in Africa before 1900 in terms of "sound." [6]

This conclusion is disconcerting in the extreme. It might be useful to try another, more systematic approach. The lines of attack traditionally adopted by music historians are therefore set out here, in diagram form, against the various levels of historical investigation at which students in Africa will have to work. In Figure 21, the traditional lines of approach adopted by music historians are represented by the vertical arrows (I–IV), and the levels of historical investigation are indicated by horizontal rectangles (A–E).

Music historians, given opportunity and experience, ought to be thoroughly at home with level A at all its intersections with the four arrows. It is here that their contribution will naturally be at its best. At level B much will depend on the informant's awareness of musical sound and his ability to put his knowledge into words. In oral tradition, in Africa as anywhere else, this is notoriously difficult, and it becomes progressively more so as one moves to levels C and D; especially at their intersections with arrow III, the quest for information will mostly be in vain. Consequently, any data found along arrow IV that may have survived in speech are likely to remain musically meaningless. At level E music historians may take refuge in the assumption that oral tradition can be extremely stable, so stable indeed that experience at level A might make it legitimate for them to speculate on and to construct working hypotheses with regard to the earlier stages of any musical culture.

At the beginning of this century so little was known at any

---

5. P. Fr. Witte, "Lieder und Gesänge der Ehwe Neger," *Anthropos*, I (1906), 65–81, 194–209; Jan Czekanowski, *Forschung im Nil-Kongo-Zwischengebiet*, Wissenschaftliche Ergebnisse der deutschen Zentralafrika Expedition, Vol. VI, pt. 1, Ethnographie–Anthropologie (Leipzig, 1917).
6. Klaus P. Wachsmann, "The Earliest Sources of Folk Music in Africa," *Studia Musicologica*, VII (1965), 181–86.

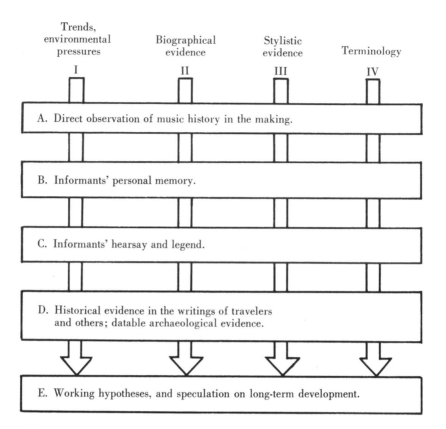

FIGURE 21. Scheme of investigation for ethnomusicology

level that students could interpret their observations in time-depth with impunity. Yet African music was certainly not absolutely stable even before the impact of Western music was felt. In fact, many field workers have found that changes in music are frequent and that musicians of the simpler and illiterate societies, in spite of the continuity of their traditions, are often conscious of the effect of change.

However theoretical these considerations may seem, they have nevertheless influenced the planning of this paper. A strong case can be made for a twofold procedure in dealing with the music of East Africa. We will begin with material at level A, giving a close-up view of music in Buganda; starting from the most recent times it might be feasible to reach back into the past through levels B and C, and possibly even further. This will be followed by a selection of data regarding East Africa in its widest sense, as the setting in which Buganda belongs. But here the procedure will have been reversed; instead of starting from a close-up view at level A, a long-distance view will be tried, working up from the lower levels of the diagram toward the top. It is hoped that a picture will emerge of the present state of knowledge of music history in East Africa.

MUSICAL INSTRUMENTS IN KIGANDA TRADITION

THE ENDINGIDI

During a prolonged stay with an expert Muganda craftsman and musician, the question of who would continue his trade arose. His son was mentioned, but the father remarked with some bitterness that his son was a child of the *mirembe gy'endingidi*, the age of the bowed lute.

To understand this reference to the bowed lute, or tube-fiddle, *endingidi*, it might be useful to compare it with other comments. Kaggwa does not include the *endingidi* in his catalogue of musical instruments, which was written in 1905 before the instrument itself had made its debut.[7] Another writer, Byangwa, who in 1925 was asked by the kabaka to collect Kiganda songs suitable for the use of young people, included in his collection a special group called *endingidi* songs;[8] he thought that they required censoring because they were tainted by the depraved customs of the strangers who introduced the songs in the reign of Ssuuna II. An anonymous writer has named these foreigners as Arabs and Coast Swahili. Sempebwa published a love song in which a young woman praises her beloved: "I play the *olutamba*, he will listen." Musicians use this term either for an *endingidi* in low pitch or for the most important string in the so-called *endingidi* group

7. Sir Apolo Kagwa [Kaggwa], *Ekitabo kye Mpisa za Baganda* [The Book of the Customs of Buganda] (1905; reprint ed., London: Sheldon Press, 1934), pp. 263–78 (hereafter cited as *Mpisa*); Margaret Trowell and Klaus P. Wachsmann, *Tribal Crafts of Uganda* (London and New York: Oxford University Press, 1953), pls. 96, 115.
8. Y. Byangwa, *Enyimba ze gwanga enkulu* (Kampala, 1931[?]), p. 7.

of low-pitched notes on the lyre. Whatever its musical meaning, Sempebwa's translation of this term as "banjo" is a
happy choice, since it conveys the aura of innovation that
surrounds both the banjo and the *endingidi*.[9] Finally, there is
the remark of a famous retired *endingidi* player that it would
not be dignified at his age to play the instrument, an attitude
that one does not find with players of other traditional instruments.

It is possible that the *ennanga* mentioned as one of the
notable items brought to Buganda in 1852 was in fact a bowed
instrument. It is even likely that among the Swahili there had
been men from Usaramo or from other parts of the coast, such
as Kilwa, where bowed fiddles were in vogue. One can dis-
count Wood's 1868 picture of a "fiddle" from Karagwe, which
is most likely a fantasy inspired by the flat-bar-zither, *zeze*.[10]
In due course the southern link with the coast was superseded
by the Mombasa route. Here acquaintance with bowed music
was possible through the *mbebe* (from Arabic *rebab?*) of the
eastern Kamba—the instrument certainly existed in Kamba
country by 1900 [11]—or by direct contact with Indian musicians
in the labor force employed on the construction of the railway
from Mombasa to Kisumu between 1896 and 1901. However,
Asiatic fiddles are played in a vertical position, whereas the
endingidi and the *mbebe* are held horizontally against the
lower ribs, and this difference in playing position makes the
explanation of direct Asian contact less convincing. Most
likely, Swahili travelers were responsible for bringing the
endingidi to the northern shore of Lake Victoria. In fact, Mr.
Nabikamba, chief of Gabula County in Busoga, stated that a
Swahili had introduced it to the capital of Busoga in 1903.
The event was especially memorable because it coincided with
an epidemic of coughing, and the authorities, suspecting a
connection between the illness and the instrument, thought of
suppressing it altogether. Whatever the route, it is unlikely
that songs sung to the accompaniment of these instruments

9. E. K. K. Sempebwa, "Baganda Folk Songs," *UJ*, XII (1948), 23–24.
10. J. G. Wood, "The Natural History of Man," *Africa*, I (1868), 444.
11. B. Ankermann, "Die Afrikanischen Musikinstrumente," *Ethnologisches Notizblatt*, Vol. III (1901), bk. 10, fig. 7.

in Swahili or Arabic could have remained unnoticed in Buganda for long. It is more likely that they were known for half a century before the local version of the bowed instrument, the *endingidi*, was invented around 1907.

The history of the invention of the *endingidi* has been told elsewhere.[12] Here it will suffice to say that, in its creation, autochthonous and foreign elements converged and the outcome was considered an invention of Kiganda inspiration. It occurred under a lucky star; a trade and industrial fair, the first ever, took place the following year. A merry-go-round was erected at a site known to this day to many people especially since the event was commemorated by the song "E-kyuma kya Bboola," which was also played on the tube-fiddle. The title of the song simply means "the machine that is turned"; *ekyuma* is both iron and machine, and *Bboola* stands for Borrup, the name of the industrial missionary associated with the introduction of cotton and cotton ginning. If one remembers that by 1904 over a hundred hand-driven cotton gins had been distributed throughout Buganda,[13] the joke in 1908 about the merry-go-round, "the machine that is turned," is easily appreciated. By 1911 the *endingidi* had been introduced by a Muganda political agent into Kigezi to the southwest. At about this time it became also known in the Congo. In the 1914–18 war it became very popular with the *askaris*.

This then is the background to the Muganda artist's comment that his son was a child of the age of the bowed lute: a modern person, yet dated; in the popular swing, yet not in the vanguard of progress. It also reveals other aspects of Kiganda musical thinking, namely, the acuteness of memories and the awareness of different origins. It also demonstrates the role played by chance, by favorable circumstances that make it possible for a new phenomenon like bowed music in Buganda to be accepted by the people as their own. In recent years field workers have often noticed the tendency of in-

12. Trowell and Wachsmann, *Tribal Crafts*, p. 407.
13. "The Uganda Company had installed a 'hand power factory' in 1904 and 62 hand gins were sold by Government to chiefs and another 43 were given away. . . . A very primitive hand gin" (C. Ehrlich, "Cotton and the Uganda Economy," *UJ*, XXI [1957], 169).

digenous musicians to acknowledge borrowings from other peoples. One might suspect that it was no more than a convention of speech and good manners to refer to alien origins in music, but it is even more probable that there is really very little that any community can claim to be of its own invention.

For anyone familiar with the Buganda of recent decades, it is difficult to realize how fierce the Arab and Swahili impact must have been in the nineteenth century. In a comment about a song in praise of Kabaka Kyabaggu, Kyagambiddwa[14] credits him with having obtained the first imports of the Arab trade, presumably through middlemen, in the second half of the eighteenth century. This view was already held by Kaggwa.[15] Thus almost a century of mystery preceded the actual arrival of the strangers bringing their goods. The year 1852 has already been mentioned as the first certain date for this event. As to the effect of contact in later years, A. Mackay,[16] in his journal in 1879, remarked of the Baganda that he found "not a few begging blank note books in which to write in *Arabic* character the Swahili prayers," and "today wrote out the Lord's Prayer in Ruganda. Edi had written it with much other matter (I think from Stanley's dictation) in *Arabic* character. I am really astonished to find many copies of this sort about." Of the Swahili version of the Gospels by Rebman, Mackay mentioned that it had to be rendered "into the *Zanzibar* dialect" before it could be used. Yet the Arabs had not been unaware of the attraction of Luganda speech. Burton learned from Snay, the widely traveled Arab trader, that "their language was, to use an Arab phrase, like that of the birds, soft and quickly spoken." [17]

There is no reference to the manner in which the earlier hymns were sung. However, on October 8, 1879, Mackay wrote triumphantly: "Litchfield has begun this week to teach the

14. Joseph Kyagambiddwa, *African Music from the Sources of the Nile* (New York: Praeger, 1955), p. 197.

15. *Basekabaka*, p. 88.

16. *Mr. Mackay's Journal in Uganda Covering Jan. 1st 1879 to Jan. 31st, 1880* (n.p., 1880 or 1881[?]), pp. 3, 5, 12, 21.

17. Sir Richard F. Burton, *Lake Region of Central Africa*, 2 vols. (New York, 1860; reprint ed., New York: Horizon Press, 1961), II, 196.

leading boys, who are daily with him, some singing. I should like to see him make real progress in this and hope he will have much success in it." This is a truly important date; with it began, for better or worse, an intense and enlightened interest in Western music. In 1885 the first hymns in Luganda were printed.[18] In 1900 Cyril Gordon set new vernacular texts to indigenous canoe songs and drum beats for use as children's tunes on Buggala Island,[19] but this experiment does not seem to have found any imitators.

The musical currents that were set in motion in those days, and which have persisted until today, find an almost symbolical expression in a ceremony described by Ashe.[20] On July 31, 1892, the first cathedral was opened at Nnamirembe. "Mwanga and his suite waited in the vestry . . . until the beating of the church drum announced the time for the beginning of the service." In a footnote Ashe added: "The tattoo for the prayer drum in Uganda is the ordinary Unyamwezi caravan drum beat, probably introduced from Usambiro, the C.M.S. station in Unyamwezi." An illustration in Ashe's book shows the drum between altar and font. By 1908 the number of drums had been increased to six and were housed in the porch.[21] Today the set of drums is kept in a special hut placed well apart from the cathedral. Pagan associations were not a monopoly of Protestants. Of the drums of the spirit Mukasa, Kaggwa records that the lake spirit's drum beat was like that at the Roman Catholic mission at Rubaga, where it was used to call the faithful.[22] The drum beats and their meanings give eloquent witness to the tensions of the earlier days.

If borrowing has been common throughout history, then conflict leading to tensions and demanding adjustment has been equally common. In more recent times, conflicting musical trends in Buganda have shown the ambivalent nature of

18. John Vernon Taylor, *The Growth of the Church in Buganda* (London: SCM Press, 1958), p. 220.

19. *Ibid.*, p. 221.

20. Robert Pickering Ashe, *Chronicles of Uganda* (London: Hodder and Stoughton, 1894), pp. 344, 351.

21. Charles W. Hattersley, *The Baganda at Home* (London: Religious Tract Society, 1908), pl. facing p. 205.

22. *Mpisa*, p. 216.

borrowing: on the one hand there is an enrichment of musical experience; on the other there is the shock of newness. Since the trends are criteria of diffusion and of musical history and thus concern this volume, three instances will be briefly touched upon here.

New trends become noticeable first of all in instrumental tunings. In 1948 an improved design of xylophone was constructed and offered to the Uganda Museum by Petero Kivumbi. The inventor did not aim at traditional patterns but at the Western major scale. He impressed his contemporaries because he demonstrated that these and other improvements could be incorporated in an instrument that was so essentially Kiganda. This trend is likely to succeed.

Then there are new attitudes toward speech and melody. Although the Luganda hymnbook had provided excellent material for many decades, there were also criticisms of the distortion that occurred between the sound values of the Luganda texts and those of the Western tunes. Awareness of the problem has been a stimulating experience to Baganda "Sunday composers." The stimulus arose from Professor A. N. Tucker's work on Luganda orthography, yet those who now enjoy the fruits of the experiments along these lines may not be conscious of their debt to him.

Problems of song lead inevitably to questions of vocal manner. It is difficult to discern trends of voice production and even more difficult to describe them. Two incidents might throw some light on the kinds of tensions that come to the surface in vocal manner in Buganda. The first occurred during a conference on singing, where it was agreed that *bel canto* was not in the Kiganda manner of vocal behavior and therefore was not pleasing. The other incident was the spontaneous exclamation of a Muganda prime minister on hearing a well-trained and beautiful European voice that it made him feel as if honey were running down his own throat.

It will be interesting to see how Baganda musicians resolve conflicting musical judgments in the future.

As the *endingidi* story shows, it is not only because of Western contacts that feelings are ambivalent. What is new to music historians in Africa is that, for once, not only is the finally accomplished conquest recorded but also the protests that accompanied it. In the case of another instrument, the so-called *sansa,* which consists of sets of plucked lamellae, the struggle is still on.[23] It is fair to say that in Buganda its association with migrating laborers may prevent its acceptance, in spite of the pleasure it gives to many people. The position is similar with regard to the braced gourd-bow of the Bakiga laborers, which, although seen less frequently than the *sansa,* entertains a few lesser Baganda chiefs.

THE BOWL-LYRE

No social prejudice barred the way of the bowl-lyre. If there were protests they were not recorded, but one can read between the lines that someone must have felt the competition that this newcomer brought with it. Kaggwa[24] remarked on the decrease of the popularity of the bow-harp and went straight on to praise the bowl-lyre's excellence without drawing the inference that the one must have occurred at the expense of the other, a point that was clearly made by Roscoe.[25]

The comparison between *sansa* and bowl-lyre is worth following in some detail. The original point of entry of the former into Uganda was apparently the Alur country. The Baganda have two names for the *sansa.* The older name, *akadongo k'Abalulu,* points to the Nilotic Alur laborers or to the so-called Alur tuning of the Acholi *sansa* (the root, *dongo,* indicates the Basoga middlemen who have become its most efficient carriers). The other, more recent name in Luganda, *likembe,* was presumably introduced by Bantu laborers from Rwanda and Burundi.

The bowl-lyre became known in Buganda as *endongo* or *entongooli.* The traces of its migration lead back toward eastern Uganda. Basoga musicians have definite views on the recent travels of the lyre; for example, one of the Lusoga terms, *Namugwe,* indicates the Bagwe (the eastern neigh-

23. On the *sansa,* see Trowell and Wachsmann, *Tribal Crafts,* pl. 78, pp. 327–28; on the braced gourd-bow, see *ibid.,* pl. 109, pp. 382–83; on the bowl-lyre, see *ibid.,* pls. 95, 115/a, pp. 400–405.
24. *Mpisa,* p. 277.
25. John Roscoe, *The Baganda* (London: Macmillan, 1911), p. 33.

bors of the Basoga) as a donor group. The migration of the lyre seems to have taken place over a period of a few generations rather than one of centuries. As to the date of its entry into Buganda, there is some doubt; some Basoga think it happened in Mwanga's days, but some Baganda assign it to Muteesa's reign. Both camps name the men involved and speak of their descendants and the circumstances of the transaction. According to one tradition, the ruler of Gabula chieftainship visited the kabaka's court accompanied by a lyre player and a dancer; their skill pleased the kabaka and he retained the artists. Kaggwa merely records the fact that the bowl-lyre came from Busoga, boasts that the Baganda had become even better lyre players than the Basoga, and adds—as an honest reporter of musical innovation will always be obliged to report—that it was of special attraction to young people.[26] Roscoe laments the obscenity of the lyre songs.[27]

Kaggwa himself was fond of lyre music. In 1896, when the Austrian traveler Max Schoeller exchanged presents with Kabaka Mwanga and with Kaggwa, the prime minister, the kabaka sent his own instrument, inscribed in his own hand with a dated dedication.[28] Kaggwa did the same, except that his instrument was of inferior quality. It should be possible to check the authenticity of the signatures; both instruments are pictured in Schoeller's book.

In Buganda the lyre is used both as a solo instrument and in consort with others;[29] Linant de Bellefonds saw at Muteesa's court, in 1875, a consort of six lyres, played by a group of Basoga musicians. The solo style is not unlike that of the bow-harp. On both instruments musicians seem to establish their fame by a particular song. Thus the lyre player Mundu was famous for his rendering of the story of the hippopotamus that killed Chief Namwama, who disobeyed the

26. *Mpisa*, p. 278.
27. *The Baganda*, p. 35.
28. Max Schoeller, *Mitteilungen über meine Reise nach Aequatorial Ostafrika und Uganda 1896–97* (Berlin: Dietrich Reimer, 1904), II, 178.
29. Kyagambiddwa, *African Music*, p. 108; Trowell and Wachsmann, *Tribal Crafts*, p. 404.

law by failing to carry a lamp in the dark.[30] In a similar fashion, the harpist Mayanja was renowned for his moving performances of *Ssematimba*. Mundu's playing was also notable for a technical peculiarity that distinguishes it from that of others: occasionally he executed arpeggios with the thumb of the right hand stroking the fourth through eighth strings. Data on this style of lyre playing are astonishingly rare.

TRUMPETS AND DRUMS

Even the highest patronage is no guarantee of acceptance and survival—as can be gathered from the fate of the bands of European drums and bugles in Muteesa's days. According to Thoonen: "Among the things which took Muteesa's fancy during the visits of Stanley, Linant de Bellefonds, and Emin Pasha, were the European drums of their escorts, and it was not long before he had begged or bought a dozen of the coveted instruments." [31] Muteesa employed a knowledgeable retainer, who had once been in the service of the sultan of Zanzibar, to train young men in the music of the drums. The drums were beaten "on festive occasions, such as grand levees and the reception of distinguished visitors." Cymbal players were also included. As to the bugles or trumpets, Baker remarked with glee how welcome they were as presents when he traveled through Bariland in 1871.[32] Mackay found out, to his expense, that they required frequent repairs, and he had something to say about them in the journal for 1879. Some of them were copper, and of English manufacture; others were of "native made brass." [33] Mwanga was as fond of these bands as was his predecessor, and he tried to imitate the music of the Zanzibar court. He had heard that the bands there were manned by Goanese, and therefore he created a court office, *kigoowa*, in order to establish his own "music of Goanese bandsmen" (the root of the word *kigoowa* is pre-

30. See Kyagambiddwa, *African Music*, p. 141, for text and tune.
31. J. P. Thoonen, *Black Martyrs* (London: Sheed and Ward, 1941), pp. 45, 47, 88.
32. Sir Samuel Baker, *Ismailia*, 2 vols. (New York, 1875; reprint ed., New York: Negro Universities Press, 1969), I, 403.
33. *Mr. Mackay's Journal*, entry for January 17, 1879.

sumably Goa).[34] No trace of the European bands and bugles has survived.

Contrary to expectations, the copper kettledrum with the gracefully bent, upright wires around the edge from which clapper bells are suspended is not a relic of this episode. It was already in use at the kabaka's palace when Speke had his first audience in 1862.[35] This drum is still occasionally used in the palace. Another recent innovation is the little frame-drum, *mataali*, with which Baganda Muslims accompany their ritual.[36]

It is common knowledge that the rulers of Buganda were exceedingly antagonistic to strangers who approached their realm from the east, but this certainly did not apply to music. Thus there is yet another musical institution with its own style of performance which could earn for itself the attribute *Basoga* from Roscoe's pen, namely, the sets of side-blown trumpets, *amakondeere*.[37] I have never heard them called Basoga but on several occasions have come across the term *Bamogera*.

The country of Bumogera is mentioned more than once in the history of the clans. Some informants said it was Samia; Nsimbi says it was near Kisumu.[38] Presumably, Bamogera is the Luo (Crazzolara spells this *Lwoo*) term for Baganda. As Crazzolara found among the Jo-Padhola, "these Wagende or Baganda are now called Jo-Magere but were known in earlier history as the Jo-Ngaaya, a very interesting reminder of the Jo-Pa-Gaya of Acooli [Acholi] and other countries." [39] Whatever their origin, they did not come via the mainland; on arrival in Buganda, Mubiru, the founder of the lungfish clan, announced to his people: *"Ffe tuli bantu ba ku nnyanja"*

34. Thoonen, *Black Martyrs*, p. 88.
35. John Hanning Speke, *Journal of the Discovery of the Sources of the Nile* (New York: Harper and Brothers, 1864), p. 291.
36. See Trowell and Wachsmann, *Tribal Crafts*, p. 375, on *mataali*.
37. *The Baganda*, p. 31.
38. M. B. Nsimbi, *Amannya amaganda n'ennono zaago* [Ganda Names and Their Meanings] (Kampala: East African Literature Bureau, for the Uganda Society, 1956), p. 252.
39. J. Pasquale Crazzolara, *The Lwoo* (Verona: Missioni Africane, 1951), pp. 320, 323.

(We are lake people).[40] According to Nsimbi, Mubiru gave
the task of blowing the *amakondeere* to his grandchildren.[41]
Another term connected with the trumpeters, *abakanga,* is
associated with a site, Bukanga, in Mmengo at which Mubiru
settled. There are similar words for trumpets in the Luo
region. The strange single, end-blown instrument *kawunde* is
blown for the kabaka by the *Mukanga ow'omu Kikanga.* The
history of the clans ascribes the arrival of the Bamogera to
the Kintu era; there are other traditions of the travels of the
lungfish clan, but they need not concern us here. None con-
tradicts the impression that the trumpets of Buganda were
carried by the Luo migration and that they entered their
new home from the east.

Presumably these trumpets had, at this early stage,
reached their full development in sets. Each instrument has
a name that indicates its place in the set. Some of the names
have a Nilotic ring, but these are aspects for the linguist to
study.[42] In my view, the Nilotic practice of using trumpets as
regalia was welcomed with enthusiasm by a people who
were mucn given to hunting. The sound of the animal-horn
trumpets is an integral part of the hunt, and, as I have
described elsewhere, the hunt provides an ideal setting for
the growth of concerted music of the hocket type.[43] Notes
are heard in isolation, from different directions; players
need produce no more than one, or at the most two, tones on
their instruments, and there are blocks of simultaneous
sounds over the kill when individual sounds need no longer
be distinguished.

To suggest that the form of the set as it is known today
was developed after its arrival in Buganda would raise difficult problems with regard to the origin of the Kinyoro trum-

40. Sir Apolo Kagwa [Kaggwa], *Ekitabo kye ᴅɪᴋᴀ bya Buganda* [The
Book of the Clans of Buganda] (1908[?]; reprint ed., Kampala: Uganda
Bookshop and Uganda Society, 1949), p. 38 (hereafter cited as *Bika*).
41. Nsimbi, *Amannya amaganda,* p. 260, n. 10; Trowell and Wachsmann, *Tribal Crafts,* p. 349, n. 3.
42. Trowell and Wachsmann, *Tribal Crafts,* pp. 357–58.
43. Klaus P. Wachsmann, *Folk Musicians in Uganda,* Uganda Museum
Occasional Paper no. 2 (Kampala, 1956), pp. 7–8.

pets and of other sets as well. It would be more consistent to assume that both Buganda and Bunyoro received the sets independently of each other in the course of the Luo migration. In this respect they differ from the *entenga* drum-chimes, which according to tradition did not reach their present full development until they changed from peasant spectacle to royal entertainment. I realize that I have been led to conclusions in search of a premise, namely the Bumogera origin, and, in order to return to a slightly less speculative level, I hasten to report that by Kyabaggu's time the *amakondeere* performed songs whose subjects and words had been given by no less a person than the king himself, whom the trumpeters accompanied during his campaigns.

THE ENTENGA DRUM-CHIMES

One more musical ensemble of great interest must be mentioned, the drum-chimes, *entenga,* which were also borrowed from eastern Buganda. A description of the drum-chimes and their history can be found elsewhere.[44] They were invented, according to clan tradition, at Bukerere in Kyaggwe, the east county of Buganda, and were first used as a village pastime. The *entenga* were used, for example, to divert the bleak thoughts of a man with a fatal disease—according to the song *"Munyi alwadde kookolo, leero takyawona,"* "Munyi is ill with *kookolo,* now he will not recover." [45] Munyi, a priest of the spirit of Nnende, became the patron of the drum-chimes. Nnende was known to have spoken Lusoga, and some say that he was a Musoga. Eventually the team of musicians and its drum-chimes were acquired in about 1800 by Kabaka Kyabaggu; he had become enamored of their sound during a visit to the court by Nnende, who had included the instruments in his own entourage. This pattern is familiar: the bowl-lyre, too, came to Buganda when the ruler of Gabula, now a county in north Busoga, paid homage at the court accompanied by his own lyre player and dancer.

44. Klaus P. Wachsmann, "Some Speculation on a Drum Chime from Buganda," *Man,* LXV (1965), art. 1.
45. Kagwa, *Bika,* pp. 47–48.

In Busoga, in the Nasuti area, people think that *entenga* was really borrowed from them, that *Lutenga* is in any case a word that denotes Lusoga speech (excluding the kind of Lusoga spoken in Busiki chieftainship). Further east of Busoga, the *namaddu*,[46] a set of six drums, of the Bagwere may well have been a precursor of the larger *entenga*. The Bagwere still play *namaddu*. Kiganda tradition specifically mentions that the number of drums was increased in later times. Is it possible that the earlier *entenga* chime was actually a *namaddu* set that was adapted to the playing technique of the twelve-key xylophone, *entaala?* The Bagwere themselves think of the *namaddu* as intimately connected with the xylophone, and indeed the playing of the *entenga* in Buganda is also compared to the music of the xylophone.

XYLOPHONES

Buganda in its earlier stages was a small country with its back to the lake, surrounded by regions that were largely the domain of Bunyoro rulers. The twelve-key xylophone, *entaala* or *amadinda*, is distributed today throughout these inner or original counties, but it has no traditions of foreign origin. Kaggwa[47] mentions three songs that Kabaka Mawanda asked the *entaala* musicians to play for him, presumably in the eighteenth century, one of which happens to contain the earliest reference to a symptom of treponematoses.[48] The *entaala* appears to be unique. No changes are reported, no stylistic evidence points to its neighbors, and no individual names can be cited to give even a semblance of historical perspective. Its most characteristic stylistic element, the *amakoonezi* technique, has so far (1962) not been traced in any other Kiganda performance.

The twelve-key *entaala* is not the only Kiganda xylophone. Another type, the *akadinda*, which in the 1950s apparently existed in only one or two specimens,[49] was in the care of

46. Trowell and Wachsmann, *Tribal Crafts*, pp. 319, 373.
47. Kagwa, *Mpisa*, p. 264.
48. I am obligated to Dr. A. J. Duggan of the Wellcome Foundation for this identification of the disease.
49. Trowell and Wachsmann, *Tribal Crafts*, pp. 319–20; Klaus P. Wachsmann, "Musicology in Uganda," *Journal of the Royal Anthropolog-

the elephant clan; *Namutalira* was the title of the official in charge of the instrument. This clan also acted as the king's herdsmen and participated in the initiation of a new king at his accession by handing him the flute, *takiwereza*, which once belonged to Kabaka Kimera—possibly in the sixteenth century—who played on it while herding.[50] Roscoe calls the *akadinda* "the King's musical instrument."[51] The localities to which tradition links the instrument are close together. One is the hut Nawandigi, above the river of the same name at the clan seat of Buligi, which the people described as Kintu's residence and the birthplace of the *akadinda;* the other locality is the clan land along the northwestern shore of Lake Victoria. In the 1940s, the elephant clan could no longer supply these musicians; members of the monkey clan began to take over.

Skirting the twelve-key *entaala* area in a wide arc are the larger xylophones, like the *akadinda,* with styles that are different. The arc spans the *akadinda* sites in the southwest, through Bunyoro, Buruli, and Bunyala in the north, and the Kisoga instruments in the east. With most of the larger types, three customs of the past are preserved: supplementing the sounds of the xylophone with ensembles of drums, dancing to their music in a manner now almost forgotten, and sacrificing a cock over the instrument. However, it is likely that similar practices once accompanied the twelve-key *entaala* also. An ancient idea of sacrifice survives in the words of the *entaala* song *"Nnyina Mukuma twamulya, twamukuba entaala,"* in which the monkeys sing "We ate Mukuma's mother and used her bones as beaters on the xylophone."[52]

---

ical Institute, LXXXIII (1953), 52. Some interesting and original theories are presented in Kyagambiddwa, *African Music,* p. 7. The investigation was repeated with the same informant, but without being aware of Kyagambiddwa's discoveries, by Gerhard Kubik; see "The Structure of Kiganda Xylophone Music," *African Music,* II, no. 3 (1960), 6–30.

50. Nsimbi, *Amannya amaganda,* p. 249; Roscoe, *The Baganda,* p. 147.
51. Roscoe, *The Baganda,* p. 147.
52. Personal communication from Nsimbi, May 19, 1949. I was able to record this song when it was performed by an *akadinda* ensemble in August of the same year. The players on this occasion simply referred to the song as *"Mukuma."*

It would be of great interest, but beyond the scope of this paper, to describe in detail the customs associated with the playing of the larger xylophones. It must suffice here to concentrate on one cluster of practices only. In one place an instrument of sixteen keys consisted of three groups of keys: the lowest in pitch, keys 12–16, were considered to be male; the central keys, 7–11, female; and the top section, 1–6, young girls. Keys 7 and 12 were the "leaders" of their respective groups, marked as such by buckles [53] carved on their upper surfaces, like the buckles of certain gongs or the keys of the *saron-slentem;* [54] The leading key of the "young girls" section did not have this feature. As the people in another village explained, there was no need for the "girls" to have a leader with this anthropomorphic mark since the leading dancer herself would at one stage lift up the first key and hold it high for all to see.

This is an ingenious argument; it draws attention to the importance of the dance, as if the keys themselves were dancers or the dancers were keys. The movements, executed in a counterclockwise circle, were gentle and shuffling, with slow and apparently relaxed muscular action, utterly different from the attack and tempo of the manner that prevails today—or so at least it must seem to the layman. As for the modern style, it demands "tossing the head, jerking the neck, making the chest dance, dancing as if walking slowly, and looking back as if in fright." This is a translation of a description by an indigenous writer of the dominant *baakisimba* style as danced by a kabaka.[55] The king of Bunyoro, Winyi I, is said to have asked Kabaka Kayima, in the sixteenth or seventeenth century, for an *entaala,* but it is of course not certain whether this was the kind of instrument known by that name today.

53. In Luganda the word *makundi* (plural) means both buckle and the large navel caused by an umbilical hernia. Sacrifices were poured over the keys of the xylophones, and A. Southall reports that the "use of people with umbilical hernia for sacrifice is at any rate common . . . to Bunyoro," and he includes neighboring tribes ("The Alur Legend of Sir Samuel Baker and Mukama Kabarega," *UJ,* XV [1951], 187, n. 1).

54. J. Kunst, *Music in Java* (The Hague: Martinus Nijhoff, 1949), II, 426, fig. 70.

55. B. Musoke Zimbe, *Buganda ne Kabaka* (Mengo, 1939), p. 319.

Winyi henceforth acquired the nickname Rubembekantara,[56] which may refer to a style of dancing to xylophone music. It implies walking slowly and putting the heels down first,[57] but these instructions presumably convey little to a choreographer. In any case, they refer to a dance that has been almost entirely forgotten. Modern agencies such as the demonstration team of the Uganda Museum may do much for the survival of instrumental techniques; so far they have done little to encourage skilled dancing.

THE ENNANGA, BOW-HARP

The word *ennanga*, if applied to the musical instruments of traditional Buganda, can mean only one thing: a harp of eight strings, with tuning pegs and devices attached to the neck that must be adjusted carefully to achieve the desired pitch and timbre effects.[58] The instrument has been the greatest favorite in the past, as entertainment for chiefs rather than for the common man. Perhaps the transfer of the name *ennanga* to keyboard instruments and the violin (but not to the guitar) reflects the high esteem in which these Western newcomers were and are still held. It is probably in this light that Kaggwa's mention of an *ennanga* as an early Arab import can be understood. Attempts to keep alive the art of playing the harp are being made by the musicians at the Uganda Museum, and interest in the harp has spread from there in many directions. Yet it still remains to be seen whether the art can be kept alive much longer. At the turn of the twentieth century, Roscoe was aware of its fading importance,[59] and the music historian of that period in Buganda is faced with

56. K.W. [Sir Tito Winyi], "Kings of Bunyoro," *UJ*, IV (1940), 78. *Entaala, endara*, and similar words refer only to certain Uganda xylophones and their immediate neighbors across the Congo border. Compare this with *stranatra*, xylophone, in Madagascar, and with *antara*, an interval of a single step, in Sanskrit and High Javanese. Compare also, on this, Kunst, *Music in Java*, pp. 54, n. 1, and 101.

57. However, note that in this context *ntara* may be "a cow with long horns extending sideways," indicating "walking in a stately manner" (personal communication from Dr. John Beattie).

58. *Ennanga* also serves as a term for trough-zithers in the region from Acholi to Ciga and in Ziba. Placed in the *ki* class, it refers in Ziba to the women's musical bow played with the chin stop.

59. *The Baganda*, p. 33.

the paradox that an instrument can be the favorite of a nation and yet lose ground at the same time. Did it require more skill and attention than the younger generation could give it? Had its art become so esoteric that in 1950 a country of some one and a half million inhabitants could raise hardly a handful of expert players? Or had the heroic style of harp music lost touch with the present?

Kyagambiddwa tried to explain what made the style of the bow-harp so different.[60] Furthermore, the traditions surrounding the instrument explain why its music was considered heroic. It is linked with a most moving instant in Kiganda history. Kabaka Nyakibinge, in the fifteenth or sixteenth century, had gone to Ssese Island because his soothsayers had told him that there he would find the man who would save his people from their enemies. When Nyakibinge set eyes on the chosen hero, Kibuuka, he saw a youth who "played the harp and had a birthmark on his shoulder." [61] The reference to the birthmark has survived in the name *Lugandankovu*, which a famous player, Ssebigajju, gave his instrument in the days of Ssuuna II. Kibuuka's instrument was called *Tannalabankondwe*, and it was kept in the temple of Kibuuka's spirit, together with other objects commemorating his person, until it vanished when the shrine was destroyed in 1893.[62] Among these objects were "two gourd rattles in the special care of a man called Tonondaba." The rattles were used "to the rhythm of the drum and harp on special occasions." [63] This kind of ensemble is unknown in present-day Buganda, but it existed in 1945 in the old chieftainship of Busiki in eastern Busoga.[64] It is perhaps noteworthy that Kibuuka and the official in charge of the temple, as well as the most famous of harpists, Mayanja, all belonged to the sheep clan, which, like the lungfish clan, claimed to have immigrated from Bumogera.[65] Whatever the

60. *African Music*, pp. 216–17.
61. Père R. P. Le Veux, *Manuel de langue Luganda* (Algiers: Maison-Carrée, 1917), p. 329.
62. E. B. Haddon, "Kibuka," *UJ*, XXI (1957), 118.
63. Roscoe, *The Baganda*, p. 307.
64. Trowell and Wachsmann, *Tribal Crafts*, p. 398, pl. 113B.
65. Kagwa, *Bika*, p. 67.

facts of the Kibuuka episode may be, according to Haddon [66] he was killed in battle shortly before 1576, but Sir J. M. Gray [67] argues that it happened either shortly before 1462 or 1492. Thus the references to Kibuuka's harp may possibly take the music historian back five centuries.

ROYAL DRUMS

No mention has yet been made of the royal drums and their origins. Their names and dates are linked with the long list of rulers' names even more closely than are those of other instruments and songs. It is interesting to note that Kaggwa listed the songs of Buganda according to the ruler with which they were associated.[68] The most economical arrangement for listing the drum data would be to set out a catalogue of rulers and drums in a similar fashion.

The drums most important for the legitimate succession of kings are *Ttimba, Kawulugumo,* and *Nnamanyonyi.*[69] Speculation on their combination as a group of special prestige within the larger group of regalia drums and on the significance of the frequent appearance of regalia drums in pairs, sometimes even coupled together physically, has been offered elsewhere.[70] It is interesting that *Ttimba* was brought from the northwest of Buganda, as tradition records at great length.[71]

SUMMARY

Thus the narrative of Buganda's history, viewed through her musical instruments, has come almost full circle. In several cases what may have been involved was not merely the simple importation of an instrument but the poetic and embroidered record of its institutionalization in some form. Who knows? The stories reflect the growth of a community, its ambitions, and its attraction to others. Is it in any way sur-

---

66. "Kibuka," p. 116.
67. "Kibuka," *UJ,* XX (1956), 54.
68. *Mpisa,* pp. 264 ff.
69. Nsimbi, *Amannya amaganda,* pp. 55, 289; Trowell and Wachsmann, *Tribal Crafts,* p. 369.
70. Trowell and Wachsmann, *Tribal Crafts,* p. 373.
71. Kagwa, *Bika,* pp. 48–49, 99.

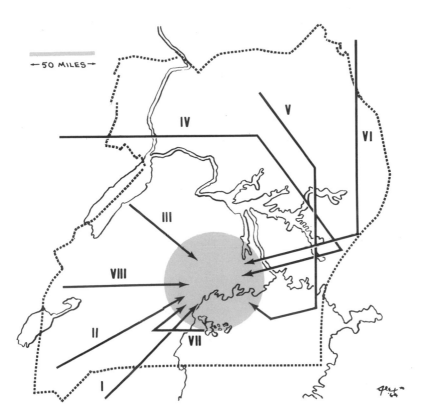

MAP 2. Uganda. The course of the arrows indicates the presumed paths of migration of musical instruments. The circle represents the ancient heartland of Buganda.

I. Bowed lute
II. Braced gourd-bow
III. Drum *Ttimba*
IV. *Sansa* (thumb piano) *aka-dongo k'Abalulu*
V. Trumpet set
VI. Bowl-lyre
VII. Xylophone *akadinda*
VIII. *Sansa* (*likembe*)

prising that so many of the musical instruments and the attitudes toward them are found to be credited to strangers, mythical and real?

Naturally, only those Kiganda musical phenomena which have traditions of their origin have been touched upon. (A summary of the instrumental traditions discussed here is shown in Map 2.) Bull-roarers, rock gongs, reed-box rattles, the earth-bow, notched flutes, children's songs, and others were all omitted for this reason. Some of these could no doubt be compared to similar forms of musical practice in other regions of Africa on the basis of stylistic evidence alone. Admittedly, comparisons do not add up to history; but, together with the hypothesis that at least a few phenomena are survivals from most ancient times, they deserve discussion.

BUGANDA MUSICAL INSTRUMENTS
IN THE EAST AFRICAN SCENE

Common sense suggests that it must be futile to speculate on the earliest music-making without the evidence of sounds, let alone to relate such speculation to East Africa. Yet prehistorians have dealt with an aspect of man's mentality which music historians have noted. If the tools of human beings "improved so slowly that 1,000 centuries might go by with only the slightest changes," [72] it is easy to see that these conditions might also have applied to man's acoustic activities. Whether the foundations of music lie in the psychosomatic make-up of man or are almost totally a matter of cultural conditioning makes no difference: The deeper one probes into the past, the stronger the element of stability in music appears. This view also makes sense if stated in reverse: The most rapid patterns of change in music yet seen are the most recent, namely, those in Western music of this century. Here change has become a trend to such rapidity and force that at long last it has become potentially destructive of everything that went before—or so it may appear to a modern observer.

This argument needed stating in extreme terms in order to account for the conclusions and premises that students of the earliest phases of music have adopted. On the one hand, they have felt that they should rely only on music that was free of Western influence or other recent developments; like archaeologists who hate to see their sites disturbed, music ethnologists prefer their material untouched by the latest and most destructive changes. On the other hand, music eth-

72. J. Hawkes, "The Arrival of Man," *Observer*, September 27, 1960.

nologists have searched for methods by which they could view their finds as an arrangement of layers—when in fact they know that no layers have been found. Three assumptions have provided such a method: first, that the centers of musical inventions are exceedingly few; second, that invention is rare everywhere in any case; and third, that the lengths of the radii of diffusion can be taken as the record of a chronological sequence. As Hornbostel put it, "The relative range of distribution indicates the relative age." [73] Sachs,[74] in 1929, and Hornbostel,[75] applying Sachs's findings to Africa in 1933, adopted these principles in the study of musical instruments. Hornbostel has stated the case in a clear and exhaustive way, and no more can be said here in its defense.[76] For music historians the system has from time to time provided useful working hypotheses, which have been borne out by observation at level A of Figure 21 above. Schaeffner,[77] for instance, found among the Dogon that independent evidence corroborated Sachs's sequences.

Yet the Hornbostel-Sachs strata and groupings are crude tools when it comes to the consideration of history from a closer distance and on a locally applied time-scale. The postulated primary center of diffusion is too remote and hypothetical, as a rule, to be connected to the local phenomena by a chain of historical data. Yet it is with these secondary and tertiary stages of diffusion that music historians in Africa are concerned.

How is a music historian to identify the secondary centers? The procedure adopted here is both naïve and desperate. Since there is no history—let alone music history—in the true sense, any musical information that archaeologists or anthropologists may find will come in handy if it promises a glimpse behind the curtain.

73. Erich M. von Hornbostel, "The Ethnology of African Sound-Instruments," *Africa*, VI (April–July, 1933), 148.
74. Curt Sachs, *Geist und Werden der Musikinstrumente* (Berlin: Dietrich Reimer, 1929).
75. "African Sound-Instruments," pp. 129–57, 277–311.
76. *Ibid.*, pp. 147–57.
77. André Schaeffner, "Ethnologie musicale ou musicologie comparée?" in *Les Colloques de Wégimont*, ed. Paul Collaer (Brussels: Elsevier, 1956), pp. 29–30.

AULOI *AT MEROË, AND OTHER REED INSTRUMENTS*

The first and indeed most surprising fact for music historians is the discovery that *auloi* (oboe-like instruments having, however, a cylindrical bore) of Corinthian or Alexandrian manufacture were known at Meroë in the second decade B.C.[78] These *auloi* are the southernmost musical finds in the Nile Valley and provide the only datable musical phenomenon connected with Africa until A.D. 724—for which date Schaeffner has proved the existence of Negro musicians in Sumatra.[79]

At Meroë two lots of auloi were found, one in the town site, the other in the northern cemetery. Statues of *auletes* (*aulos* players) add to the wealth of the finds. At the time of the more important find, dating from the reign of Queen Amanishakhete, 12–2 B.C.,[80] *auloi* had been played in the Mediterranean world for some six to eight centuries. The Meroë finds represent the most advanced designs and craftsmanship. The main components were metal and ivory. The bore was narrow and cylindrical. No reeds have survived. It has been generally assumed that their sound was piercing, like that of modern oriental reeds. Recently this view has been critically examined and doubted.[81] Presumably the *auloi* could be played in pairs and were blown with extended cheeks, possibly with the aid of the *phorbeia* and with different throat positions. As to the latter, Eichhorn's [82] description of the attitudes of a *msomari* reed player of the Shambala

78. N. B. Bodley, "The Auloi of Meroë, A Study of the Greek-Egyptian Auloi found at Meroë, Egypt," *American Journal of Archaeology*, 2d ser., L (1946), 217–40; Kathleen Schlesinger, *The Greek Aulos* (London: Methuen, 1939), pp. 78–79. I gratefully acknowledge the advice received from David M. Dixon, then of the Wellcome Foundation, on the material and the literature regarding Meroë (see also Chapter 6).

79. "Ethnologie musicale," p. 22.

80. Dated in accordance with Arkell's reckoning; see Anthony J. Arkell, *A History of the Sudan to 1821*, 2d ed. (London and New York: Oxford University Press, 1961), p. 158. See also David M. Dixon and Klaus P. Wachsmann, "A Sandstone Statue of an Auletes from Meroë," *Kush*, XII (1964), 119–25.

81. J. MacGillivray, "The Cylindrical Reed Pipe from Antiquity to the 20th Century, Its Classification and Scope," in *Hinrichsen's Eleventh Music Book, Music Libraries, and Instruments* (London: Hinrichsen Edition, 1961), pp. 218–20.

82. A. Karasak, "Beiträge zur Kenntnis der Waschambaa III," ed. A. Eichhorn, *Baessler Archiv*, VII (1918–22), 63.

matches with quotations from Kathleen Schlesinger's *The Greek Aulos.*[83]

In spite of the similarities, too little is known to suggest a link with any of the many types of reed instruments that are used today in Africa, and it is especially improbable that *aulos* practices from Meroë survived in any form in modern East Africa. The sources of the East African reed instruments have in fact been sought in quite a different direction. Generally one thinks of Arab countries and Arab middlemen, but Grottanelli, for instance, thinks it likely that the Somali double-reed *parapanda* is derived from a Southeast Asian (if not a Chinese) prototype.[84] He assumed that Indonesian seafarers made a landfall at the Somali coast before turning south. In addition to this traffic,[85] other agencies were involved, as Grottanelli reminds his readers: "The Chinese are known to have imported *zang* (Negro) slaves as early as the beginning of the 9th century," and in Jubaland he finds the *parapanda* exclusively used by "Somali ex-slaves of Negro origins." The fascination of this line of thought does not lie so much in the contribution to the Hornbostel-Sachs hypothesis of Far Eastern musical contacts as in the opening up of yet another vista of the complexity of East African music history: the diffusion of musical traits through liberated slaves. For East Africa the significance of these contact agents has been known since 1917, when Skene investigated the "Arab and Swahili Dances and Ceremonies." [86] Grottanelli has now taken the range of these influences well beyond the East Coast of Africa. The word *parapanda* was known at Sofala in 1586, but according to Kirby it referred to a trumpet.[87] Sachs [88] thinks of two different terms, *zummara* and *zamr,* and most

83. Schlesinger, *The Greek Aulos*, pp. 56–57.
84. V. L. Grottanelli, "Asiatic Influences on Somali Culture," *Ethnos,* XII (1947), 176–77.
85. M. D. W. Jeffreys, "Negro Influences in Indonesia," *African Music,* X (1961), 10–16.
86. R. Skene, "Arab and Swahili Dances and Ceremonies," *Journal of the Royal Anthropological Institute,* XLVII (1917), 413–34.
87. Pervical R. Kirby, *The Musical Instruments of the Native Races of South Africa* (London: Oxford University Press, 1934; reprint ed., Johannesburg: Witwatersrand University Press, 1953), p. 73.
88. Curt Sachs, *Les Instruments de musique de Madagascar* (Paris: Institut d'Ethnologie, 1938), p. 24.

East African reed instruments, including the Madagascan *anjomara*,[89] can be derived from one or the other. Trumpet and reed terms mix in confusion; for example, in Ethiopia [90] there are the trumpets *simbar* and the reed instrument *simbar matundi,* and Grottanelli [91] reports an oboe *simbar* from the region of Merca.

Turning away from the coast, one realizes that, quite apart from the Meroitic sphere of influence in the south, there may have been quite extensive contacts between tribes in spite of the difficulty of terrain, the complexity of tribal frontiers, and the local political barriers that existed between Meroë and the Great Lakes region. The history of the Nile Valley may give the impression of its being separated from the source of the Nile, but the musical instruments of the two regions have much in common (see Chapter 6).

THE BOW-HARP

The bow-, or arched, harp is a case in point. It does not occur below the equator except for spurious and recent transplantation. It served frequently as a subject in ancient Egyptian paintings and reliefs. In East Africa and the Sudan the instrument is characteristic of the tribes that the Luo migration affected, linking the Great Lakes with the Southern Sudan. The features common to the African specimens have been described elsewhere; [92] they are no closer to each other than they are to harp designs from Southeast Asia. Ancient Javanese reliefs illustrate pegs that are presumably immobile, like the pegs in ancient Egyptian examples. In the most Western harp in Africa, the *ardin* of Mauritania,[93] the pegs are strikingly small in comparison with those in the Nile valley. The need for short pegs arises from the technique of playing the instrument: the neck of the *ardin* rests against the player's body and his fingers pluck the strings close to the pegs.

89. *Ibid.*
90. Guglielmo Barblan, *Musiche e strumenti musicali dell'Africa Orientale Italiana* (Naples: Triennale d'Oltremare, 1941), pp. 72, 74.
91. "Asiatic Influences," p. 178.
92. Trowell and Wachsmann, *Tribal Crafts,* pp. 393–95.
93. Klaus P. Wachsmann, "Human Migration and African Harps," *Journal of the International Folk Music Council,* XVI (1964), 84–88.

Obviously, in this position long pegs would restrict the player's freedom of movement. The method of tying the string to the peg varies from tradition to tradition. In some cases it is laid in elaborate loops, which make subtle adjustments possible. (Does this allow certain general conclusions regarding attitudes to fine nuances in tuning in a culture?) Modern harps from Burma have a string attachment that relies on friction against the curved neck without having recourse to suspension pegs, but the instrument of the Karen people of southern Burma has genuine tuning pegs like its sister in modern Africa. Sachs, even in 1929, had looked to Asia as the source of this device.[94]

TUNINGS

Comparisons of construction lead inevitably to comparisons of tuning. Thus we become involved, whether we like it or not, in an issue that was first raised by Hornbostel in 1919.[95] He dealt with tonal sequences and tuning procedures in Brazilian panpipes which differed markedly from those that the West has come to accept as natural. The issue was that tonal sequences provided points of comparison over wide geographical distances and could be used for the identification of distinct musical cultures. From this it seemed an easy step to speculate on common origins. Hornbostel[96] was thus led in 1920 and again in 1933 to state that "[the] origin in Burma, Siam, or Java [of the African xylophone] is demonstrated beyond doubt by the identity of the standard pitch and the tonal system." By 1940, Sachs also did not think that certain similarities could be mere coincidences, and he accepted the hypothesis that communication across the Indian Ocean had been responsible for them.[97] He was wise in re-

94. *Geist und Werden der Musikinstrumente*, p. 145; Hornbostel, "African Sound-Instruments," p. 139.

95. Erich M. von Hornbostel, "Über ein akustisches Kriterium für Kulturzusammenhänge," *Zeitschrift für Ethnologie*, XLIII (1911), 60–62; Hornbostel to P. G. Schmidt, *Anthropos*, XIV–XV (1919–20), 569–70.

96. Erich M. von Hornbostel, "Xylophon," in *Deutsches Kolonial Lexikon* (Leipzig, 1920), III, 733; Hornbostel, "African Sound-Instruments," p. 287.

97. Curt Sachs, *The History of Musical Instruments* (London: J. M. Dent; New York: Norton, 1942), p. 239.

stricting the hypothesis to "instruments in a well-defined area of African Bantu districts" and named the Zambezi Valley as a probable route. Kunst supported these theories wholeheartedly.[98] Then in the late 1950s, Dr. A. M. Jones (see Chapter 4) revived the interest in Sachs's and Hornbostel's thesis.

For musicologists the thesis, once it has been stated, is less important than a sober assessment of the musical features that are involved in these comparisons. Standard pitch and tonal systems are not the only musical data handled by musicians. There are other features—for instance, in the xylophone practices of East Africa and Southeast Asia—that deserve just as much attention. Although they do provide circumstantial evidence for contact between peoples, there is no room to treat these issues in this paper.

The argument is in danger of getting out of hand—as is inevitable where musical discussion begins from an investigation at level E of Figure 21. To restore a semblance, at least, of documented historical consideration, I will now turn to three different sources, all from Ethiopia: observations on music by Ludolphus, published in 1681;[99] a series of colored illustrations in the Ethiopian MS. Or. 533 of the Revelation of St. John the Divine, of not later than 1730;[100] and James Bruce's letter to Charles Burney, in 1774, on Ethiopian music.[101] These sources offer an opportunity for a well-grounded discussion of East African musical practices.

DRUMS

To begin with the kettledrum, or timpani, Ludolphus finds fault with the Ethiopian priests because of the dancing and skipping in the liturgy, although he acknowledges the scriptural authority derived from 2 Sam. 6:14–15 of "David

98. J. Kunst, *Around von Hornbostel's Theory of the Cycle of Blown Fifths*, Koninklijke Vereeniging Indische Instituut, publication no. 76 (Folk Music, no. 27) (Amsterdam, 1948).

99. J. Ludolphus, *Historia Aethiopica* (Frankfurt, 1681), bk. 4, p. 6.

100. This manuscript in the British Museum was brought to my attention through E. S. Pankhurst, *Ethiopia, A Cultural History* (Essex: Lalibela House, 1955), pp. 185 ff.

101. Charles Burney, *A General History of Music* (London, 1776), I, 214–20.

dancing and leaping before the Ark with all his might." [102]
In the few references to music in the *Historia Aethiopica*, it
becomes clear that Ludolphus' informants described matters
that struck them as characteristic of their homeland in contrast to their experiences in Europe. Dancing to the sound
of the drums at the feast of Epiphany would have greatly
upset Ludolphus. At the extreme southern end of greater
East Africa, Sicard observed that among the Venda the drum
ngoma lungundu had ceased to be a sound instrument and
been assigned a role similar to that of the ark of the cove-
nant.[103]

Many writers have stated that drums in East Africa are
objects of political and spiritual power, and they usually refer to the drums of Ankole, Buganda, and Bunyoro in support
of this view. Certain drums in Ethiopia have individual
names; according to Ludophus, "their war like musick for
the horse are Drums much bigger than ours and the King's
which are the biggest, go by the names of *Bear* and the
Lyon." [104] The kettledrum has equally important functions in
some of the West African kingdoms, for instance with the
chiefs of Bussa.[105] However, it should be understood here that
drums often go by the name of kettledrum even though (1)
they may not have the characteristic "bowl- or dish-shaped
body"; [106] (2) they have a second skin, hard and relatively
nonsonorous, which is alien to the kettledrum proper; (3)
they are played singly or in drum-chimes instead of in pairs;
or (4) they are sometimes struck with the bare hands instead of the sticks.

There is a remarkable parallel between the drumsticks in
the hands of the angels depicted in the Ethiopian MS. Or. 533

102. *Historia Aethiopica*, bk. 3, chap. 6, pp. 87–89.
103. H. von Sicard, *Ngoma Lungundu: Eine afrikanische Bundeslade*,
Studia Ethnographica Upsaliensia, no. 5 (Uppsala: University of
Uppsala, 1952).
104. J. Ludolphus, *A New History of Ethiopia Made English by J. P.
Gent* (London, 1682), p. 218.
105. D. F. Heath, "Bussa Regalia," *Man*, XXXVII (1937), art. 91.
106. Erich M. von Hornbostel and Curt Sachs, "Classification of
Musical Instruments," trans. Anthony Baines and Klaus P. Wachsmann,
Galpin Society Journal, XIV (1961), 17.

(see Chapter 3, Fig. 22), those photographed on the steps of the church at Aksum,[107] and those used on the *entenga* chimes of Buganda. The beaters are thin, long, and curved, and touch the drumskin with the convex part of the stick. In this they resemble the drumsticks that are "hooked or coiled in the form of a bishop's crozier," which according to Sachs "still exist in Tibet, South India, Sumatra, and Borneo while they have disappeared from Europe, northern India and Persia." [108] Unfortunately it is impossible to decide from the data at my disposal whether the Ethiopian drums in this context are true kettledrums. If they were, they would be called *negarit*, a common term in the large North African area in which the true kettledrum reigns supreme. Barblan states that the Emperor himself was preceded by forty-four pairs of such instruments and that a Ras was allowed half this number.[109] Bruce informs Burney that they were called "*nagareet*, because all proclamations are made by the sound of this drum . . . [and] if made by the king, they are for all Abyssinia." [110] The illustrator of MS. Or. 533 could hardly have found a better way for emphasizing the force and authority with which the seven angels manipulate the universe than making them strike these drums. Bruce also told Burney that there were forty-five of them for the king—which would please the musicians in the region of the Great Lakes because they, too, claim that the regalia drums existed in multiples of nine.

There are other drums, both in the church and for the Emperor's music, that do not fit the definition of the kettledrum. Instead of a bowl- or dish-shaped form, they have a body that looks like an egg truncated at both ends, and instead of being placed before the drummer like kettledrums proper, they are worn in Ethiopia across the stomach, suspended from a belt over the neck or shoulder; the sound skins at either end are

107. *The Times* (London), weekly ed., August 22, 1945; H. V. Harlan, "A Caravan Journey through Abyssinia," *National Geographic Magazine*, XLVII, no. 6 (1925), 617.
108. *The History of Musical Instruments*, p. 157.
109. *Musiche e strumenti musicali*, p. 68.
110. Burney, *A General History of Music*, pp. 215–16.

beaten with the bare hands. This method of suspension and of playing the drum is like that of the barrel-shaped instruments of ancient Egypt.[111] Those also had convex sides, and their lacing was in an X-shaped pattern; they too were worn on a sling passed over the right shoulder and under the left one. Wild called them the favorite instruments of the Nubians.[112]

It is in the "truncated egg" form—with a more or less curvilinear profile [113]—that the so-called kettledrums are found in Buganda and Bunyoro, but they differ from their Ethiopian counterparts in the manner and in the position in which they are played. The customs in drumming represent a complex picture in which many strands between East Africa and Ethiopia cross and intertwine. With one exception that I know of, namely the kabaka's copper kettles seen by Speke, kettledrums proper never reached Uganda, but the practices associated with them in Ethiopia are sufficiently close to those in the interlacustrine kingdoms to make one speculate on the likelihood of cultural intercourse at some time in history. It is impossible to say whether it all goes back to an early widespread use of barrel-shaped drums or whether the far more recent true kettledrums developed into the "truncated egg" type, either locally or under some external stimulus.

A third type of Ethiopian drum is truly cylindrical; according to Barblan, such drums are played by Somali musicians.[114] They also occur as regalia drums in the city-states of the East African coast [115] but are not found in Buganda.

The idea of early widespread instrumental usages in both the whole of North Africa and the regions immediately to the north of the equator could be applied with some justifi-

111. H. Hickmann, *Aegypten: Musikgeschichte in Bildern* (Wiesbaden: Breitkopf, 1962), II, 43, 73.
112. H. Wild, "Une Danse nubienne d'époque pharaonique," *Kush,* VII (1959), 90.
113. Trowell and Wachsmann, *Tribal Crafts,* pls. 88/b, 88/d.
114. *Musiche e strumenti musicali,* figs. 19, 26, 58.
115. T. A. Dixon, "The Regalia of the Wa-Vumba," *Man,* XXI (1921), art. 20: "These drums are stated to have been made . . . about 1630 A.D."

cation to a more primitive and universal instrument, the percussion or concussion stick. Harvesters at the time of the fifth dynasty and Lybian mercenaries at the time of the New Empire are shown dancing with such sticks. According to the authorities of the Musée de l'Homme, "c'est à peu près dans tout le Sahara que sont repandues les danses du baton." [116] This can be said also of large tracts of the Nile-Congo watershed. The Pygmies of the eastern Ituri,[117] the Amba, the Lega, the Madi, and the Lugbara all use percussion sticks; so do the Ingessana of Dar-Fung,[118] and the Bodi and Male of Southern Ethiopia.[119]

The remarks on the percussion sticks are a digression that was provoked by the hypothesis of a widespread early usage north of the equator including parts of the interlacustrine region. It is defensible only because of the absence of data and other historical evidence, but at least it raises the issue of chronological sequence.

LYRES

The lyres present a more compact picture. Today lyres occur in the Nile Valley from Cairo to Lake Victoria, in Ethiopia, and among a number of tribes farther to the southwest. In the latter region and in Uganda, southwest Kenya, and northern Tanzania, it is possible to map their progress of migration to some extent and to link it with the movement of populations from the time of the Luo migration onward, through the era of Arab influence in the nineteenth century in the Southern Sudan to the latest diffusion of the instrument in Uganda. In the neighborhood of Lake Rudolph there is a gap some 200 to 300 miles wide in the spread of the lyre, which may be at least partly due to the material poverty of the tribes inhabiting this region today.

116. *La Vie du Sahara* (Paris: Musée de l'Homme, 1960), p. 75.
117. B. Costermans, "Muziek-Instrumenten van Watsa Gombari en Omstreken," *Zaïre*, I (June, 1947), 653–55.
118. H. Hilke, "Die Ingessana im Dar-Fung," *Zeitschrift für Ethnologie*, LXXXIV (1961), 212.
119. A. E. Jensen, *Altvölker Süd-Aethiopiens* (Stuttgart: Kohlhammer, 1959), pl. 21, no. 1 (Bodi); pl. 39, no. 3 (Male).

It is difficult, in spite of the compactness of the area of distribution and the uniformity of the structural elements of the lyre, to speak of a single style of lyre music. It seems that wherever the lyre was accepted it was at the same time adapted to the level of local craftsmanship and to the local taste in timbre and musical structure. Linguistically, several consistent terms can be quoted. As for design, there is the fundamental difference between the box-lyre and the bowl-lyre, which has a parallel in ancient Greece between the *kithara* and *lyra*. Like the instrument discovered in Ur, some Ethiopian instruments have tuning levers tied to the tuning bulges on the yoke of the lyre. There is a tendency in most places to decorate the terminals of the yoke, especially in Ethiopia and in ancient Egypt. As to tuning, two main areas can be distinguished: an eastern type, having a gapped scale that strongly suggests a common source for both the *bagana* type of Ethiopia and the *obuxana* type of the Luo with its cousins, the Kisoga and Kiganda tunings (and an occasional exception like the tuning of the six-string lyre of the Gwe) ; and a western type, usually with fewer strings tuned in regular sequence from highest to lowest note. It also seems to be represented in Ethiopia in the *kerar* type of lyre, which is simpler and smaller than the *bagana,* as was the *lyra* in relation to the *kithara.*

Whereas the ancient Greeks probably played the instrument with a plectrum, the African data are puzzling. Many lyres in lower Egypt and in the Sudan have plectra of leather or of horn; can one take it for granted that where plectra occur the strings are always stopped? Three out of five lyre players in MS. Or. 533 hold a plectrum in the right hand, while the left-hand fingers stretch out behind the plane of strings as if the finger tips were ready to stop a note here and there—or were they poised to pluck the strings as harpists pluck their instruments in the twentieth-century orchestra? (see Chapter 3, Fig. 23). Bruce never mentioned a plectrum. In fact, his linguistic explanation for *mesinko,* which he (probably mistakenly) cites as the Ethiopian term for one of the smaller kinds of lyre, is that the verb *sinko* means "striking a string with the finger," [120] that is, not with a plectrum. Plectra in Uganda and Kenya are freaks, and even the arpeggio technique elsewhere associated with the plectrum-cum-stopped-strings was seen only once in Buganda, and on that occasion the strings were played open. In Sebei a plectrum has been observed, but that was in a performance altogether inspired by modern guitar music.

Bruce has several interesting things to say of the lyres. They had five, six, or usually seven strings, whereas today the bagana has eight to ten strings.[121] Strings were manufactured by a process identical with that used in Busoga and Buganda today. Bruce also reports that he had "seen several of these instruments very elegantly made of horns," that the arms were made of the horns of the "Agazan, a kind of goat," but that, with the arrival of firearms and with deforestation in Tigre, the animal had become scarce. This, according to Bruce, explained why the fashion of naturally curved arms had come to an end, and was now replaced by "a light red wood . . . always cut into a spiral twisted form, in imitation of the ancient materials.[122] Modern *bagana* have spiral patterns carved in relief on the surfaces of the arms. In connection with this story, it is interesting to note that, in Madi and Nuer country even today, the straight wooden arms of the lyre have tips that are sheathed with the minute horn tips of a small buck.[123] One may also ask whether the *ebikuzzi*, tassels of long goat's hair which decorate the ends of the yoke in Kisoga and Kiganda instruments, have a similar origin. In most instruments in European collections the *ebikuzzi* are missing; their value exceeds that of the lyre itself, and they are usually removed by the musician when he parts with his instrument. Bruce's story may also explain, at least in part, why the artist of MS. Or. 533 painted his lyres in such curvilinear designs. Incidentally, the picture folio 18B of David on the throne playing the lyre has a fascinating

120. Burney, *A General History of Music*, p. 218.
121. The spelling of Ethiopian terms is according to Edward Ullendorff, *The Ethiopians* (London and New York: Oxford University Press, 1960), pp. 171–72.
122. Burney, *A General History of Music*, p. 218.
123. Personal communication from A. N. Tucker.

likeness that may indeed have a common source of inspiration in Byzantium.

The lyre also has strong zoomorphic associations in other ways. Bruce, for instance, calls the lyre *beg* and claims that the word means "sheep" in Amharic.[124] The ancient Ur instrument was decorated with a bull's head;[125] in ancient Egypt the heads of ducks were carved near the yoke, and the elaborate scrolls in other lyres may be survivals of this kind of figure. Perhaps the string-holder, in the form of an animal, in a Nubian lyre in the Pitt-Rivers Museum at Oxford also belongs in this category.[126]

On Asian soil the lyre seems to have fallen into disuse. Farmer says that "off the beaten track, in the Yemen and the Hijaz, the more primitive lyre or kithara (?) known as the *mi'zaf* was still favored in the tenth century. In Baghdad it was laughed at as a 'rat trap,' although Al-Farabi recognized it."[127] On African soil it spread in recent times farther south and west. The southernmost people reached are the Wagaia tribe of Ukererwe Island.

Bruce also mentions the bowed lute but has no local names for it: "[It] is sometimes seen in the hands of the Mahometans, but they have brought it with them from Arabia."[128] The modern name for the bowed lute is *masanko,* a word that Bruce knows in the spelling *mesinko* as a term for the lyre. MS. Or. 533 includes two scenes with players of bowed lutes in them; the instrument is pictured in the form and vertical attitude employed in modern times (see Figure 23). Thus the bowed lute must have been popular in Ethiopia before the year 1730, which is the earliest date on record of its occurrence in East Africa. Whatever the age of the instrument it did not share in any contact that might have taken place between Ethiopia and the regions to the south.

124. Burney, *A General History of Music,* p. 218.
125. André Parrot, "Nineveh and Babylon," in *The Arts of Mankind,* ed. André Malraux and G. Salles (London: Thames and Hudson, 1961).
126. Reg. no. 131.C.1.
127. H. G. Farmer, "The Music of Islam," in *The New Oxford History of Music,* Vol. I, ed. Egon Wellesz (London and New York: Oxford University Press, 1957), p. 444.
128. Burney, *A General History of Music,* p. 218.

TRUMPETS

The transmission of musical phenomena is highly selective. Although MS. Or. 533 includes the bowed lute, it has nothing to contribute on instruments as important as the trumpet. Ludolphus, in spite of the very general nature of his few comments on instruments, does say that "the Trumpeters and Hornwinders . . . have their particular Country and Mansions by themselves." [129] This remark has a familiar ring for people like the Baganda and others in the region of the Great Lakes. In Buganda as recently as 1945, royal trumpeters lived together as a group in at least one village, to which the local people referred as "the official residence of the trumpeters," *kitongo ky 'abakondeere*. They spoke of several of these settlements in different parts of the country and gave their names.

In East Africa, the interlacustrine region and Ethiopia have in common a flair for trumpet ensembles of more than two instruments. On the coast of West Africa, similar conditions must have prevailed if the reports of the first missionaries are reliable—but did these missionaries, when they described their reception at the ancient kingdom of the Congo in 1491, really have in mind ivory trumpets sounding in musical consort? At any rate the instruments were symbols of authority, and we are told that they alone could broadcast the death of a king.[130] In Ghana, a set of ivory trumpets reaffirm an ancient link with political authority at the opening of the parliament. In addition, sets of end-blown gourd trumpets play for the initiation ceremonies among the Banda.

On the coast of East Africa the large instruments, *ziwa*, are usually played singly, but their functions are similar to those of the sets. "[They] enshrine not only the strength but the spirit of the people." [131] In Zanzibar, says Ingram, in 1931 "the sacred horn was blown last, three days after the death

129. *A New History of Ethiopia*, p. 59.
130. A. Ihle, *Das alte Königreich Kongo* (Leipzig, 1929), pp. 59, 165–66, 169.
131. Gervase Mathew, "The Land of Zanj," in *The Dawn of African History*, ed. Roland Oliver (London and New York: Oxford University Press, 1961), p. 51.

of the Mwenyi Mkuu." [132] In the interior, single trumpets, often side-blown, occur in several places. They often belong to death rituals. One would like to understand the historical relationship of the various trumpet phenomena and to place the Kiganda trumpet sets correctly in the East African scene. Alas, apart from the clan traditions already cited there are no data even remotely like historical fact. In several respects the use of trumpets in sets differs from their use singly or in pairs. Yet at the same time, trumpets in Africa have much in common, and thus the lines of demarcation between the different types and usages tend to blur. One would like to distinguish the various elements that go into the make-up of the sets to relate these elements to trumpet types and trumpet usages in general, and to list their occurrences on a geographical basis. This was the method by which Sachs and Hornbostel, forty years ago, arrived at their groupings of musical instruments and at the sequence in which the groups are ranked, with an interpretation in terms of chronology. This is an example of a working hypothesis and of speculation at level E in Figure 21 above. A restatement of the questions here touched upon will now be attempted in the form of a diagram, Figure 24.

The *vertical strip* VII at the right side of the diagram represents the Kiganda sets and their interlacustrine cousins. Each *square* stands for a different cluster of features in trumpet usage, and the *circle* represents the reed-flute ensembles whose music has so much in common with the trumpets. The *levels* at which the squares and the circles are placed alongside the strip follow the sequence in which Hornbostel grouped the African musical instruments.[133] Thus I, at the bottom, occurs in Hornbostel's group 1, his earliest, universal stratum; II occurs in his group 4, which reaches from East Africa to Oceania; III occurs in his group 7, which reaches from ancient southwest Asia to ancient Egypt and includes the bow-harp and the barrel-shaped drum; V and VI occur in his group 9, which reaches from the Sudan and Arabia to

132. William Harold Ingrams, *Zanzibar* (London: H. F. & G. Witherby, 1931), p. 151.
133. "African Sound-Instruments," pp. 278–95.

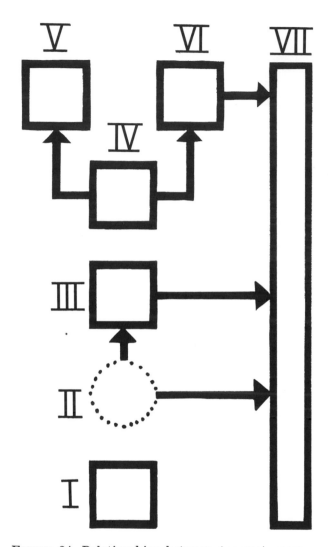

FIGURE 24. Relationships between trumpet usages

   I. Universal usage of trumpets blown singly, as a rule
  II. Sets of stopped flutes, the so-called reed-flute ensembles, played
      in hocket style
 III. Communication on trumpets during the hunt, on side-blown in-
      struments of animal horn
 IV. Trumpet usages widely documented in Asia
  V. The "sacred horns" of the city-states on the East African coast
 VI. Tall, end-blown trumpets, generally in pairs, of North Africa
VII. Regalia trumpet sets of the interlacustrine states

East Asia. IV, being non-African, has no place in Hornbostel's scheme.

The arrows relate some of the clusters to each other and indicate the direction of a "postulated" impact. Thus the interlacustrine sets, VII, are shown without links to I, the "death" trumpets, because no specifically musical link can be shown between them. The reed-flute ensemble, II, has been included in the diagram of trumpet usages because of the hocket style of performance that is common to both.[134] II also joins up with the signal horns, III, because the exigencies of the hunt demand from the hunters the kind of acoustic co-operation [135] that is characteristic of hocket. Only III and VII occur in Buganda. As for the function of the trumpet sets in East Africa as regalia, it is tempting to think that it was stimulated at least in part by contact with VI, the tall end-blown trumpets used, as a rule, in pairs at some North and West African courts. (It should be noted, however, that in the extreme north of Ghana the sets are funerary ensembles rather than regalia.) Ensembles of the tall North African type of trumpet tend to become larger either by employing more trumpets or by adding a set of flutes or conical reed instruments; they were also associated with kettledrums.[136] It now remains to comment on V, the *siwa* of the East African Coast. They fail to connect up with any other group and yet there are family likenesses between them and the others, and these may well point to a source, IV, common to V and VI but outside Africa. The diagram poses interesting problems, but it must be admitted that it may well be based on wrong facts and faulty argument.

The music historian who has been persistent enough to read this far may feel that there is not much fun in working on a jigsaw puzzle in which so many pieces are missing. The music anthropologist may suspect that the few pieces bandied about really belong to different pictures. In spite of these

---

134. J. H. K. Nketia, "The Hocket-Technique in African Music," *Journal of the International Folk Music Council,* XIV (1962), 44–52.

135. Wachsmann, *Folk Musicians in Uganda,* p. 7.

136. André Schaeffner, "Timbales et longues trompettes," *IFAN*, XIV (1952), 1475–76.

shortcomings, however, the quest for music and history in East Africa goes on. We certainly hope that this book may have added a few of the missing pieces and helped to identify the pictures to which they belong.

6.

A Note on
Kushite Contact
with the South

DAVID M. DIXON

Editor's Note: The study of music history in Africa has been much influenced by the hypothesis of its external roots in Southeast Asia, an idea that was put forward by Hornbostel as early as 1911. Dr. Dixon's comments, though made primarily in response to the preceding paper on traditions of musical instruments in Buganda, focuses attention on the Nile Valley as a possible internal source of musical culture in tropical Africa. This aspect has hitherto been neglected in the field of music.

ON THE *auloi* found by Garstang on the town-site at Meroë there is little to be said. For various reasons his chronology was badly adrift, and little attention seems to have been paid to stratigraphy. He does not even mention these *auloi* in his "interim reports" on the site. They were published by Southgate,[1] who does not, and doubtless could not, indicate their exact provenance.

Although the pyramid of Queen Amanishakhete had been plundered, there is little doubt that the *auloi* formed part of the burial equipment of this tomb, for they were found in the original filling of the stairway.[2] Judging by the size of the pyramid, there was an increase in the prosperity of Meroë at this time (ca. 18–2 B.C.). It was in this tomb that Ferlini in 1834 found the famous treasure which up to 1939 was in the museums of Berlin and Munich.[3] The reign of Amanishakhete's son-in-law and successor, Natakamani (2 B.C.–A.D. 23), witnessed considerable building activity in Kush, and Egyptian craftsmen were imported who revived there for the last time the dying Egyptian tradition. The *auloi* are only some of the many Hellenistic objects found in tombs of the time of Amanishakhete and Natakamani. Most of them arrived at Meroë either by trade or as gifts brought home by returning Kushite envoys to Roman Egypt. The *auloi* perhaps fall into the latter category.

The fragmentary statue of the *auletes*, however, is of native manufacture.[4] Though a rather crude piece of work, it is not devoid of some artistic merit. It is of friable Nubian sandstone; the player has been painted pink, or flesh color, and his instrument yellow. The details are clear enough in the drawing, but mention might be made of the puffed cheeks. (See the drawing on the title page of this volume.) The statue, which is now in the Petrie Museum, University College London (at present unnumbered), was found in the "royal baths"

1. T. Lea Southgate, "Ancient Flutes from Egypt," *Journal of Hellenic Studies*, XXXV (1915), 12–21.

2. Dows Dunham, *Royal Tombs at Meroë and Barkal*, Vol. IV of *The Royal Cemeteries of Kush*, 5 vols. (Boston: Museum of Fine Arts, 1957), p. 109.

3. Heinrich Schäfer, "Der Goldschatz einer Königin von Meroë," in *Aegyptische Goldschmiedearbeiten*, Mitteilungen aus der ägyptischen Sammlung, Königliche Museen zu Berlin (Berlin, 1910), I, 93–188; "Ferlinis Ausgrabungsbericht und Katalog," *ibid.*, app. 2, pp. 213–38.

4. For a fuller discussion, with photographs and reconstructions, see David M. Dixon and Klaus P. Wachsmann, "A Sandstone Statue of an Auletes from Meroë," *Kush*, XII (1964), 119–25.

at Meroë along with another, similar figure which is still there.[5]

Turning now to the question of a Meroitic sphere of influence in the South, attention was drawn some years ago to "a suggestive link between the lacustrine area and Meroë" furnished by "the striking resemblance of some Bunyoro milkware, and of ware found on the Bigo and Ntusi sites in Uganda to Meroitic, and especially late Meroitic, ware." [6] This Uganda pottery postdates by a considerable period the Kingdom of Kush itself, but there is no reason why contact should not have existed between Meroë and the Lakes during the Meroitic period (ca. 591 B.C.–A.D. 350). Here I can mention only some of the main points (detailed discussion will be found in my forthcoming study, *The Kushite Empire in the South*, from which Map 3 is taken). Between the Blue and White Niles the Wellcome expedition of 1910–14 uncovered at Jebel Moya a site contemporary with the late Meroitic period.[7] On the White Nile the southernmost site of a definitely Meroitic date that is known at present is Fiki Mahmoud, on the east bank about two miles south of Geteina.[8] But among the pottery fragments collected from a number of (unexcavated) occupation mounds that exist on both banks, especially from the vicinity of Jebelein at least as far south as Malakal,[9] are burnished red and black shards bearing impressed, and perhaps incised, designs of animals, birds, and plants. The impressions on the black ware are filled with red pigment.[10] These wares are clearly related to, though not identical with,

5. J. Garstang, "Third Interim Report on the Excavations at Meroë in Ethiopia," *Annals of Archaeology and Anthropology*, V (1912), 79–80.

6. *History and Archaeology in Africa, 1953* (London: School of Oriental and African Studies, 1955), p. 19.

7. F. Addison, *Jebel Moya*, Vols. I and II of *The Wellcome Excavations in the Sudan* (London: Oxford University Press, 1949); F. Addison, "Second Thoughts on Jebel Moya," *Kush*, IV (1956), 4–18.

8. O. G. S. Crawford, "Field Archaeology of The Middle Nile Region," *Kush*, I (1953), 26–27.

9. O. G. S. Crawford, "People without a History," *Antiquity*, XXII (1948), 9–12.

10. Anthony J. Arkell, "More about Fung Origins," *Sudan Notes and Records*, XXVII (1946), 96; Arkell, *A History of the Sudan from the Earliest Times to 1821*, 2d ed. (London and New York: Oxford University Press, 1961), p. 209.

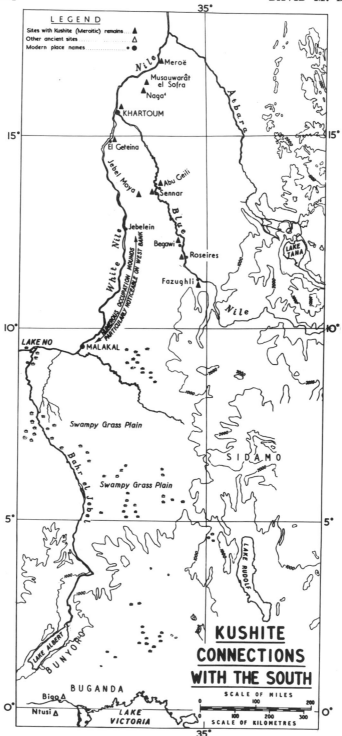

LEGEND
Sites with Kushite (Meroitic) remains....▲
Other ancient sites ....▲
Modern place names ....●

MAP 3. Kushite connections with the South

the black burnished ware with red- or yellow-filled designs found at Meroë itself and in Meroitic graves at Khartoum. That the Kushites were acquainted with the swamps of the Sudd is clear from the assistance they were able to render (in the form of an escort and letters of recommendation to neighboring tribes) to the Roman reconnoitering party sent up the Nile by Nero in A.D. 61.[11] Although the road directly south to the Great Lakes is broken by the Sudd, this would not have constituted an absolutely impenetrable barrier, and it is quite possible that a trickle of goods and influences did find its way through or around.

The main route to the Lakes, however, would probably have followed the Blue Nile and skirted the foothills of Ethiopia. Remains, dating from about the second century A.D., of a cemetery belonging to what was apparently a wealthy and prosperous community were uncovered by chance on the east bank of the Blue Nile at Sennar in 1921,[12] and shards showing Meroitic influence have been picked up on sites as far upstream as Roseires. A Kushite (?) settlement, dating perhaps from the second and third centuries A.D., existed at Begawi, some 50 miles north of Roseires,[13] and it may have been connected with the gold of the Fazoqli district.[14] It is probably not overrash to say that when, or if, excavation is undertaken in the vast area between Khartoum and the Lakes, the archaeological gap between them may well be considerably narrowed, if not closed.

11. Pliny *Natural History* 6. 29. 181, 184–86; Seneca *Naturales Quaestiones* 6. 8. 3; cf. W. Schur, *Die Orientpolitik des Kaisers Nero*, (*Klio*, Vol. II, supp. 15 [1923]) ; J. C. C. Anderson, in *Cambridge Ancient History*, (Cambridge: At the University Press, n.d.), X, 778–79, 880 ff.; L. P. Kirwan, "Rome beyond the Southern Egyptian Frontier," *Geographical Journal*, CXXIII (1957), 16–17; F. Hintze, *Studien zur meroïtischen Chronologie und zu den Opfertafeln aus den Pyramiden von Meroë* (Berlin: Akademie-Verlag, 1959), pp. 27 ff.

12. F. Addison, "Antiquities at Sennar," *Sudan Notes and Records*, XVIII (1935), 288 ff.; F. Addison, "Archaeological Discoveries on the Blue Nile," *Antiquity*, XXIV (1950), 12 ff.; David M. Dixon, "A Meroitic Cemetery at Sennar (Makwar)," *Kush*, XI (1963), 227–34.

13. J. D. P. Chataway and F. Addison, "Archaeology in the Southern Sudan," *Sudan Notes and Records*, XIII (1930), 259 ff.

14. Cf. G. A. Wainright, "Cosmas and the Gold Trade of Fazoqli," *Man*, XLII (1942), 30; Anthony J. Arkell, "Cosmas and the Gold Trade of Fazoqli," *Man*, XLIV (1944), 30–31; R. C. E. Long, "Cosmas and the Gold Trade of Fazoqli," *Man*, XLIV (1944), 104.

Islam and
African Music

7.

The Interrelation
of African and Arab Musics:
Some Preliminary
Considerations

LOIS ANN ANDERSON

I HAVE ALWAYS BEEN FASCINATED with the concept of Arab influence in African music, especially since this concept appears with some regularity in publications on African music. To find some bona fide evidence to support this concept is not an easy task. For one thing, since music in Africa is not homogeneous and since the characteristics of the music of any one African society cannot, therefore, be considered without identifying that particular music with a particular society, we may ask which African music should provide the test

Research in Uganda during the summer of 1969 was made possible through grants from the American Philosophical Society and the University of Wisconsin Graduate School. The author would also like to acknowledge the suggestions and help given by the following in the preparation of this paper: A. Lukwago, S. Kafeero, T. Debalkie, J. Snyder, E. Akarli, R. el-Khater, M. Rashdan, M. Partowmah, and J. Harries.

case for illustrating Arab influence. The music of Arabic-speaking nations is also very diversified, and it includes at least two different types: folk music, which is probably pre-Islamic in origin and is geographically restricted according to different ethnic groups; and Arab classical music, which is represented by at least three different historical traditions.

African communities that are predominantly Islamic provide a good test case for possible Arab influence. The *mu'adh-dhin's* call to prayer and the reading of the Koran, although differing in each locality where Islam is found, have been recorded in North Africa, the Middle East, and sub-Saharan Africa. In North Africa, Negro communities, composed of the descendants of former slaves, provide music for Islamic religious cults and are of interest for the study of our problem here. Does this music maintain characteristics of the area from which the people came, or have these people been influenced by the music of surrounding Arabic-speaking peoples? Countries bordering North Africa likewise qualify as possibilities for discovering evidence of Arab influence. Musical instruments said to have been introduced into Africa by the Arabs surely provide pointers, at least, to where research into this topic would be fruitful. In this paper I shall make some relevant observations and suggestions about the question.

One preliminary remark should be made. I have often been rather amused when students, on being introduced to non-Western music, identified new sounds with other sounds from their own experience of Western music. However, I also found this in discussions with European Africanist colleagues who had little or no musical interests; they too identified musical sounds from Africa with sounds from their personal experiences. For example, the resemblance of *kora* music from Senegal to Spanish flamenco guitar music has been mentioned to me. Do ethnomusicologists working with African music also try to identify a musical sound which is new in their experience of African music with sounds from another musical tradition, in this case Arab music?

"ARAB INFLUENCE" AND VOCAL PRODUCTION

On several occasions I have read record reviews of African music which described individual pieces as showing "Arab influence." Being interested in finding out what this influence sounded like, I have often played these recorded selections and immediately afterwards played an Arab piece to see if there was indeed, to my ears, any similarity. The first contrasting feature I found was the pitch vocabulary. A so-called Arab-influenced selection from Africa generally had a different pitch vocabulary from a selection from Saudi Arabia, for example.

Was it the type of voice production, then, which produced the idea of Arab influence? An example from Ethiopia,[1] which was cited in a review as showing "considerable Arabic influence," immediately reminded me of voice production as I knew it among the Kiga of southeastern Uganda. In this example from the Wollamo of Sidamo Province, Ethiopia, the singer uses a rapid syllabic delivery of the text on one pitch, accompanied by the *masinko*. A Kiga example, however, illustrates a rapid delivery of text in a descending direction, with the singer utilizing a technique midway between speech and song.[2] On the basis of these two examples, a case could be made for some type of similarity in voice production. While the Kiga have not had any close contact with the Wollamo, this similarity should still be noted.

I would also like to mention here that I once asked an Ethiopian (Amhara) interested in the study of his traditional music whether Ethiopian and Arab musics could be compared. His immediate reaction was that there was no basis for comparison. On further thought, he said that the Imam Ahmad ibn Ibrahīm al-Ghazī (nicknamed by the Europeans Ahmad Grañ, "the left-handed"), from the area of Harar, who sacked and burned Ethiopian churches and monasteries from A.D.

1. *"Masenqo* player, singing the News," *The Music of Ethiopia—Music of the Cushitic Peoples of Southwest Ethiopia,* UNESCO Anthology of African Music, no. 5, BM 30 L 2305, side 2, band 11, recording and notes by Jean Jenkins, 1965.
2. "Ruminyora" (*ekyevugo* with *omukuri* flute), tape 36, item 2 in the author's collection.

1526 to 1543,[3] introduced the *anchihoy* mode into Amhara music. The scale used in this mode consists of intervals of less than a semitone, more than a major third, a minor second, more than a major second, and more than a minor third.[4] My informant specifically emphasized the interval of less than a semitone, which might offer some basis of relationship between Amhara music in this mode and Arab music.

RELIGIOUS MUSIC OF ISLAM

In the recitation of the Koran and the call to prayer by the *mu'adhdhin,* there is neither a standardized method of psalmody nor any type of fixed music notation. Thus, the reading of the Koran and the call to prayer will vary according to the individual as well as from country to country. Yet one would like to ask whether there are any elements which identify aspects of this oral tradition and whether they are present wherever Islam is found.

From the beginning of Islam, there has been a controversy over the use of music in worship. In regard to secular song and instrumental music, authorities of the four schools of law declared that "listening to music was religiously 'unworthy' of a Muslim," while liberal theologians felt that listening to music should be allowed. In pre-Islamic Arabia it was thought that the *jinn* and the spirit world could be called up by music, and it was even claimed that some music was derived from the *jinn* and even *shaitān* himself. Both the pagan magicians and the poets, who were also soothsayers, "hummed and chanted their oracles and verses," practices which were forbidden by the legal authorities of Islam. Thus, it was necessary to make a clear distinction between music associated with Islam and secular music, in order to avoid the connotations of

3. Richard Pankhurst, ed., *Travellers in Ethiopia* (London: Oxford University Press, 1965), pp. 31, 35, 36; A. H. M. Jones and Elizabeth Monroe, *A History of Ethiopia* (Oxford: Clarendon Press, 1965), p. 82; Asa J. Davis, "The Sixteenth Century Jihād in Ethiopia and the Impact on Its Culture (Part One)," *Journal of the Historical Society of Nigeria,* II, no. 4 (1963), 569, 578.

4. Ashenafi Kebede, "The Krar," *Ethiopia Observer,* XI, no. 3 (1968), 159, 160.

secular music. According to H. G. Farmer, the term *ta'bīr* (interpreting) was adopted for the singing of religious music to distinguish it from *ghinā* (singing in secular life).[5] Amnon Shiloah gives a more restricted definition of *ta'bīr*, stating that it is used to distinguish the reading of the Koran from *ghinā* (singing), which was applied to secular music.[6]

In examining the recitation of the Koran, it is necessary to consider the history of the writing down of the Koran text itself. Variants existed in the readings and in the pronunciation used in recitation. Today, seven readings of the text (*qirā'a*) are recognized. Phonology of the Arabic language, which developed in respect to the reading of the Koran, affected the psalmodization used in recitation, since the text itself is the most important feature of recitation and rules of recitation must be followed with respect to the text.

During Muhammad's life, his scribes wrote down his revelations from Allah. The successor to Muhammad, Abū Bakr, ordered the collection of these writings, and the third Caliph, 'Uthmān (d. A.D. 656), ordered an authentic text to be prepared. When copies of this text were made, one copy was kept in Medina and three others were sent as standard texts to Kufa, Basra, and Damascus. Later, another copy was sent to Mecca. Differences in readings of the text persisted. The reciters of the Koran (*kurrā'*), who had the readings committed to memory, would not always alter variant readings even when there was a written text in front of them. The carelessness of copyists and the deficiencies of the Arabic script gave rise to unlimited liberty in reading. An attempt was made to eliminate the defects, and only those variants were allowed which were based on recognized authorities, preferably those who received their readings from successors of the companions of the Prophet. The art of reading the Koran, up to this time transmitted orally, was replaced by critical writings which dealt with variant readings.[7] At first, seven schools of readings

5. H. G. Farmer, "The Religious Music of Islam," *Journal of the Royal Asiatic Society*, pts. 1 and 2 (1952), pp. 60, 61, 62, 64.
6. "L'Islam et la musique," in *Encyclopédie des musiques sacrées*, ed. Jacques Porte (Paris: Editions Labergerie, 1968), I, 418.
7. F. Buhl, "Kur'an" in *The Shorter Encyclopedia of Islam*, ed. H. A. R. Gibb and J. H. Kramers (Leiden: E. J. Brill, 1953), pp. 277–83.

were recognized, then ten, then fourteen, and finally seven again.[8] Abū Bakr, b. Mudjāhid (d. A.H. 324/A.D. 936), chose seven men who were well-known teachers and declared them authoritative Koran readers, and, with each of these, two men were recognized as transmitters.[9] Thus, an official line of transmission was established for the readings of the Koran.[10] This had an effect on the actual recitation of the Koran since psalmodization, which was also part of the recitation, was passed on orally from teacher to pupil.

The seven recognized teachers are given below together with the geographical location of each school or style of reading and its spread to various parts of the Islamic world.[11]

Teacher	Location	Areas of Transmission
1. Nāfi' (d. A.H. 169/ A.D. 785)	Medina	Egypt, Tunisia, Sicily Algeria, Spain
2. Ibn Kathīr (d. A.H. 120/A.D. 737)	Mecca	
3. Abū 'Amr al-'Alā (d. A.H. 154/A.D. 770)	Basra	
4. Ibn 'Amir (d. A.H. 118/A.D. 736)	Damascus	Syria
5. Abū Bakr 'Āsim	Kufa	Most used in Muslim world, including Egypt.
6. Hamza (d. A.H. 156/A.D. 772)	Kufa	Morocco
7. Al-Kīsā'ī (d. A.H. 189/A.D. 804)	Kufa	Eastern Arabia, Iraq, various countries of Middle East.

At the present time, two methods of reading are in general use—that of Hafs, the transmitter of 'Āsim, and, in North Africa (except Egypt), that of Nāfi'.[12]

Rules of vocal articulation were established by As-Sakkakī

---

8. Si Hamza Boubakeur, "Psalmodie coranique," in *Encyclopédie des musiques sacrées*, I, 392.
9. Buhl, "Kur'an," p 283.
10. Boubakeur, "Psalmodie coranique," p. 392.
11. *Ibid., pp.* 392–93; Buhl, "Kur'an," p. 283.
12. Buhl, "Kur'an," p. 283.

(d. A.H. 626/A.D. 1229), and treatises on this subject were also written by Ibn al-Jazarī and Ibn Haddād.[13] Ibn al-Jazarī (b. A.H. 751/A.D. 1350 in Damascus), who had mastered seven ways of reading the Koran in A.H. 768/A.D. 1367, made the pilgrimage to Mecca and then went to Cairo. By A.H. 769/A.D. 1368, he had mastered thirteen ways of reading.[14] He set down rules which strictly govern the "prosodic vocalization and punctuation of the Qur'ān [Koran]." [15]

The melodic characteristics of recitation were not restricted and no attempt was made to invent any type of musical notation. The reading of the Koran has evolved gradually into a system whereby different types of recitation are distinguished. Ibn Qutaiba (d. A.D. 889) mentions the use of various musical characteristics at different stages in the history of recitation. According to him, recitation of the Koran was a "dirge-like cantillation" at an early stage in this development. 'Ubaidallāh ibn Abī Bakr, who flourished before A.D. 700, was the earliest "reader" to use melodies (alhān) in reciting the Koran. By the ninth century, the melodies of popular songs were being used.[16]

Si Hamza Boubakeur distinguishes four methods used in reading aloud or reciting the Koran by memory: (1) qirā'a, simple recitation or cursory reading (with or without text); (2) tajwīd, rhythmical delivery, accentuation of long and short syllables, and observance of pauses (with or without text); (3) tilāwa, recitation with inflection of the voice (by memory); and (4) tartīl, psalmody (by memory).[17] It is of interest to note here that Farmer states that the term tartīl is used in secular folk music to differentiate unmeasured songs from those which are measured.[18]

A further distinction in the delivery of the Koran text can be made in that qirā'a is simply reading from the text,

13. Boubakeur, "Psalmodie coranique," p. 396.
14. T. H. Weir, "Ibn al-Djazari," in *The Encyclopedia of Islam*, ed. M. Th. Houtsma *et al.* (Leiden: E. J. Brill, 1927), II, 372.
15. Farmer, "Religious Music of Islam," p. 63.
16. *Ibid.*
17. Boubakeur, "Psalmodie coranique," p. 388.
18. H. G. Farmer, "Ghinā'," in *Encyclopedia of Islam*, Supplement (1938), p. 81.

while *tilāwa, tartīl* and *tajwīd* are types of recitation which can be performed with the text or from memory. In recitation of the Koran the rules of recitation must be observed, while in reading (*qirā'a*) these rules do not apply.[19] The controversy over the use of music in Islam may be the reason why both *tartīl and tajwīd*, which utilize musical characteristics, are considered styles of recitation rather than musical styles. Recitation is said to be the ornamentation or embellishment of reading.[20]

Tilāwa is a generic term for the act of recitation which can be applied to the Koran as well as to other texts, while *tartīl* and *tajwīd* are used only in recitation of the Koran. The term *tartīl* is used for performing *tilāwa* (recitation) of the Koran, while recitation in the *tajwīd* style is considered a musical form of recitation.[21] In either of these types of recitation (*tartīl* or *tajwīd*), the reciter follows conventional signs in the text which indicate the elongations, pauses, and liaisons (rules of recitation), as well as the passages after which the reciter should prostrate himself.[22]

Al-Hussari, a well-known reciter from Egypt whose recitation of the complete Koran has been recorded on tape, specializes in the *tartīl* style. A restricted range, of predominantly a fifth, is used, and the melodic characteristics of each line basically follow a similar melodic outline. There is a steady pulse in a medium tempo and each syllable is given equal stress in terms of pulse as well as dynamics. For each new verse, there is a change in the basic melodic outline.

Tajwīd is considered "an art, the art of reading and of reciting the Koran to perfection, of embellishing the voice and of psalmodizing the Koran according to the rules and laws of phonetics" of the Arabic language.[23] The reciter who performs *tajwīd* exercises free musical interpretation and can produce great emotional response in the listener.[24] Certain standards of performance are considered essential for an ef-

19. Personal communication from M. Rashdan.
20. Boubakeur, "Psalmodie coranique," p. 403.
21. Personal communication from M. Rashdan.
22. Boubakeur, "Psalmodie coranique," p. 402.
23. *Ibid.*, p. 394.
24. Personal communication from M. Rashdan.

fective setting of the text in the *tajwīd* style. These include:
(1) *istrisāl*, prolonging the sound without allowing the
voice to drop; (2) *tarkhīm*, softening the sound without ruin-
ing the intonation; (3) *tafkhīm*, amplifying the sound in order to embellish it; (4) *taqdīr al'anfās*, breathing at natural
pauses; and (5) *tajrīd*, knowing how to go from loud sounds
to soft sounds and the reverse.[25]

Abdul Bassit, an Egyptian who currently is considered to
have the best voice in recitation, specializes in *tajwīd*. Characteristics of his *tajwīd* include a wide range of pitches, vocal
ornaments, melismatic treatment of the text, and a variation
in dynamics. There is no consistent melodic outline for each
line of text. A slow tempo and a steady pulse are utilized and
the stress of particular syllables by a longer duration produces a rhythmical organization of the recitation. Stress is
given to particular syllables by duration, intensity (dynamics), and melisma.

While I was in Uganda in the summer of 1969, recordings
were made of the recitation of the Koran by a Muganda Muslim. Islam does not have a long history in Uganda, having
only been introduced there in the mid-nineteenth century.
While the Buganda region in the south is predominantly
Christian, in at least two of the eighteen counties the majority
of the people is Muslim. I recorded recitations of the Koran
performed by a man who is considered to be the best reciter
in his community, Kitayita, in Busiro County. I asked specifically that the same verse be recited in different ways. The
examples given include two styles of recitation and a reading
of the Koran. Each performance begins with the customary
invocation to the Prophet. The first example, which is the
current manner of singing the Koran in Buganda, consists
of two melodic phrases, with the first sung at a higher pitch
level than the second; the first phrase ends with several
syllables sung in the same pitch, while the second ends with
a melismatic formula.[26] The second example, a simple reading

25. Boubakeur, "Psalmodie coranique," p. 403.
26. "Suurat Mu-auminu," recitation of Koran, chap. 23, by Mwalimu
Saziri Kafeero, Kitayita, Busiro County, Buganda, tape U69, item 6
in the author's collection.

of the text, is recited on one pitch level, with a characteristic ascending pitch on the penultimate syllable.[27] The third example represents an older style of recitation that is no longer used.[28] The first two phrases of the text (the invocation to the Prophet) are similar in melody, but there is more variation in the following lines, although the ends of phrases generally utilize one of two different pitches. In comparison with the first of these examples, more melisma is used and some vibrato is noticeable. When I asked my informant for terms to describe the style of recitation used in these three examples, he said that the first and third examples are different *tajawiti* (*tajwīd*) and that a further distinction could be made in that one can "beat time" with the first example, which is the current style used. The second example represents a method of reading the Koran.

When these examples were played to Muslim Arabs, an immediate reaction was that the reciter was non-Arab. The type of voice was cited as one difference while other distinctions were the reciter's pronunciation of Arabic sounds, stresses on syllables which would not have been stressed by an Arab, and stresses which were longer than they would be if performed by an Arab. Most listeners identified the reciter as African, and two listeners thought that it was a Sudanese style of recitation.

In both the first and third examples given above (i.e., the recited versions), a melismatic treatment is given to the text. This characteristic is not found in the traditional music of Buganda, and the presence of some vibrato, especially in the third example, is also foreign to Kiganda music. In an examination of the recorded examples of the recitation of the Koran (in the *tajwīd* style) and the call to prayer from various countries, a common characteristic is the use of melisma in the melodic treatment of the text. This is also a characteristic of classical singing by a soloist in the Arab tradition. This element has been incorporated into Koranic recitation and the call to prayer and thus can be cited as Arab influence in non-

27. *Ibid.*, tape U69, item 7.
28. *Ibid.*, tape U69, item 8.

Arab countries. In Buganda, as in other areas, one learns to recite the Koran according to the method used by one's teacher, and it is said that the style used in recitation indicates the sheik with whom the singer studied. In the context of one society, a valuable comparative study could be made of recitations of the same text of the Koran by the same individual on different occasions, by different individuals who studied with the same sheik, and by individuals who studied with other teachers. Further investigation could be made by comparing the recitation of the Koran in an African society and in the area of the Arab world from which Islam is said to have been introduced.

The recitation of the Koran by Arabs living in African countries should also be examined and compared with recitation from their areas of origin. Arabs in East Africa came principally from the Hadhramaut in southern Yemen. Ingrams states that there are a great number of Hadhramis from Shihr, the Tamimi tribe, and the tribes of Hajr province in Kenya, Tanzania, and Zanzibar.[29] On the East African coast, Arabs from the Hadhramaut, especially the Tarīm-Saiwūn region, established a religious domination and had great influence on Swahili culture, as illustrated by the "prevalence of the Shāfi'ite *madhhab* [school of law], methods of teaching and manuals used, the derivation of the content of Swahili narrative and didactic poems, traditional hereditary clans of religious leaders, respect for *Sharīfs* [those who claim descent from the Prophet], and many aspects of material culture." [30]

An example of Koranic recitation, presumably from Turkey (recorded at a meeting of dervishes in London but only identified as "Islamic"),[31] illustrates the use of different pitch material and a different vocal quality than in the preceding three examples from Uganda. Vibrato is used, and the melodic

29. Harold Ingrams, *Arabia and the Isles*, 3d ed. (New York: Praeger, 1966), p. 162.
30. J. Spencer Trimingham, *Islam in East Africa* (Oxford: Clarendon Press, 1964), p. 73.
31. "Suratu 'r-Rahman," recitation of Koran, chap. 55, *Islamic Liturgy: Song and Dance at a Meeting of Dervishes*, Folkways FR 8943, side 1, band 1, recorded in London by John Levy, notes by Martin Lings.

setting of the text is melismatic in nature. This performance is also in the *tajwīd* style of recitation.

Muhammad declared that the human voice was the most proper means to call people to prayer, and after this decision he ordered one of his faithful, Bilal, to proclaim the *shahāda* (formula of the profession of faith). Bilal had been an Abyssinian slave, whose master, Abu Lahab, beat him often because of the slave's attraction to Islam. Amer ben Khattab, a rich Arab chief who had been converted to Islam, bought Bilal from Abu Lahab and gave him his freedom. Bilal then devoted himself to the cause of Islam and became the first *mu'-adhdhin*.[32]

The call to prayer (*adhān*), like the recitation of the Koran, is not standardized in musical content. While it may sometimes be a simple chantlike delivery, more often it is melismatic in nature, based on particular *maqams*, although the Hanbalites, Wahhābīs (a puritanical sect founded in Saudi Arabia in the eighteenth century), and Ibādīs are not allowed to use any melody for the *adhān*.[33] The *maqams* used in the call differ from those used in the recitation of the Koran, since the former, whose aim is to attract the attention of the faithful, represent an external form of prayer while the latter aim to produce internal prayer.[34] Mauguin states that particular *maqams* are preferred for the call to prayer in different Arab countries: in Syria and Jordan, *hijaz;* in Egypt, *rast,* sometimes modulating to *sikah;* and, in the Maghrib, *rast-dhil.* In Turkey, the preferred *maqam* varies with the five different calls to prayer each day:[35]

1. Call of the morning: *saba*
2. Call at midday: *hijaz-ushak*

---

32. Bernard Mauguin, "L'Appel à la prière dans l'Islam," in *Encyclopédie des musiques sacrées*, p. 404; Nelly Caron, "La Musique shiite en Iran," *ibid.*, p. 430.

33. Mauguin, "L'Appel à la prière dans l'Islam," p. 405; Th. W. Juynboll, "Adhān," in *The Encyclopedia of Islam*, ed. H. A. R. Gibb *et al.* (Leiden: E. J. Brill, 1960), I, 188; and Bernard Lewis, *The Arabs in History* (New York: Harper & Row, 1967), p. 160.

34. Mauguin, "L'Appel à la prière dans l'Islam," p. 405.

35. *Ibid.*, pp. 405–8.

3. Call of the afternoon: *hijaz-ushak, saba*
4. Call at sunset: various *maqams*
5. Call of the evening: *hijaz, rast, beyati-ushak*

Caron says that, in Persia, *dastgah Shur* and its derivatives, especially *avaz Bayāt-é Tork,* are most generally used.[36] In the Maghrib, Mauguin says that by virtue of the ethnic plurality there is a great diversity in the melody of the call. While the call of the Hanifi rite is said to be a very ornamental melisma, the call of the Mālikī rite exhibits a severe style and restricted ambitus.[37] No information is available on the melodic resources of the *mu'adhdhin* in Black Africa, where Islam has been introduced in different areas at different times in history by various members of the Arab world or by Black Africans who were in contact with Muslims in the Maghrib.

Three examples of the call to prayer are discussed here, one from Upper Volta and two from Tunisia. The example from Upper Volta, near the border of Ivory Coast, uses repeated phrases in sections, with changes in the pitch level of each section.[38] Its overall range is one octave. The first example from Tunisia is sung by a twenty-two-year-old man.[39] The range is nearly an octave, more melisma is used than in the preceding example, and vibrato is exploited in the ornaments. While the vocal quality in the example from Upper Volta can be inadequately termed "forced," the Tunisian example reveals a more relaxed vocal quality. Another example from Tunisia is sung by a seventy-year-old man.[40] He uses a restricted range and incorporates some vibrato. Different voice qualities, as well as varying degrees of melisma, are found in each of these three examples.

In all the examples of Islamic music given here, are there

36. Caron, "La Musique shiite en Iran," p. 430.
37. Mauguin, "L'Appel à la prière dans l'Islam," p. 406.
38. "Call to Prayer," *French West Africa,* Columbia World Library of Folk and Primitive Music, Columbia KL–205, side 1, band 2.
39. "Call to Prayer," *Tunisia,* Vol. II, *Religious Songs and Cantillations,* Folkways FW 8862 (1962), side 1, band 1, recording and notes by Wolfgang Laade.
40. "Call to Prayer," *ibid.,* band 4.

general characteristics which are a part of Islamic religious
musical tradition? The melismatic treatment of the text by
African Muslims may perhaps be cited as showing Islamic,
Arab, or, more precisely, Islamic-Arab influence. However, in
the case of African Muslims, one would also be interested in
determining, by more detailed analyses, whether the pitch
material used in each case is, in fact, drawn from the musical
tradition of the society of which the individual is a member
or from Arab tradition. We have already noted the difference in vocal quality in the African and Arab examples given.
Does an African Muslim imitate a particular Arab *maqam* in
the call to prayer or in the *tajwīd* style of recitation of the
Koran? If so, would there be a certain limitation in musical
interpretation by an African since the characteristics of im-
provisation within the *maqam* system are foreign to him?
Or is there an emphasis on the imitation of a particular individual's interpretation which would be orally transmitted
from generation to generation?

The songs used at Islamic feasts and sung by the congre-
gation would be another source of examining Arab influence
in Islamic music within African societies. Do these songs
have characteristics which are more local or regional in
nature? In the Buganda region of Uganda, sets of different-
sized *mataali* frame-drums without jingles are used to provide the rhythm for songs sung by the faithful at Islamic
celebrations. The rhythms used are said to be from the "Swahili style" of Islamic songs. Among a group of former royal
musicians from Buganda who are Muslim and who are from
two interrelated families, one man plays the frame-drum for
Islamic festivities. Yet, with this group of traditional musicians, no attempt has been made to incorporate the use of
the frame-drum in traditional Kiganda instrumental music.
Has an African feature been added to these Islamic instruments in that a set of frame-drums includes instruments of
graduated sizes?

Other types of Islamic features in African Islam—including *maulidi* (Arabic: *mawlid*), poem recitals in honor of the
Prophet's birthday; *qasīdas* (praise poems); and musical
forms used in the *tarīqa* (mystical religious order) rites, some

of which are accompanied by musical instruments—should be investigated to see whether characteristics of Arab poetry and music predominate or whether there is a fusion of African and Arab. Trimingham mentions that in Swahili culture each center, quarter, and social class has "its own recitals of *qasīdas* and *maulidis,* its own dances, music, and amusements."[41]

What unique elements are present, if any, in the traditional music of those African societies which are predominantly Muslim? Are there musical elements from Arab tradition which have been incorporated? Or have the traditional African forms and styles of music prevailed so that a distinction is maintained in the various types of music associated with Islam and traditional music?

NEGRO COMMUNITIES IN THE MAGHRIB

The music of North Africa includes folk music as well as classical Arab music, with the latter being represented by at least two different traditions. While there is evidence that a modal system existed in Arab music by the time of al-Kindi (d. A.H. 248/A.D. 862),[42] some of the Persian modes, including their indigenous names and formations, were utilized in Arab music by the tenth or eleventh centuries. By the thirteenth century, the whole structure of the old Arab modes had changed, and twelve *maqamat,* six *avāzāt,* and subsidiary modes (*shu'ab*) were systematized by Safī al-Dīn (d. A.H. 656/A.D. 1258).[43] The new modal system dominated the music of the Middle East from Sarakhs (Iran) to Cairo and Istanbul, excluding Al-Andalus (Spain) and the Maghrib.[44] With the expulsion of the Moors from Spain, the Andalusian-Arab classical tradition was brought to the Maghrib in North Africa where it is still maintained today in urban centers while the older folk tradition is a feature of rural areas.

What effect, if any, did the folk music of pre-Islamic North

41. Trimingham, *Islam in East Africa,* p. 74.
42. Boubakeur, "Psalmodie coranique," p. 390.
43. *Ibid.*
44. H. G. Farmer, "The Old Arabian Melodic Modes," *Journal of the Royal Asiatic Society,* pts. 1 and 2 (1965), pp. 99–100.

Africa have on Arab classical music? Are the two traditions mutually exclusive?

The music of various Berber groups, especially those closest to Black Africa, should be examined to see whether there has been any exchange of musical features between Berber and African societies. Alexis Chottin, in a discussion of the instruments of the Berbers of South Morocco, the Shluh (Chleuh), distinguishes three "modes" and their respective scales in Shluh music: (1) the "Chleuh" (*darb aselhi*), which is autochthonous in origin; (2) the "Guinean" (*darb agnawi*); and (3) "makkel" (contrary, opposite). *Darb agnawi*, according to Chottin, has a distinct character, and he includes specific features such as its tonic, five pitches within an octave which can be divided into two similar, disjunct tetrachords composed of a major third and fourth, the use of an ascending formula at the beginning of a melody, and the frequent use of an "augmented fourth." [45] *Agnawi* is a Berber term for Negroes, who will be discussed further below.[46] Chottin says that the "modes" above are used by the Shluh and thus the "mode" *darb agnawi* may be direct evidence of the assimilation of a Negro African feature in Shluh music.

Chottin gives the tunings of the *ribab* (one-stringed bowed lute) for each of the three modes in relation to the tuning of the *lutar* (*gumbri*), a three-stringed plucked lute, in the Shluh instrumental ensemble.[47] The illustrations of the *ribab* and an older type of *gumbri* [48] show a flexible metal plaque, with rings attached, fixed to the top of the neck of each instrument—a typical buzzing device used on instruments in West Africa. He notes a special device on the *ribab* which gives the production of its tone a particular color: several rows of beads across the skin which sound when the instru-

45. Alexis Chottin, "Instruments, musique et danse chleuhs," *Zeitschrift für vergleichende Musikwissenschaft*, I, no. 1 (1933), 12, 14.
46. Fr. Esteban Ibáñez, O.F.M., *Diccionario Rifeño-Espagñol* (*Etimologico*) (Madrid: Instituto de Estudios Africanos, 1949), p. 16.
47. Chottin, "Instruments, musique et danse chleuhs," p. 12.
48. *Ibid.*, Figs. 1 and 3,, opposite p. 17.

ment is played.[49] This device will be noted again in connection with the lute in Mauritania.

In the Maghrib (Morocco, Algeria, and Tunisia), one particular musical instrument is found exclusively with those Negroes who are called *Gnawa* (Berber: *Agnawi*) or with masquerade figures representing Negroes who appear at celebrations of important feasts in the Islamic calendar.[50] This instrument may have been introduced by the Hausa during the slave trade when Hausa were being brought as slaves to North Africa. Made of iron and consisting of a pair of cymbals with a straight bar between them, this instrument resembles the shape of a dumbbell. One instrument is attached to another by a cord so that one pair of instruments is held in each hand and, in effect, four sets of cymbals are played by one man. A second cord is attached to the middle of each instrument for the manipulation of the instrument in playing. The last three fingers pass through the cord loop of the bottom instrument, allowing the finger tips to activate the cymbal part. The thumb in the cord loop on the top instrument holds the cord taut while controlling the cymbal part opposite that controlled by the fingers. The instrument may be held in either a horizontal or a vertical position.[51]

This instrument is called by various names in Arabic, Gnawa, and Berber, with variants of the Arabic and Gnawa terms being used indiscriminately by various writers. They are called *qarqaba* in Arabic.[52] In Morocco, Thornton calls them *tjaktjaka;*[53] Westermann specifies *tsaqtsâqa* as the

49. *Ibid.*, p. 12.
50. For a discussion of the masquerade figures of Blacks, see E. Laoust, "Noms et cérémonies des feux de joie chez les Berbères du Haut et de l'Anti-Atlas," *Hesperis*, I (1921), 280, 299–301.
51. See illustrations in: Philip Thornton, *The Voice of Atlas* (London: Alexander Maclehose, 1936), pl. opposite p. 94; Christopher Wanklyn, *Music of Morocco*, Folkways FE 4339 (1966), recording and notes by C. Wanklyn, Notes, p. 2; and Wolfgang Laade, *Tunisia*, Vol. II, *Religious Songs and Cantillations*, Folkways FW 8862 (1962), recording and notes by W. Laade, Notes, pp. 7, 8.
52. Edward Westermarck, *Ritual and Belief in Morocco* (New Hyde Park, N.Y.: University Books, 1968), I, 502; Wanklyn, *Music of Morocco*, Notes, p. 2.
53. Thornton, *The Voice of Atlas*, p. 94.

Gnawa term;[54] and *tiqerqawin* is the Berber term.[55] Laade uses *chakchaga* for the instrument in Tunisia.[56]

A possible Turkish origin for the name of the instrument should not be overlooked. Helen Hause believes that the Sudanic terms for calabash rattles (*segesege, seke, sekele, seke seke, asakasaka*) are derived from *shaqshaq*, a Turkish term, which she feels could have entered North Africa with the Ottoman occupation in the sixteenth century.[57] When the Turks ruled North Africa, the Turkish shadow plays, *Karagöz*, were introduced. Included among the characters of different nationalities in the shadow plays in Tunisia (for which there is the most documentation) were Negroes, who also featured in the shadow plays in Turkey.[58] Martinovitch mentions *shak-shak*, "a large castanet," used in Turkish theatrical forms.[59] Hony gives the meaning of *saksak* in Turkish as "a slap stick, a large castanet." The root word *sak* means a "clacking noise, such as wood against wood." *Sakur* is a rattle, and other derivatives from the same root include the connotation of noisy or rattling sounds.[60]

Among the Hausa communities in Tunis and Tripoli, Tremearne specifies the term *karakab* used for these double cymbals in the Bori possession rites. He says that they, as well as other instruments used by the Hausa in Tunisia, are an Arab instrument although he makes no mention of their use by the Arabs.[61] This same instrument has been cited among the Hausa in Nigeria, where it is called *sambani*. An illus-

54. Westermarck, *Ritual and Belief in Morocco*, I, 347.

55. E. Laoust, *Cours de Berbère Marocain. Dialectes du Sous du Haut et de l'Anti-Atlas* (Paris: Augustin Challamel, Editeur, 1921), p. 234.

56. Laade, *Tunisia*, Vol. II, *Religious Songs and Cantillations*, Notes, p. 5.

57. Helen Engle Hause, "Terms for Musical Instruments in the Sudanic Languages," *Journal of the American Oriental Society*, LXVIII, no. 1 (1948), supp. 7, 20.

58. Jacob M. Landau, *Studies in the Arab Theater and Cinema* (Philadelphia: University of Pennsylvania Press, 1958), pp. 40, 42–45.

59. Nicholas N. Martinovitch, *The Turkish Theatre* (New York: Theatre Arts, 1933), p. 124.

60. H. C. Hony, *A Turkish-English Dictionary*, 2d ed. (Oxford: Clarendon Press, 1957), pp. 330–31.

61. A. J. N. Tremearne, *The Ban of the Bori: Demons and Demon-Dancing in West and North Africa* (London: Heath, Cranton and Ouseley, 1914), pp. 281–84.

tration of a Hausa woman in Nigeria playing it is the only reference to its being played by a woman.[62] It should also be noted that *ba-sambani* in Hausa (the prefix indicating occupation) refers to a slave of Arab traders.[63]

The Negro Muslim cults of the Maghrib are called Gnawa or, in Berber, Agnawi,[64] a term said to be derived from Guinea. Negroes came as slaves to Tunisia by two different routes: from the Eastern Sudan and Fezzan via Ghadames or Tripoli; and from the Western Sudan and Guinea to the oasis of Tozeur, where they were sold to merchants of the north and then brought to Béja, where they were sold to Tunis and its vicinity. Those from the Eastern Sudan and Fezzan are now found in the region of Medinine and Gabes in southeastern Tunisia, where they consider themselves subtribes of their former masters' tribe. Such groups as the Hamruni in Gabes region and the Ghebunten in Medinine region are quite isolated in the desert, and their music and dances are said to be very little influenced by their "Arab surrounding." Negroes found in other regions are scattered and do not form tribal communities of their own but are united under the guise of Islam in the form of Muslim cults called Gnawa. The cults were formed from the groups which came via Tozeur, and these people and the same institutions are also found in Algeria and Morocco.[65]

The patron of the Tunisian Gnawa is Sīdi Marzūq, according to Laade, and an annual celebration is held at his tomb at Tozeur and also at Nefta. The language used in the ritual songs of the Gnawa is said to be neither Arabic nor Berber; it is called *ajmi* (an Arabic term meaning foreign) by the Tunisian Negroes, who no longer know its origin. The songs are in response form, with a leader and chorus.[66] In a recording of Gnawa cult music of the "Msarha" type for Sīdi Marzūq at Nefta, the leader of the group plays the *benga* drum,

62. Akin Euba, "Preface to a Study of Nigerian Music," *Ibadan*, XXII (1965), 54.
63. G. P. Bargery, *A Hausa-English Dictionary and English-Hausa Vocabulary* (London: Oxford University Press, 1934), p. 91.
64. Ibáñez, *Diccionario Rifeño-Espagñol*, p. 16.
65. Laade, *Tunisia*, Vol. II, *Religious Songs and Cantillations*, Notes, p. 4.
66. *Ibid.*, pp. 4–5.

a cylindrical drum with two laced heads, played with one stick and the hand. There is an introductory pattern on the drum; then the drum and *chakchagas* (double cymbals), played by the chorus, are heard in unison with the same rhythmic pattern. A second *benga* drum is also used. The singing is inaudible in this recording.[67]

Stambali ("reunion" or "gathering"), as gatherings of Gnawa celebrants are called, is held on Friday, at *mawlid* (a feast celebrating the birth of the Prophet) functions and at weddings, in addition to the annual celebration at the Saint's tomb.[68] In a recorded example of *stambali* music from Béja, an introduction is given by a bowed lute, followed by the entrance of the *chakchagas,* the solo singer and then the responding singer who plays the *tabl* drum. At first the bowed lute answers the soloist and then drops out when the responding singer enters. The same melodic line is repeated by the soloist and responding singer. The leader of the group here is the principal singer, who plays the *chakchagas* in a steady pulse. The drumming resembles Arab drumming in that two different pitches, resembling the low *dum* and the high *tek,* are used in a simple rhythmic pattern which is maintained throughout.[69]

The ritual music and dancing of the Gnawa religious cult is much in demand by Moroccans for the exorcizing of *jnūn,* the purification of houses after death, and at weddings and festivals. Legey gives a description of exorcizing in which the musicians (the leader plays the *gembri* lute, and others the *qarqaba* cymbals) play an important part. The instruments are incensed during the ceremony, and drops of milk are rubbed on the *gembri* and *qarqaba.* The patient, in response to the singing, dancing, incense, and perfumes, begins to dance while the musicians make a "deafening din" to drive out the evil spirits.[70] Westermarck gives a description of ex-

67. *Ibid.,* side 2, band 3.
68. *Ibid.,* Notes, p. 4.
69. *Ibid.,* side 2, band 2.
70. Dr. Françoise Legey, *The Folklore of Morocco,* trans. Lucy Hotz (London: George Allen & Unwin, 1935), pp. 207–9.

pelling *jnūn* from a sick female in the course of which a group of female Gnawa play *agwal* drums, *bendīr* (frame-drums), and *ganga* (Westermarck says this is the Gnawa term for the small, two-stringed *gembri* lute,[71] while Grame reserves *ganga* for the Gnawa term for a drum).[72] In a description of a Gnawa performance to cure a sick person at Tangier, Westermarck says that two large drums (*t-tabel de gnawa*) and many iron cymbals (*tsaqtsâqa*) are used.[73]

Commercial recordings of Gnawa from Morocco are usually from the Jmā al-Fna Plaza in Marrakesh, where various types of music and theater are performed. In one recording, there are four *tabl* drums, each struck with a pair of curved sticks, and at least four players of *qarqaba* cymbals.[74] While the *qarqaba* maintain a steady pulse, one drum introduces an additive rhythmic pattern which is reminiscent of a pattern found in Ghana, but which may be similar to an Arab or Berber pattern or reserved for the Gnawa. The other drums play a steady pulse at a higher pitch. The rhythmic variation in the main drum part also suggests the freedom exemplified by the master drummer in West African drum ensembles. Midway in the recording the main drum and the *qarqaba* play rhythmic patterns in unison, separated by rests, while the other drummers maintain a steady, fast pulse.

An example recorded by C. Wanklyn at the *mawsim* (annual feast at saint's shrine) of Mulai Ibrahim at Asni in the Grand Atlas Mountains is called *Ah'ouach,* the term for a Berber dance.[75] The instruments used include *bnader* (singular: *bendir*), frame-drums and *quarqaba.* Female singers repeat the same two melodic phrases while the cymbals and frame-drums play a simple rhythmic phrase in unison, high and low pitches being used on the drums. The performers may be Gnawa, although they are not mentioned in the notes. Westermarck says

---

71. Westermarck, *Ritual and Belief in Morocco,* I, 345–47.
72. Theodore C. Grame, "Music in the Jmā al-Fna of Marrakesh," *Musical Quarterly,* LVI, no. 1 (1970), p. 79.
73. Westermarck, *Ritual and Belief in Morocco,* I, 347.
74. Wanklyn, *Music of Morocco,* side 1, band 2.
75. *Ibid.,* side 2, band 4.

that the Gnawa are among the groups who entertain people at a feast of a Muslim saint.[76]

Gnawa or masquerade figures representing them are a feature of important feasts during the Islamic year. A performance called *bsāt,* arranged by the Sultan's soldiers on the eve of *Asūr* (the tenth day of the first month of the Islamic calendar) and performed before the Sultan in Fez, includes the performance of Gnawa and the use of *qarqaba* cymbals. An essential feature of the performance is a large replica of a saint's tomb, *bsāt* (which gives its name to the celebration), carried by the soldiers. The procession which follows the miniature replica of the tomb includes a large number of persons dressed up as different kinds of people, spirits, animals, and other objects. Included in the groups of musicians in the procession are twenty to thirty *mwalīn d-daqqa* with *bnader* (plain frame-drums), *agwālāt* (short clay cylinders with skin), and *qarqaba* (cymbals) ; and some Gnawa, one with a *handqa* (the Fez name for the small two-stringed lute) and the others with *qarqaba.* When the group visits a house, the *bsāt* is carried in first; then the masqueraders enter in separate groups and perform. The different figures are soldiers or hired performers.[77]

The appearance of these masqueraders during the month of Asūr, as well as during other important feasts of the Islamic year, have been recorded from other parts of southern Morocco, from Algeria, and from Tunis.[78] Tremearne says that the masquerades are mainly performed by Arabs, and the only one in which the Hausas in North Africa take part is the *Bu Sadiya,* in which a man dresses up in a mask decorated with birds' feathers and wears vulture wings on his shoulders and a coat made of various skins. He says that the masquerade which is performed at the *Babbar Salla,* or Great Prayer (and feast), the tenth day of *Dhul Hajj* in North and West Africa, may take place at any time, the main purpose

76. Westermarck, *Ritual and Belief in Morocco,* I, 177.
77. *Ibid.,* II, 81–83.
78. *Ibid.,* II, 83–85, 133–47; Laoust, "Noms et cérémonies des feux de joie," pp. 280, 299–301.

being to take a collection from the spectators. In his illustration of the *Bu Sadiya* figure, the masquerader carries the iron cymbals, as do two of his companions, while the third companion carries a *gimbiri* lute.[79]

The use of double iron cymbals by the Gnawa in the Maghrib poses a problem for further investigation. Anthony King, in a personal communication to me, says that among the Hausa in Nigeria this instrument is always played by women for semi-religious songs on the occasion of major and some minor religious feasts. He also indicates that it is probably of non-Hausa origin. Instruments played by women in African societies are usually never played by men, and vice versa. However, in the Maghrib, these cymbals are played only by men and are an important feature of Bori possession rites. Yet the instrument is not used for the same rites in Nigeria. The question arises whether the opposition of sex of the players of this instrument in the Maghrib and Nigeria, as well as the use of the instrument for Bori rites in the Maghrib and the exclusion of it for similar rites in Nigeria, indicates the possibility of different sources for the instrument in each area.

Rouanet, in his article on the music of the Maghrib, says that the *qarqaba* (cymbal) players at Laghouat in southern Algeria distinguish three different types of rhythms: eastern, northern, and western. He says that the instrument is used frequently in regions near the desert and that it was imported by Negroes of Gouarara and the Sudan, who have kept it as a specialty. In his list of Maghrib ensembles, Negro festivities in Algeria include the use of frame-drums (*taria*) and *qarqaba* in Biskra and Algiers, dancers with *qarqaba* in Gouarara, and *qarqaba* and *gembri* (lute) in Algiers.[80]

Rouanet also notes that *schenachek* is the term used for a pair of small metal cymbals attached to a forked stick, which is held in the hand. They are used in street diversions, espe-

79. Tremearne, *The Ban of the Bori*, pp. 235, 241, pl. 27 opposite p. 40.
80. Jules Rouanet, "La Musique dans le Maghrib," in *Encyclopédie de la musique*, ed. A. Lavignac (Paris: Librairie Delagrave, 1922), V, 2910, 2936, 2937.

cially by Negroes.[81] Sachs says that these cymbal-clappers were used during the late Coptic epoch (A.D. 324–640) in Egypt.[82]

MUSIC AND POETRY IN MAURITANIA

In Mauritania, there is definite evidence in musical tradition to show the influence of Black Africa on Moorish music. The Moors say that the "white" contribution is the distinction of four musical modes, while the "black" contribution is the division into two artistic styles. Moorish scholars agree on a recent origin for Moorish poetry and vocal music. Among those who codified the tradition, one of the earliest and most celebrated is Ali Uld Manu, ancestor of the present Manu *griots*. He was the personal *griot* of Ali Chandora (emir of Trarza, who died in 1727). Later, the Blacks also contributed to the form of present Moorish music. Ali Waraka, of Wolof origin, and Ehl Bubhan, of Toucouleur origin, both from Trarza, are the best known, and their descendants are still considered among the famous singers.[83]

For the Shinqiti Arabs, Saddim Wult Njartu is credited with joining the *qasida* form to a new musical style divided into two aspects, one "white," Arab in origin, and the other "black," inspired and influenced by Negro music from the east and from across the Senegal River. In addition to introducing the Sudanic form of singing, Saddim is also noted for his systemization of poetic meter and rhyme.[84]

Lekhal, the black "way" or "road," is said to be coarser and stronger than *lebiadh*, the white "way." It is said to be forced and is characterized by the frequent elongation of

81. Jules Rouanet, "La Musique arabe," *ibid.*, V, 2793; see illustration in *Die Musik in Geschichte und Gegenwart*, VII (Kassel: Bärenreiter, 1958), pl. 41, fig. 2.

82. Curt Sachs, *The History of Musical Instruments* (New York: Norton, 1940), p. 104.

83. G. Balandier and P. Mercier, "Notes sur les théories musicales maures à propos de chants enregistrés," in *International West African Conference, II, Bissau, 1947* (Lisbon: Ministério das Colónias, Junta de Investigacões Coloniais, 1952), V, 140, 138.

84. H. T. Norris, *Shinqiti Folk Literature and Song* (London: Oxford University Press, 1968), pp. 36, 55.

pitches. It is considered to be the easiest to perform. The white way, *lebiadh,* is the most subtle and is considered the "road" of the masters.[85]

Each of the four Moorish modes can be expressed in either the black or the white style, while only one of these modes, *signim,* is used in the intermediate style, *zrag,* which is said to incorporate qualities of both the white and black styles.[86]

In two examples, the first being the *senai kerr* mode of the black way [87] and the second being *Vagho arraisruz* in the white way,[88] one notes the different pitch vocabularies used, the different tunings of the *tidinit* lute, and the greater use of vibrato in the second example. It is apparent that an in-depth study of these traditions would be necessary to define the characteristics of each of the four Moorish modes as well as features of the white and black styles.

Moorish singers utilize both Arabic and vernacular languages. In both, there is a correspondence between the musical modes and the different poetic meters—that is, different meters are related to individual musical modes. However, the Moorish meters are less numerous and have a less rigorous correspondence than Arabic meters. The singers experiment, before starting to sing, to determine the mode which best fits the meter of their text. The rules are relaxed to such a degree that singers can utilize texts composed in languages of a different character (Wolof, for example) and without a well-defined metrical system.[89]

Other poetic traditions, such as in Hausa and Swahili, that draw on an Arabic background should be investigated from the musical point of view in order to determine whether the recitation of poetry has adopted musical ideas from the Arabic tradition or whether there has been a synthesis of musical traditions.

In the musician class among the Shinqiti Arabs of Mauritania, the male musician is called *iggiw* and the female

85. Balandier and Mercier, "Notes sur les théories," pp. 146–47.
86. *Ibid.,* p. 147.
87. *Musique Maure,* OCORA 28, side 1, band 1.
88. *Ibid.,* side 2, band 1.
89. Balandier and Mercier, "Notes sur les théories," pp. 154, 155.

tiggiwit. Norris says that *iggiw* is a word borrowed from communities across the Senegal River, where the term for a *griot* is *gewel* in Wolof and *gawlo* in Toucouleur. The Sarakolle of Guidimakka, who live in the river regions of Mauritania, also have a musician class, the *diarou.* Each noble family has its own *diarou,* who sings the story of the family and its genealogy and who, in the past, accompanied the men to battle and praised their victories. Norris feels that it may be assumed that this type of society was typical of Mauritania prior to the Hassani invasion, since culturally far more of the country was Sudanic then than now. In addition to the *griot,* Norris says that there was a type of musician in Mauritania similar to those of other Saharan nomads, typical of the bard found in other Arab lands, and a descendant of the great poets of pre-Islamic Arabia. In Norris' opinion, the Sudanic character of the name of the musician class in Mauritania and the fact that this class is not found in the central Sahara support the supposition that, in this respect, Moorish society, at least in the Trarza and the Hawd, had been greatly influenced by the culture of Mali and its neighbors.[90]

The two chief instruments in Mauritania are the *tidinit* lute, and the *ardin* harp. The *tidinit,* which is similar to lutes found in West Africa, differs from the examples found in Senegal, its nearest neighbor, in that the Mauritanian instrument has four strings while the Senegalese instrument has five.[91] The *tidinit* is also related to the West African lutes by the use of extra sound devices. Metal chains lie across the sound-skin of the *tidinit,* and a flexible metal piece with iron rings fastened to its edges is attached to the top of the neck.[92] This last device is similar to those found on many different types of instruments in West Africa.

Contacts between Black Africa and the Arabic-speaking nations across the Sahara, as well as across the Red Sea and the Indian Ocean, have a long tradition, and the study of various aspects of these contacts, which include the interaction of musical traditions, is urgently needed. The religious

90. Norris, *Shinqiti Folk Literature and Song,* pp. 35, 53, 54.
91. *Ibid.,* p. 61.
92. Balandier and Mercier, "Notes sur les théories," pp. 159–60.

music of Islamic communities in Africa must be studied in the context of and in comparison with the indigenous musical traditions of those societies. The music of Black African communities in North Africa and on the Arabian peninsula must be studied as musical traditions in their own right before they are compared with other musical traditions of neighboring peoples in order to determine the influence of one upon the other.

8.

Islamic Musical Culture
among the Yoruba:
A Preliminary Survey

AKIN EUBA

THE YORUBA, in their folklore, claim descent from that part of the Middle East which was the source of Islam.[1] This would seem to imply a common origin between Yoruba and Arab musical cultures. The migration of the Yoruba southward to their present territory was, according to traditional history, occasioned by the conflict that arose in Mecca when Oduduwa, the founder of Yorubaland, and his followers abandoned the Islamic faith and reverted to idolatry.[2] This raises the possibility that, at the time of their arrival in the area we now know as Yoruba country, the Yoruba may have had

1. Samuel Johnson, *The History of the Yorubas from the Earliest Times to the Beginning of the British Protectorate* (Lagos: C.M.S. Bookshop, 1937; reprint ed., London: Routledge and Kegan Paul, 1966), p. 3.
2. *Ibid.*, pp. 3–4.

a music similar to that of Arab culture prior to the founding
of Islam. The Yoruba musical culture thus initially deviated
from post-Islamic Arab musical culture but later on came
again under Islamic influence.

The above deductions seem fairly reasonable, provided we
can accept oral tradition as it stands. The oral tradition
concerning the history of the Yoruba may be open to question on several points, but historians have not discounted it
entirely.[3] In the absence of strong evidence to the contrary,
it is difficult to reject the theory that the Yoruba originally
came from the east.[4]

However, it is possible to surmise that the pure traditional
music of the contemporary Yoruba is a synthesis of the music
of pre-Islamic Arab culture and that of the original aborigines of Yoruba country. This raises the question of which
elements in Yoruba music are pre-Islamic Arab in origin
and which elements are aboriginal. This is indeed a difficult
question, and it cannot be answered until we know more
about the cultural history of the people who now inhabit
Yorubaland. It would be more profitable, in present circumstances, to investigate Arabic elements that came into Yoruba music following what we may consider, by deduction
from oral traditional evidence, as the re-Islamization of the
Yoruba.

The Fulani had been settling peacefully in northern Nigeria
at least since the middle of the fourteenth century,[5] and there
is no doubt that trade contacts between the northern Nigerian kingdoms and Yorubaland were already well established by that time.[6] Islam had become a factor in Yoruba
country before the Fulani Jihad of 1804 and had gained a
foothold as far as the coast.[7] Nevertheless, the Islamic in-

3. *Ibid.*, p. 5; see also S. O. Biobaku, *The Egba and Their Neighbours*
(London: Oxford University Press, 1957), p. 1.

4. Johnson, *History of the Yorubas*, p. 5.

5. Michael Crowder, *The Story of Nigeria* (London: Faber & Faber,
1962), p. 80.

6. F. H. El-Masri, "Islam," in *The City of Ibadan*, ed. P. C. Lloyd,
A. L. Mabogunje, and B. Awe (Cambridge: At the University Press,
1967), p. 250.

7. *Ibid.*, p. 249.

cursion before the jihad, although extensive in terms of distance, may not have been significant.[8] After the jihad, a more thorough Islamization of Yoruba country was achieved by peaceful means.[9]

Before the arrival of Christianity, Islam had spread to almost all parts of Yoruba country.[10] This, together with the fact that "the Islamic doctrine was more appealing and acceptable to the traditional Yoruba," [11] may explain why elements of Arab musical culture have been more easily integrated into Yoruba traditional music than have those of Western musical culture.

At the present time, more Yoruba are Muslims than are Christians, and it is even possible that Islam has more followers than do the indigenous religions of the Yoruba. This pattern is reflected among the musicians who practice the traditional styles of Yoruba music: there are far more Muslims than Christians. In my own field work, I have not yet encountered traditional musicians who are Christians, although I have been informed by two traditional drummers, themselves Muslims, that there are Christians among their colleagues. What is probably more surprising is that there are more Muslim traditional musicians than musicians of the indigenous faiths. One of my informants, a traditional drummer who became a Muslim at about the age of fifteen, considers conversion to Islam as a steppingstone to civilization. According to this informant, most of the younger drummers are Muslims; traditional drummers who still worship òrìsà are not only in the minority but are mostly old men.

There is among Nigerians today an attitude of tolerance in religious matters, a fact which is borne out by the professional practice of Yoruba traditional musicians. A traditional drummer, regardless of his religion, is not discouraged from playing in any situation for which his services might be required. Muslim musicians play for Muslims and non-

8. G. J. A. Ojo, *Yoruba Culture* (London: University of Ife and University of London Press, 1966), p. 186.

9. Johnson, *History of the Yorubas*, p. 38.

10. Ojo, *Yoruba Culture*, p. 186.

11. *Ibid.*, p. 187.

Muslims alike; they are called upon to perform in the worship of Yoruba gods, and their repertoire embraces all forms of music appropriate to the various deities. In this respect, Muslim musicians not only participate in so-called pagan ceremonies but are in fact the chief custodians of one of the most important areas of traditional religious worship.

This situation seems perfectly acceptable to Yoruba Muslim theologians, and they have not actively discouraged Muslim musicians from performing traditional religious music. As one Yoruba drummer put it, Muslim religious leaders raise no objection because "music is our profession and we can practice it this way or that way." This attitude illustrates the tolerance of Muslim leaders, which even extends to the many Yoruba Muslims who make a syncretism of Islam and the traditional forms of worship.[12]

A comparison between the Christian and Islamic viewpoints concerning traditional culture is relevant here. Much has been said about the influence of Christianity upon traditional culture, especially in those aspects connected with indigenous religious practices. Paganism is incompatible with Christianity, and, since music and the other traditional arts are so closely linked with the indigenous religions, these arts must be forsaken by those who have converted to Christianity.

The Islamic attitude toward traditional religious practice and its artistic expression is, *in theory*, identical with the Christian attitude. But, in practice, Yoruba Muslims have tended to preserve traditional culture more than have Yoruba Christians. The agencies responsible for the dissemination of Christianity among the Yoruba have been active in other cultural spheres besides religion. As one writer puts it, the cultural personalities of the agents of Christianity have outshone those of the agents of Islam.[13] In accepting Christianity, the Yoruba have also emulated the general culture of the people who converted them. Christianity has opened the door

12. Kevin Carroll, *Yoruba Religious Carving: Pagan and Christian Sculpture in Nigeria and Dahomey* (New York: Praeger, 1967), p. 106; P. A. Allison, "Newly Discovered Stone Figures from the Yoruba Village of Ijara, Northern Nigeria," *Man*, LXIII (June, 1963), 94.

13. Ojo, *Yoruba Culture*, p. 187.

to Western education, and being well-educated in Western terms also means being able to understand the language of Western artistic culture. As already stated, there are far fewer Christians than Muslims among professional traditional musicians. However, of the Yoruba musicians that practice Western art music professionally, none, so far as I am aware, is a Muslim.

In the days before political awareness and national consciousness began to reopen the eyes of the Western-educated Yoruba to the values of their cultural heritage, there was a tendency among these people to regard many aspects of traditional culture as being synonymous with Islamic culture. For example, in a place like Lagos, which had the largest concentration of Western-educated Yoruba, it was usually the Muslims who wore traditional clothes and patronized traditional music. Many people therefore came to look upon traditional clothes and traditional music as belonging to the Muslims.

Yoruba Christians were much quicker than Yoruba Muslims to accept Western education and cultural values. According to one leader, it was only recently that Yoruba Muslims began to seek the same level of Western education as Yoruba Christians.[14] Previously, Christians tended to enter and continue schooling while Muslims generally went into commerce.

This trend may have had important consequences for the practice of traditional music. Christians with Western education automatically went into civil-service jobs and were less affluent than Muslims who went into business. The Muslims, therefore, had more money to spend on social ceremonies—such as marriage, funeral, and child-naming rites— and could better afford to contribute to the financial sustenance of traditional musicians, who are indispensable for such occasions.

The orthodox Islamic attitude toward music, as expressed in the doctrines of the four chief legists,[15] would seem, in

14. Personal communication from A. R. Shitta-Bey, *Seriki Muslumi* V of Lagos.
15. H. G. Farmer, *A History of Arabian Music* (London, 1929; reprint ed., London: Luzac, 1967), p. 29.

practice, to find no support among Yoruba Muslims. But the official attitude of Yoruba Muslim leaders does partially corroborate that of the legists, particularly that of al-Shāfiʻī.[16] Although there are some who condemn music totally, the general attitude of Yoruba Muslim leaders is that music is acceptable if it is put to proper use. There is approval of all music that expresses religious sentiments and condemnation of music that is used in practices considered incompatible with good religious behavior. One Yoruba Muslim musician, now deceased, was nicknamed "the Preacher" because his songs, although belonging to a form of neo-traditional Yoruba secular music, were religious and philosophical in tone. The works of this musician were very popular and were considered appropriate for listening by Muslims. Conversely, music that is associated with the night club—and even that used in the theater—is, theoretically, disapproved of. Furthermore, although music is not condemned when it is used to celebrate Muslim religious festivals, Yoruba Muslim leaders would still counsel moderation on such occasions. For example, a Muslim who, at the celebration marking the end of the fasting period, indulges himself in music to excess would thereby negate the very purpose for which he fasted.

Traditional music is to be found only in the social activities of Yoruba Muslims and not in actual religious worship. When music is used in Muslim worship, it is invariably the orthodox Arab music used throughout the Muslim world.

This situation calls for further comparison between Islamic and Christian practices among the Yoruba. When the Yoruba were converted to Christianity, they initially moved away from traditional forms of music; but these have now found a place in church worship, and the singing of hymns based upon Yoruba traditional musical style has become quite popular.

Muslim religious festivals are social occasions during which much traditional music may be heard. At *Id-el Fitr* and *Id-el Kebir*, an important Muslim personage would engage a traditional drum orchestra to accompany his procession to

16. *Ibid.*, pp. 29–30.

and from the prayer-ground.[17] Upon his return home from worship, the drummers would stay on to play for his family and friends to dance. At *Id-el Fitr* the musicians are retained just for the day, but at *Id-el Kebir* they may be engaged to play for up to five days—in the case of very wealthy chiefs, sometimes up to two weeks.

In the old days, during the fasting period, drummers used to parade from house to house to awaken people for the early morning meal.[18] They started playing around ten o'clock at night, at which time the women of the house usually began preparing the morning meal. The drummers continued playing until about four o'clock in the morning, when they returned home for their own meals.

The favorite orchestra for these festivities is the *dùndún* tension-drum orchestra. The music itself does not seem to have any particular style that could be considered exclusive to Islam. The drum patterns are taken from the general repertoire of Yoruba traditional music. The main difference is in the language of the *iyálù* [19] talking drum, which on these occasions assumes a prayerful tone appropriate to the Islamic religion. The *iyálù* is of course also used to recite the praise poetry of important persons attending the festivities.

At least three forms of neo-traditional music have developed as a result of the incidence of Islamic culture among the Yoruba. Two of these have direct links with the actual practice of the religion, while the third may be regarded as Islamic by virtue of its association with Muslim musicians. The three musical types are known as *wákà, sákárà,* and *àpàlà.*

Wákà was originally performed at socioreligious ceremonies, such as marriage, and was also used to welcome Muslims returning from the pilgrimage to Mecca. At first, *wákà*

17. During Muslim festivals, when the mosques are too small to accommodate all desiring to worship, Yoruba Muslims usually pray in the open air, at specially appointed grounds.
18. This meal, called *sàrì*, is normally eaten between 2:00 and 4:00 A.M.
19. Literally, "mother drum," the leading instrument of the *dùndún* orchestra.

songs were religious in sentiment and were meant for the spiritual inspiration of participants in *wáká* ceremonies. The songs were accompanied with simple musical instruments consisting of pairs of circular tin-foil idiophones with jingles, which were struck against one another. In recent times, *wáká* has tended to depart from its original religious function, and its instrumental resources have been augmented by drums. As may be imagined, since this transformation from religious simplicity to secular sophistication does not conform to the notions of Islamic orthodoxy, it has met with disapproval from Yoruba Muslim leaders. They have not actually banned the *wáká* songs, but they no longer recognize them as vehicles for religious inspiration. For example, the producer in charge of Muslim religious programs at the Nigerian Broadcasting Corporation in the Western State of Nigeria informed me that he used to feature *wáká* artists in his programs, but when *wáká* changed character he stopped inviting *wáká* musicians for broadcasts. Nowadays, whenever a *wáká* musician applies, he is referred to the corporation's music department.[20]

Apàlà began much the same way as did *wáká*. During the fasting season, young Muslims got together to perform music to awaken people for the early morning meal. The most gifted singer among them was dressed up like a Muslim priest, and he led the others in singing. The musical instruments used at the beginning consisted of bamboo rhythm sticks. The original performers of *àpàlà* were young amateurs, but later the form was taken up by professional musicians, who enlarged the instrumental resources by adding drums of the *dùndún* family. From then on, *àpàlà* became mere entertainment music. It also was performed in the early evening rather than in the early morning. Another instrument that is now usually included in the *àpàlà* group is the *agídígbo*, a *sansa* type with a rectangular wooden sound-box and metal keys.

Sákárà may be considered to derive from Islamic culture, not only because its style closely resembles that of *wáká* and

---

20. It is of some interest that the producer in charge of traditional music is himself a practicing Muslim.

àpàlà but also because it has been created chiefly by Muslim musicians. The musical instruments of sákárà include drums of the dùndún family and a single-string fiddle, gòjé (also found among the Hausa of northern Nigeria as goge), which almost certainly came from Arab musical culture.

Historically, wákà is thought to predate both sákárà and àpàlà, and, of the three forms, àpàlà appears to be the most recent. One Ibadan Muslim drummer believes that sákárà originated in Ilorin [21] and that it came to Ibadan during the reign of Bálè Shittu, who was Olúbàdàn from 1914 to 1925.

Apart from the gòjé, there are other instruments which may have come into Yoruba music through the influx of Islamic culture.

The bèmbé is a cylindrical double-headed drum with a snare. It is played with a curved stick similar to that used for the dùndún tension drums. Bèmbé drums also exist among the Hausa of northern Nigeria and may have a common origin with identical drums from the Middle East, as described by Curt Sachs.[22]

The Yoruba historian Samuel Johnson mentions an ivory trumpet used by the kings of Old Oyo and which he believed to have been introduced to the Oyo Yoruba from the Hausa and Nupe of northern Nigeria.[23] In addition, Johnson noted the existence of the long trumpet kàkàkí (the most characteristic musical instrument of royalty among present-day Hausa), which was also played for the kings of Old Oyo.

Some people believe that the Yoruba tension drum of the dùndún family came from the north.[24] The distribution of the hourglass tension drum in West Africa provides some support for this notion, for the drum is common along the northern belt and other Islamized areas of West Africa.[25] The

21. A predominantly Yoruba community in northern Nigeria and the center from which Islam spread to other Yoruba-speaking communities.
22. *The History of Musical Instruments* (New York: Norton, 1940), p. 249.
23. Johnson, *History of the Yorubas*, p. 121.
24. See, for example, Carroll, *Yoruba Religious Carving*, p. 67.
25. For details of the West African distribution of the hourglass tension drum, see Darius L. Thieme, "A Descriptive Catalogue of Yoruba Musical Instruments" (Ph.D. diss., Catholic University of America, 1969), p. 12.

Hausa tension drum, *kalangu,* may be a relative of the Yoruba *kànàngó,* the smallest of the *dùndún* tension drums.

The *kotso* of the Hausa is similar to the Yoruba *kósó,* which, according to Johnson, was played in Old Oyo "to wake up the king every morning at 4 A.M." [26] The *kósó,* a single-headed open-end tension drum played with the bare hand, is rare among present-day Yoruba. Legend has it that the instrument came from the north and was introduced into Yoruba music at the time of the founding of Ile-Ife.[27]

According to Ifa oral literature, *dùndún* drums were the seventh kind of drums to be created by Ayàn, the first Yoruba drummer; afterwards came *gángan* and then *kósó.*[28] The *gángan* differs little from the *dùndún* drums and must have been created to enlarge the *dùndún* family. Nowadays it is used as an occasional member of the *dùndún* band.

Anthony King's view that the *kósó* family is probably "the earliest extant group of [Yoruba] portative drums" [29] is not supported by Ifa oral literature as interpreted by my own informant, Chief Fágbèmí Ajànàkú. The *kósó* legend in Ifa literature, according to the chief, goes as follows:

When Agbejimoko [probably a Yoruba chief] was going to heaven, his *dùndún* drummer insisted on accompanying him. Halfway up to heaven, his drum fell down; one of the heads became torn and the tensioning thongs came loose. Agbejimoko's drummer was not to be discouraged by this. He simply picked up the drum, tied round the tensioning thongs, and continued playing the drum with his bare hand.

SUMMARY

Much remains to be known about the history of the Yoruba, but, if oral literature is accurate, they probably originated in a region north of the Sahara. They were almost certainly well acquainted with Arab culture long before the jihad of 1804,

26. Johnson, *History of the Yorubas,* p. 58.
27. A. King, *Yoruba Sacred Music from Ekiti* (Ibadan: Ibadan University Press, 1961), p. 4.
28. Personal communication from Chief Fágbèmí Ajànàkú, the *Aràbà* of Lagos.
29. King, *Yoruba Sacred Music,* p. 3.

and it is possible that their earliest musical style had affinities with pre-Islamic Arab musical culture.

Since the jihad, the majority of the Yoruba have become Muslims but have not, in practice, conformed strictly to the orthodox doctrine of the four chief legists of Islam. The tolerance with which Islamic leaders of the Yoruba have viewed the practice of traditional music by Yoruba Muslim musicians, even when this practice brings the musicians into contact with paganism, has encouraged Muslims to maintain the cultivation of traditional music. Thus Yoruba Muslims have played an important role in keeping traditional music alive, and one of the leading authorities on Yoruba music, His Highness Tìmì of Ede, believes that but for the Muslims traditional music might have died.

Southern Africa

9.

Music and
the Historical Process
in Vendaland

JOHN BLACKING

THE NON-MUSICAL "ORIGINS" OF MUSICAL SOUND

OVER THIRTY YEARS AGO, Percival Kirby discussed the history of the music of the South African Bantu.[1] He pleaded for "greater precision in the description of cultural phenomena," and in particular for accurate field observation of techniques of performance. His plea is no less relevant today; even in the field of ethnomusicology, music is often described, analyzed, and compared solely on the basis of sounds that are heard, as if a recurring interval or pattern of melody were a constant factor in all cultural contexts, quite regardless of differences in its nonmusical "origins."

1. Percival R. Kirby, "The Principle of Stratification as Applied to South African Native Music," *South African Journal of Science*, XXXII (1935), 72–90.

Just as an ethnomusicologist may observe how a people's choice and creation of music is affected by historical processes, so a historian ought to be able to learn something about its social and cultural history by studying its music. But if the sounds of music do reflect in some ways the history of the people who create them, descriptions and analyses of the sounds alone will rarely be sufficient. If musical evidence is to be used in reconstructing African history, musical styles must be carefully described both as patterns of social and cultural action and as patterns of sound. If analysis of their cultural backgrounds and techniques of performance is ignored, or is at best superficial, comparisons of apparently similar styles may be entirely unjustified, and historians could be either misled or deprived of the confirmation they need.

For example, an incomplete analysis of the music of two or more different African societies might fail to reveal that certain similar sounds are produced in entirely different ways and hence cannot be compared, or that different sounds are the product of the same process and are therefore comparable. Historians could thus be led to assume wrongly that some kind of relationship had existed between different societies or, conversely, to ignore relationships that really did exist.

Music-making is not simply an exercise in the organization of sound; it is a symbolic expression of social and cultural organization, which reflects the values and the past and present ways of life of the human beings who create it. Thus the logic and meaning of musical patterns can never be understood fully without reference to other phenomena in the culture of which they are a part. Furthermore, the link between human culture and musical sound cannot always be directly observed; the sound may be an incidental result of techniques of performance, which are determined largely by social situations and by the physical possibilities and limitations of singers, players, and their instruments, all of which may be assigned by the cultural context. The same pattern of sound may turn up accidentally in different social and cultural contexts, as the result of entirely different processes of creation. Alternatively, a melody may be radically transformed when it is "arranged" for performance by different instruments and ensembles, and the resulting variations might be described objectively by an ethnomusicologist as so many *different*, unrelated patterns of sound. This would not be a true description of the music, because it would ignore the important factor that *to the performers and listeners* the unity of theme is musically more important than the variations, which are the products of *social* situations. Without adequate study of the cultural background and of techniques of performance, an ethnomusicologist can therefore attach importance to observed differences in, say, patterns of melody, while the creators of the music are concerned primarily with a pattern of "chords," of which several different melodies are merely partial expressions.

I make no apologies for devoting half of this paper to what is essentially a discussion of methodology, and to elaborating the issues raised by Kirby. People hold on to musical styles long after they have changed or abandoned other elements of their culture. So-called traditional styles of African music may often reflect the precolonial diffusion of peoples and cultures in much the same way that the sounds of neo-African music reflect the influence of missions and urban living. But before we can progress in the study of music and history in Africa, we need more intensive ethnomusicological studies of limited areas, which relate musical styles to their social and cultural contexts.

One such study could hardly be accomplished in less than a year by an ethnomusicologist working on his own, because performances of music are invariably related to the annual course of the seasons; but in cooperation with a social anthropologist who has been among a people for some time, it should be possible to make a reasonably adequate field study of all but the most complex musical traditions within a period of six to eight weeks.[2] The anthropologist can make a paradigm of the different musical styles, with the necessary sociological

2. With the help of Raymond Apthorpe, who had done several months' field work amongst the Nsenga of the Petauke district, Zambia, I was able to record a representative sample of Nsenga music, together with the details necessary for adequate analysis, in ten days.

information, so that when the ethnomusicologist arrives the music can be "ordered" and systematically recorded. This is not ideal, of course, as performances out of context may be distorted; but at least it can be of value in our present stage of research.

If African music is studied on these lines, the results of analysis should be of considerable use in reconstructing African history. Musical relationships between different groups may be discerned after other evidence has disappeared, and differences of musical style may either confirm an ethnohistorian's doubt about the basic homogeneity of a culture or at least encourage him to examine the matter more deeply. For instance, the Venda initiation schools of *domba* and *vhusha* are sponsored entirely by rulers, and thus appear to be part of the culture of the ruling clans; but their musical style suggests, and subsequent sociological investigation tends to confirm, that they were in fact taken over from conquered clans rather than introduced by the conquerors. Knowledge of this is an essential clue to understanding the form and function of these initiations in contemporary Venda society. Similarly, variations of style in the music of the Nsenga of the Petauke district, Zambia, lend musical support to Raymond Apthorpe's ethnohistorical thesis that the Nsenga are not, as has often been supposed, an offshoot of the Cewa.[3]

The admirably objective methods of ethnomusicological analysis advocated by Hornbostel have been used and developed by Herzog, Kolinski, McAllister, Merriam, and others. In applying them to my Venda material,[4] I found that I had

3. Raymond Apthorpe and John Blacking, "Fieldwork cooperation in the study of Nsenga Music and Ritual," *Africa*, XXXII, no. 1 (1962), 72. Ethnic Folkways Library is producing three LPs of Nsenga music, to which we have added explanatory notes; the first two volumes have already appeard as record nos. FE 4201 and 4202.

4. I spent a total of twenty-two months in the field between May, 1956, and December, 1958, and worked chiefly in the Sibasa district of the Northern Transvaal. I have thanked all those who sponsored and assisted my research in *Venda Children's Songs* (Johannesburg: Witwatersrand University Press, 1967). I would also like to thank the Senate Research Committee of the University of the Witwatersrand for a research grant toward the cost of preparation of this paper. I am especially grateful to Dr. N. J. van Warmelo, Professor M. G. Marwick, and Dr. Olga Gostin, who made helpful comments on this paper: they are in no way to be held responsible for the final result.

to make several adjustments, since an objective analysis of the music per se was not always meaningful in terms of its social and cultural context. I hope that the problems raised by my experience with Venda music may be of some use to other workers and may open up a discussion on the more precise ways in which ethnomusicology can be of service to the study of African history.

In order to show how false comparisons could be made and real correspondences ignored, I will discuss first some problems that arose in describing, identifying, and classifying patterns of Venda music. I will then outline some recent, known events in Venda history and discuss the music which reflects them. Finally, I will show how an analysis of current musical styles could corroborate a pattern of events which may have taken place during an unknown period of Venda history.

SOME PROBLEMS OF DESCRIPTION, IDENTIFICATION, AND CLASSIFICATION OF VENDA MELODIES

The Venda define their music as *nyimbo dza Vhavenda,* "songs of the Venda [-speaking] people." They recognize several different styles of music within this broad category, but they define these subdivisions not in musical but in cultural terms, which refer to the music's social function.[5] There are very few Venda who, without prompting, will say that certain styles have been borrowed from other people, and there are still fewer who can describe the differences in terms of their musical characteristics.

At first, it appears that Venda music is basically homogeneous, that there is, in fact, an overall style that may be called typically Venda. Many of its features are epitomized in *tshikona,* the Venda national dance: its basic metrical

5. A full account of the different types of music recognized by the Venda is given in John Blacking, "The Role of Music in the Culture of the Venda of the Northern Transvaal," in *Studies in Ethnomusicology,* Vol. II, ed. M. Kolinski (New York: Oak Publications, 1965), pp. 20–53.

unit is one of four dotted crotchets, played at a stately
tempo of ♩. = ca. 80 M.M.; the men dance counterclockwise
round the women who are playing the drums, and each man
plays a different stopped reed-pipe of fixed pitch, so that the
whole ensemble produces a pattern of descending heptatonic
scales at intervals of the fourth and fifth.[6] The final touch of
"Venda-ness" is added when someone sings praises while the
music is being played: descending heptatonic phrases, usually
of seven syllables, are sung with a characteristic vocal tone,
interspersed with periods of chorus-singing (*u bvumela*) in
which a bass part is improvised to vocables such as *ahee, he aa,
aa ee, ahee!* L. Lanham, head of the Department of Phonetics
and General Linguistics of the University of the Witwatersrand, described this style as "glottal murmur or breathy voice,
in which the vocal folds vibrate but do not touch completely,
and the air passes through when they are swung back."

It is only when one talks with Venda about the sociological
background to musical performances that they begin to reveal the diversity which underlies this apparent homogeneity: subtle differences in musical style express both the
cleavages and alignments in Venda society, and hence the
social significance of the music and its impact on different
individuals, and some of the historical origins of those divisions. If musical evidence is to be used to support or refute
historical reconstructions, differences in musical style must
be defined as accurately as the sociological differences, and
in terms of the meaning of the music to the performers. The
nature of the contacts, if any, between the Venda and other
groups that use the same melodic or rhythmic patterns will
be revealed in correlations between the cultural antecedents
of the musical patterns and between the sounds themselves.

6. A description of the dance and the music, with a transcription, is
given in Percival R. Kirby, *The Musical Instruments of the Native
Races of South Africa* (London: Oxford University Press, 1934; reprint
ed., Johannesburg: Witwatersrand University Press, 1953), pp. 155–62;
further information is given in Blacking, *Venda Children's Songs.*

INTERVAL FREQUENCIES, SPEECH-TONE,
AND "HARMONIC" EQUIVALENCE

One well-established method of classifying musical styles is to analyze the frequency of occurrence of their different ascending and descending intervals. Provided that a rising fourth really is a rising fourth in all observed cases (and not a falling fifth transposed because of limited vocal or instrumental range), and provided that the contours of a melody are conceived as patterns of sound and are not the incidental product of other, nonmusical factors, variations in patterns of melody are *musically* significant, and valid comparisons may be made between similar patterns of sound.

In Venda music, however, there are many cases where the choice of intervals does not represent a *musical* preference, or where the particular intervals chosen are not as important as the sequence of "chords" from which they are selected.

Patterns of speech-tone are important in Venda: incorrectly sung or spoken Venda is not unintelligible, but it is not truly Venda and will therefore be criticized. By learning to sing Venda songs and by making mistakes, sometimes intentionally, I was able to learn something of their criteria for right and wrong performances.

Speech-tone may determine where a melody should rise and fall: the simple melodic pattern

may change, with different words, to

or

or

In this case, only the last variation would make any difference to an analysis of the frequency of ascending and descending intervals; but an extension of the same principle can make an interval count more an indication of the inflections of the language than of preferred patterns of musical sound.

In some cases, patterns of speech-tone may precipitate radical alterations of melodic pattern by means of the principle of harmonic equivalence. Any Venda melody may be accompanied by one or more melodies which fit "harmonically" (though not necessarily in organum). If a sentence beginning with a low-high speech-tone pattern occurs in a melody that is suited for a high-high or a high-low pattern, then the melody must be adjusted according to this principle. Thus, for the Venda there is not necessarily any *musical* difference

between

and

The frequency of descending minor thirds and ascending major thirds is, in such cases, a function of language and not an indication of musical preferences.

In many cases, linguistic factors not only influence variations in melodies but may also shape their basic patterns. The melody of the first "line" of a song may be an almost exact replica of its pattern of speech-tones, and thereafter each "line" is sung to the same melody, with a minimal number of adjustments for radical changes in speech-tone patterns.

Because of the principle of "harmonic" equivalence, two apparently different melodies may be regarded as one and the same, although the frequencies of their intervals have little in common. For example, the Venda do not recognize any difference between the following two melodies, which may

be sung to the same words and are the basic patterns of two
versions of the same song:

It will be seen that they are "harmonically" equivalent.
This might be compared to the situation in European music in
which the horn part of a symphony *is* the symphony to a horn
player, even though members of the audience might not be
able to recognize it if they heard it separately—with the
difference that for the Venda the two melodies are inter-
changeable, and one is not necessarily considered more important than the other or incomplete without it.

THE DERIVATION OF TONE-ROWS:
CAUTIONS IN USING SCALES
AS CLUES TO MUSICAL HISTORY

I distinguish between *tone-row*, the series of tones on
which a particular melody is based, and *scale*, a relatively
fixed and culturally recognized sequence of tones from which
tone-rows and melodic patterns may be derived. The Venda
have a word, *mutavha*, which refers to a set of tuned reed-
pipes or a row of keys on the xylophone or hand-piano, but
they have no word to refer to a scale as a series of intervals
dividing the octave.

Cultural factors are no less important than acoustics in determining a society's selection of intervals and scales. Sev-

eral writers have stressed that the physical potentialities and limitations of a musical instrument and its human player, and aesthetic considerations such as the spacing of holes on a flute, can influence the form of scales, and hence the patterns of vocal music. However, musical invention is also a product of social and cultural life, and it may transcend the acoustical limitations imposed by cultural products. For instance, although the "fanfare" melodies played on Venda ocarinas appear to be suggested by the physical properties of the instrument, melodies played on almost identical instruments by the Chopi of Mozambique transcend these "natural" properties.[7] Similarly, the Venda, the Nsenga, and the Tonga of the Zambezi Valley sometimes alter the tunings of their hand-pianos (i.e., *mbira*- or *sansa*-type instruments) to suit the particular melody they wish to play; conversely, they may compose a melody, or an arrangement of a melody, which is suggested by the layout of the instrument.[8]

For reasons such as these, theories of the diffusion of peoples cannot be reliably based only on the measurements of the scales of instruments, especially if they are museum specimens; the scales themselves are not as important as the tunes that are played on the instruments, how they are played, and what degrees of variation in pitch the average player will accept. It is necessary to know what the musician is aiming for when he tunes the instrument, and what will satisfy him while he is playing, and it must be remembered that he tunes by ear and not with an electronic machine.[9] Conclusions based on comparisons of scales are valid only when information is documented, as in studies by Wachsmann and Tracey, where a sufficiently large sample of tunings is supported by details of the sequence of tuning and the relevance of intervals in musical performance, especially in

7. See John Blacking, "Problems of Pitch, Pattern and Harmony in the Ocarina Music of the Venda," *African Music*, II, no. 2 (1959), 15–23, esp. p. 22.
8. See John Blacking, "Patterns of Nsenga *Kalimba* Music," *African Music*, II, no. 4 (1961), 26–43.
9. In "On the Musical Scales of Various Nations," *Journal of the Society of Arts*, XXXIII (1885), 485–527, A. J. Ellis pointed out that even the best piano tuners can be inaccurate.

relation to the tone-center of a scale.[10] Correspondences in the tuning of scales may be coincidental and is more probably an indication of the universality of laws of sound rather than of cultural diffusion. It is methodologically unsound to derive "average scales" from the tunings of a number of musical instruments and then to compare the use of these apparently similar scales in different societies, because by juggling the position of intervals in relation to the tone-center it is possible to make basically different scales look alike. As the most cursory study of European ecclesiastical modes shows, the essential differences in most scales are to be found in their musical function, and especially in the relationship of their intervals to a tone-center. It is for reasons such as this that A. M. Jones's argument about musical relationships between Indonesia and Africa is methodologically unacceptable, although his general conclusions are probably valid.[11]

Even the tunings of musical experts may need confirmation by less expert members of a society, as an example from Vendaland will show. The makers of Venda reed-pipes cut the smallest pipe first; then they cut each larger pipe in turn and tune the scale downwards by comparing the tones of adjacent pipes. Some informants have suggested that the musical intervals should be equal. I asked experts to make sets of pipes under my supervision, and when they were quite satisfied with their tunings I collected people to perform the standard melodies. It then became clear that several pipes were not properly in tune, and it was therefore necessary to retune, or throw out altogether, several "mad ones" (*mavhavhi*). The expert makers were not in any way disturbed by this "criticism" of their work. They accepted the fact that one could not be sure that the pipes were in tune until they had been tested and adjusted by means of a full performance.

Similar attention must be paid to the "origins" of sounds if

10. See Klaus P. Wachsmann, "An Equal-Stepped Tuning in a Ganda Harp," *Nature*, CLXV (1950), 40 ff; H. T. Tracey, *Chopi Musicians, Their Music, Poetry and Instruments* (London: Oxford University Press, 1948).

11. See my review of A. M. Jones, *Africa and Indonesia: The Evidence of the Xylophone and Other Musical and Cultural Factors* (Leiden: E. J. Brill, 1964), in *African Studies*, XXV, no. 1 (1966), 48.

comparisons are to be made on the basis of the number of different tones commonly used in melodies, or of intervals used in organum singing.[12] Traditional Venda music uses tone-rows having from two to seven different tones. If we are to learn something of Venda history through their music, it is essential to know, for example, whether pentatonic and hexatonic songs are merely using five or six tones of a seven-note scale or whether they are songs in pentatonic or hexatonic musical traditions. We may have a single heptatonic tradition from which all kinds of tone-rows are selected, or we may have a fusion of different musical traditions which have been adopted as a result of conquest and immigration. Both situations are found in Vendaland; there is evidence both of a fusion of peoples who used heptatonic, hexatonic, and pentatonic scales, and of the purely musical selection of six tones or less from any of these scales for particular melodies.

The way in which tone-rows are used in melodies may indicate an unsuspected scale origin. Such distinctive "fanfare" patterns as:

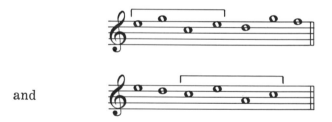

and

are, for the Venda, derived not from speech-tone patterns, not from four- or five-tone scales, nor even from a single seventone scale, but from the specific arrangement of a set (*mutavha*) of heptatonic reed-pipes which is used to play the melody of the Venda national dance, *tshikona*. The "fanfare" patterns are selected from the total pattern of two descending

12. A. M. Jones's distribution map of African harmony in *Studies in African Music* (London: Oxford University Press, 1959), facing p. 230, for instance, is a necessary and admirable pioneer study, but it should be used cautiously in any historical reconstruction.

seven-tone scales played in organum (the illustration shows only the music of the fifteen highest pitched pipes) :

Thus, it would be misleading to classify these melodic patterns as tetratonic or pentatonic or to compare them with other "fanfare" patterns, because they are both derived from a heptatonic scale and their "fanfares" are the product of a unique set of cultural and musical circumstances.

It is not even possible to calculate a single tone-center for every Venda melody, since Venda ideas about tone-centers do not always agree with the results of "objective" melodic analysis. The first tone played in the national dance (*tshikona*) is called *phala;* it is recognized as the key-note, and the melody descends from it. Similarly, in many Venda melodies based on a seven-note scale, the first tone of the melody is regarded by the Venda as the tone-center, whether or not it would seem to be so in an objective analysis of the melody. It is, of course, possible that *phala* is to be compared to middle C on the piano, and that other tone-centers are recognized, but I have not yet been able to clarify this satisfactorily.

I obtained this information by asking children and adults to imitate musical phrases which I sang to them, and to begin well-known Venda songs, given a single tone. I also asked them to sing *tshikona,* without any given pitch, and they usually sang it in the same pitch on different occasions. I was not able to make enough test recordings of the same child singing children's songs on different occasions, but I am inclined to think that they perform them on each occasion in the pitch at which they originally learned them, unless they have been diverted by the pitch of another song just before they begin. This applies also to the singing of adults, who seem to begin in, or quickly adjust to, the same pitch for each performance of the same song.

The operation of the principle of "harmonic" equivalence

was also demonstrated by these tests. If I pitched a phrase too high or too low for the subject's voice, he would unfalteringly pitch the song down or up a fourth or fifth, to suit his own vocal range, and he might even alter the pattern of the melody. This, incidentally, should be taken as a warning against relying on pitch tests as an indication of musicality, especially outside the field of European culture.

A further problem arose in connection with the diffusion of scales in Vendaland. The heptatonic reed-pipes for the national dance are made from a species of bamboo found in a sacred grove at Tshaulu, in eastern Vendaland, while the pentatonic reed-pipes used for the youths' dances (*tshikanganga, givha,* and *visa*) are made from the common river reed. The Venda say that they borrowed the pentatonic pipes from the Pedi, who live to the south of them, while the Pedi say that they borrowed their reed-pipe music from the Venda.[13] Much Venda music is heptatonic, but Pedi music is basically pentatonic. An examination of the function of reed-pipe music in Venda society led me to conclude that both stories are right: the Pedi borrowed from the Venda the idea of playing reed-pipes in ensembles and then adapted it to their own scale system; and later the Venda borrowed back the pentatonic, Pedi adaptation of their idea, so that it has now become an integral part of their own culture. The Venda recognize that the music of the two sets of pipes is different, but they do not attribute it to the different number of tones in the scales. They do not attempt to play the pentatonic music on a selection of heptatonic pipes, nor do they incorporate any of the pentatonic pipes into a heptatonic set. They simply say that the two sets of pipes, and the melodies played on them, "are different."

DISTORTION, IMITATION, AND SYNCRETISM IN THE DIFFUSION OF MUSIC

If music is to be used as supplementary evidence to support historical hypotheses, it must be remembered that the trans-

13. First mentioned in Kirby, *Musical Instruments*, pp. 162 ff., and confirmed by Y. Huskisson, "The Social and Ceremonial Music of the Pedi" (Ph.D. diss., University of the Witwatersrand, 1958), p. 27.

mission of musical styles is not always a straightforward process, because of the nature of the social situations in which borrowing takes place. Musical styles may be accidentally or deliberately distorted, because stresses and inadequacies in the learning situation may inhibit free adoption of the new music or may compel the borrowers to adapt the music to their own tastes. Similarly, music may be exactly imitated for a variety of reasons. Modern African vocal groups in Johannesburg may copy the "American style" as closely as they can, in order to identify with an international culture and feel a little less oppressed by apartheid; on the other hand, the Xhosa composer Benjamin Tyamzashe shows what he thinks of South African white culture by sandwiching between two sections of lively neo-African music the corniest of Western-style hymn music.

Thus, again, the sound of music per se may not truly reflect either the social situation in which musical styles were borrowed and incorporated into other traditions or people's preferences for certain musical features.

For example, it has often been suggested that Africans have difficulty in learning European music, especially when it is chromatic, either because they are incapable of doing so or because it does not appeal to "the African ear"—whatever that may be. I have found, however, that ability and so-called African preferences are not the crucial factors which determine how European music shall be learned and performed. Educated Africans in Johannesburg, as well as those in other South African towns and rural areas, are able to sing chromatic music quite well or very badly, depending on the ability of their trainers, the facilities available to them, and their interest in the project. Similarly, I have heard uneducated Nsenga youths master intricate chromatic progressions in jive songs—largely, I think, because they were interested in the music for its own sake and were under no compulsion to learn it. Music which is *voluntarily* borrowed by a competent performer need not differ from the original, even if the musical style in which the performer has been reared differs considerably from that which he is borrowing. I say "need not," because obviously in some cases, as in the Pedi borrowing of the Venda reed-pipe ensemble, the borrowers may wish to adapt the music to their own preferred style.

More often than not, however, European music has not been voluntarily borrowed in Africa. And that is why we cannot say, after listening to pieces of modern Venda music, that we have proof that the Venda like to revert to their traditional modes, that they prefer a staccato to a legato style of singing, that they do not mind if patterns of words and music conflict, and that they do not care about musical accuracy. Their modern music is largely the result of the way in which they have been introduced to European music rather than being a true amalgamation of European and traditional Venda music.

The sort of music that has been disseminated by Venda missions and schools has often been the worst type of European music, and even the best music has been distorted by the way in which it has been taught; but it has all become a symbol of the very best in music because of its prestige associations. The music has generally been taught syllable by syllable rather than phrase by phrase, and often by a worthy man with a singularly unmusical voice more suited to leading a rugby scrum than a church choir; this accounts for the staccato style of singing. If the singers have reverted to traditional modes, it is partly because there is no real contact with the original of the unfamiliar idiom at an early age and partly because many of the Europeans who first taught the music, and the African teachers who have carried on the tradition, have been as uncertain about the correct reading of the scores as those they have taught. The slow tempo of much new music does not necessarily indicate that the Venda like it that way; in some cases they have been advised by European "experts" at Eisteddfods and elsewhere that any music with a religious theme must be sung very slowly, and inevitably they take this by extension to refer to most European music that is not jazz, since they have little or no opportunity to hear classical music. "Experts" even assure them, like Algernon in *The Importance of Being Earnest,* that sentiment and expression are much more important than accuracy—a notion quite foreign to traditional

Venda music, in which accuracy is always expected and sentiment generally assumed, but one strong enough to have dis-
astrous results and to influence the process of borrowing of
elements of European music.

These comments are based on numerous observations and
conversations during my field work in Vendaland, especially
when I adjudicated at the annual Eisteddfods. There was a
tradition, which I ignored, that judges should give up to
fifty marks out of a hundred for interpretation—which in
some cases was supposed to include an assessment of the
choir's personal appearance—but only ten marks for a combination of accuracy, time value, and intonation! This was,
in a sense, necessary, because many of the Europeans who
were asked to judge could not read music. School choirs had
little chance of improving their performances of European
music, because the few judges who had some knowledge of
music seemed to feel compelled to hand out patronizing
praise when they must have known that the performances
were poor. Thus cultural phenomena, in this case relations
between different groups in South Africa, may have a pro-
found effect on the course of musical development.

I need hardly mention that the possibility of independent
invention can never be excluded. It cannot be assumed that
the presence of Arabic styles in African music is always a
sign of direct or indirect contact with Islam or Islamic peoples. Similarly, the use of nonsense syllables in learning drum
rhythms in both African and Indian music may be an example of independent solutions to the same problem.

On the other hand, Indonesian contacts with Madagascar
and the southeast coast of Africa can hardly be doubted,
though the direction of the contacts has been challenged.
Could there also have been Chinese or Indochinese influence
on Venda music? Attention has been drawn to parallels between the esoteric symbolism of Venda drums and the form
of the bronze drums of Tonkin. There are astonishing similarities between the sound of Venda reed-pipe ensembles and
the Laotian *khène* (or Chinese *cheng*), and originally the
music was particularly associated with death and ancestor
worship. It is not hard to imagine Africans improving on

imported music by taking a *khène* to pieces and distributing the reed-pipes to a group of people; similar sounds are then produced by subtle use of the hocket technique, with the more satisfying social situation of individuals cooperating in community. Africans have "socialized" European music in recent times; they may have done the same to other music in the past.

THE CORRELATION OF
MUSICAL AND SOCIOLOGICAL EVIDENCE
IN THE RECONSTRUCTION OF VENDA HISTORY

Having outlined some basic problems in defining musical styles, I shall now consider aspects of Venda history in which musical evidence is important. First, the evidence of song texts will be examined, and then the course of certain musical and social events during a recent, known period of history will be traced. This evidence will lend support to certain hypotheses which will be advanced about musical and social events during an earlier, unknown period of history.

It is important to know that Vendaland is not a centralized state. There are twelve chiefdoms in the Sibasa district, most of which are ruled by families who are, or claim to be, descendants of a group of people who invaded the west of Vendaland about two hundred years ago.

It appears that when the invasion began, there were a number of "aboriginal" clans scattered over Vendaland, and at least two powerful ruling houses—the people of Tshivhula (clan: *Mutwanamba*), and the Tavhatsindi (clan: *Ndou*). It was probably the invaders who imposed upon the people of Vendaland the present important class division between commoners (*vhasiwana*) and nobles (*vhakololo*).[14] It is generally assumed that it was these invaders who brought to Venda-

14. *Vhakololo* is translated by van Warmelo, in his *Tshivenda-English Dictionary* (Pretoria: Government Printer, 1937), as "the child of a chief who is still living, or of his younger brothers," but the term seems to have a wider use and refers to "any patrilineal descendant of certain chiefly families"; see also John Blacking, "Musical Expeditions of the Venda," *African Music*, III, no. 1 (1962), 54–78.

land the wealth of music and ritual practices which are a notable feature of Venda culture; and in line with this theory Kirby has suggested that the Venda heptatonic scale indicates foreign influences, possibly from people who had been in contact with Semitic modes.[15] He also compares the Venda "kettledrums," *ngoma* and *thungwa*, with the Arab drums of Darfur (Egypt) that are mounted in pairs and called *naqqareh*.

One could suggest an alternative hypothesis, which is better supported by the musical and sociological evidence. It can be argued that the early inhabitants of Vendaland were responsible for the variety of Venda culture, and that they used the heptatonic scale. Subsequent immigrants may have brought hexatonic music. It is almost certain that the later conquerors brought pentatonic music. It seems that, like many imperialists when they begin to rule a foreign people, they had little to offer culturally except skills in regional administration and the mobilization of military power. Unlike many other imperialists, they did not try to destroy what they found: they patronized the arts and made a pact with priests, magicians, and ritual experts; they married the local women and adopted some local customs. As a result, they now receive the credit for being the main authors of Venda culture.

THE ABSENCE OF HISTORICAL EVIDENCE IN SONG TEXTS

On the whole, Venda song texts tell us very little about clan history (perhaps this is a necessary outcome of the political situation). In comparison with musical traditions in other parts of Africa, there are remarkably few songs that are overtly topical and not even many that contain esoteric allusions to local events. In general, the Venda regard the ritual and the effects of performance more highly than the content of music. Musical performances per se, rather than sentiments expressed in the words of songs, are factors in the balance of social and political power. A few years ago, for instance, a dispute over a headmanship was settled by two

15. Kirby, "The Principle of Stratification."

simultaneous performances of the national dance. When it was clear that the resident headman's music was louder, and hence that the number of his followers was greater, the rival claimant withdrew without further comment.

The texts of most initiation songs are related to the instruction given, and they are only likely to be of historical value as cultural items to be considered when comparing one set of initiation rituals with another. There is one initiation text, that of the great *domba* song, which at first sounds like a saga of the Venda past; but after collecting several hundred "lines" of it during performances by different masters of initiation, I found that many "lines" were local creations of the masters and thus were not historically significant. Other, older "lines" are often collections of praises and instructions referring to the initiation mysteries, which do not throw fresh light on Venda history. Musical clues to Venda history are to be found, therefore, more in the patterns of sound than in the accompanying words.

RECENT ADDITIONS TO THE VENDA MUSICAL TRADITION

It is possible to distinguish the new sounds that were added to the Venda musical tradition not long before the arrival of European music.

First, from the southeastern areas of Rhodesia have come a number of dances of spirit-possession (*ngoma dza midzimu* —literally, drums of the ancestor-spirits), which may perhaps have the same area of origin as those dances which have spread northward to the Tonga of the Zambezi Valley. Stayt suggests that "the phenomenon of possession was rare among the Bavenda until about 1914"; [16] but this may be a conservative estimate, and it seems that the dances were established, at least in the eastern areas of Vendaland, well before the turn of the century. It is in the eastern areas that they are still the most lively, and many Venda say that "it is the people of Mutele who really know how to get possessed."

16. H. A. Stayt, *The Bavenda* (London: Oxford University Press, 1931), p. 302.

In the central and western areas of the Sibasa district, where I saw several dances, they are comparatively formal and ritualized, and even members of ruling clans join the cult groups. This was unthinkable in the past, since the possession cult was in some respects a sectarian protest against the formalism of traditional worship and an assertion of the importance of the mother's lineage in a society in which the authority of the father's lineage was an essential factor in maintaining political power. In particular, the possession cult serves as a focus of interest for powerful families who are not directly related to the ruling houses, and as a means of increasing their solidarity.

It is the rhythms and the style of drumming, rather than the content of the words and the style of singing, that give the clue to the foreign origin of the dances. The rhythms are fast, and the master drummer is a man who is hired for the occasion; in contrast, traditional Venda music is more leisurely and drums are always played by women, except in urban areas, where men play the drums for the reed-pipe dances. Furthermore, Venda women are never hired to play, and there are no real master drummer's parts in Venda music; these are distinctly Rhodesian characteristics. The tenor and alto drums can be played by women if men are not present. The conical alto drum (*murumba*) is not played with the hands, as in normal Venda drumming, but with a stick.

Second, there is little doubt about the recent northern Sotho origin of the boys' circumcision school, *murundu;* apart from the Sotho words in many texts, the music that I heard is distinctly pentatonic and non-Venda in style. Chief Makhado, who reigned in the latter part of the nineteenth century in western Vendaland, was the first Venda chief to be circumcised—probably in order to crystallize support in his political struggle against the rightful heir, his older brother Davhana. Today, the schools are attended by most commoners, and also by members of ruling families who are prepared to forfeit their chances of succession, since, in spite of Makhado's lead in western Vendaland, most of the eastern Venda insist that chiefs should be uncircumcised. The

schools have always been run semiprivately by doctors, but
they have come increasingly under the influence of headmen
who, though often uncircumcised themselves, will encourage
the circumcision of their subjects and take a part of the fees.
Headmen even express their support for the institution by
imposing a ban on communal music in areas where a school
is being held.

Third, there are girls' initiation schools, called *sungwi* or
musevhetho, which doctors run partly as an advertisement for
their practices, paying the local headman or chief an annual
fee for permission to set up the schools in his district. The
schools must be suspended if more important schools are
held (e.g., *domba* and the boys' circumcision school), but
nothing is suspended in their honor. The music is often pentatonic, and the rhythms are fast. The standard Venda tenor
and alto drums are used, but they are given special names, as
is also done when they are used in the possession dances—
a further indication of the music's foreign origin.

Although names of instruments, song types, and dances
may suggest the origins of styles, they can also arouse expectations of diversity and cultural contact where there has
been only straightforward development. For instance, the
names given to the different pitches of the pentatonic sets
of reed-pipes are clearly non-Venda and closely allied to Sotho; but the different names given to dances that are, or have
been, played on these pipes (i.e., *givha, visa, tshikanganga*)
refer only to different types of dances and dance tunes that
have been in vogue for a time and may have been superseded.
The social function of the dance, as an entertainment for
youths and girls, has always remained the same.

Of these three types of music, that of the boys' circumcision
school has been the least influenced by, or influential on, the
main stream of Venda music, and yet it is the only one which
merits cancellation by rulers of other communal activities.
The music of possession dances, in spite of its fast tempo,
is most closely related to the Venda tradition, but its performance is not encouraged by rulers. The girls' school stands
somewhere between these two extremes, both musically and
sociologically.

The different degrees of musical assimilation can be explained by the fact that the boys' school is, obviously, for males only; also, it is held in secret in the bush, there is no drumming, and the songs are not sung outside the school. The girls' school is primarily of interest to girls, to certain youths who have been to the boys' school and wish to dance in disguise, and to the relatives and friends of the doctors who run it. The special dancing platform and other paraphernalia can be seen by anyone who chooses to walk past them. Noninitiates are not supposed to watch the performances at night, but they can hear the music clearly. Girls practice the drum rhythms outside the school and interchange the rhythms of the girls' school with those of other dance-songs. Possession dances, on the other hand, are of great interest to adults and children alike, for they are related to the universal institution of ancestor worship, and their dramatic style always draws a crowd, especially on the first day or two when people are falling into trances. They therefore have a much greater impact on the musical life of the Venda than either the boys' or girls' schools.

However, in spite of its acceptance by the Venda and its prominence in Venda musical life, the possession cult has still not received the unqualified support of rulers, whereas the boys' schools have. There is a Venda saying, *musanda vha toda ngoma fhedzi*—"at the chief's village they love the big drum more than anything"—since it is beaten at the *domba* initiation, for which fees are collected from the people. The apparently obvious explanation of the situation is that the boys' schools, which could be compulsory for all men, are profitable; the girls' schools are not particularly profitable; and the possession cult is a private affair of certain families and has no financial possibilities.

There is, however, a further explanation in terms of political power. Rulers cannot sanction fully the possession cult, since it is a deviation from the traditional forms of worship which they support, and which support them. The girls' schools are not particularly important one way or the other, because the girls cannot be used to strengthen the political power of the doctors who run them, except insofar as owner-

ship of a school may bring some prestige. The boys' schools
on the other hand, could be dangerous if mishandled. Like
the girls' schools, they were introduced and are run by doctors, who are always influential men and usually commoners;
but a group of young men trained together under strenuous
conditions could be used to create disturbances and wield
political influence in a way which would not be possible with
girls. By accepting the schools as a standard Venda institution, rulers fill the gap left by the decay of formal age-sets
and of the earlier schools *thondo* and *vhutuka,* form a useful
alliance with the doctors, and achieve a balance of power
by giving commoners, and sometimes members of ruling
families, an organization that both absorbs their interests
and ensures, by the operation of circumcision, that they are
not at any time able to make a serious claim to chiefly office.

There is also an interesting spatial element in the diffusion
of these musical styles. The major ruling clans moved eastward into the Sibasa district from the areas round Nzhelele
and Louis Trichardt, and tended to drive the inhabitants of
Vendaland ahead of them. The boys' schools moved into
Vendaland by the same route. But the possession cult moved
from the opposite direction, that is, westward from the north-
east (see Map 4).

THE RECONSTRUCTION OF EARLY VENDA
MUSICAL HISTORY

An understanding of the musical and social processes involved in this *known* situation helps us to reconstruct the
growth of the complex of music and initiation rites that is
generally accepted as being pure Venda, but which, according to the musical and sociological evidence, appears to
be a synthesis of different social and cultural streams.

An important Venda instrument in the past, which is
rarely seen or played today, is the xylophone, *mbila mutondo.*
It has a heptatonic scale similar to that of the reed-pipes of
the national dance, and it appears that it is, and was, made
only by members of one of the Dau clans, who were living
in Vendaland before the arrival of the invaders.

The national dance also seems to belong to preconquest

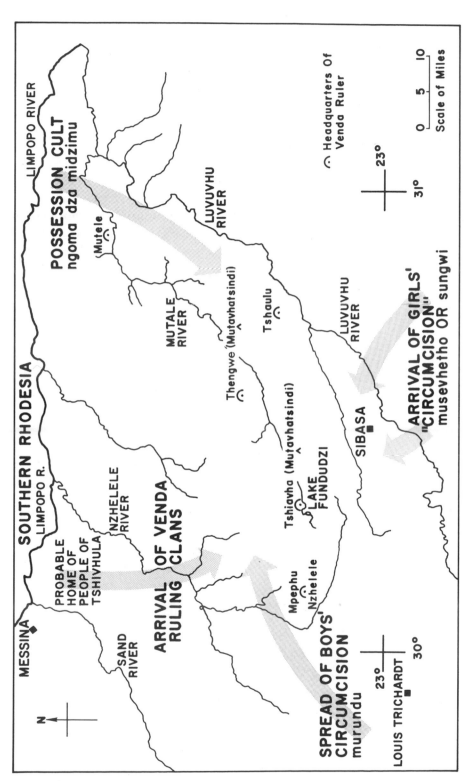

MAP 4. Vendaland, Northern Transvaal

Vendaland, and it may have been the music of the chiefs of Tshivhula or of the Tavhatsindi—probably the latter, because of their connection with Lake Fundudzi and their authority over a drum cult.

The same may be said of *domba,* a remarkable premarital initiation school with a distinctive ritual song, in which each novice sings part of a descending melodic pattern, in the same way that the national dance is played but at a much slower speed. The evidence that the core of the *domba* music and ritual is preconquest in date is even more convincing than that for the antiquity of the national dance. Some of the songs that are now publicly sung at the initiation appear to be the private songs of ancestor worship of the rain-making Mbedzi clan, whose headquarters and chieftainess are at Mianzwi, near the sacred pool of Maneledzi, to which they offer an annual sacrifice. In the great initiation song and various of the rituals there are references to the rain-makers and their pool cult; to sacred Lake Fundudzi, which is cared for by a headman of the Tavhatsindi; to a snake cult; to a drum cult; to magic and medicine; and to cultural phenomena which appear to have belonged more to the settled community in Vendaland than to their conquerors. The masters of initiation generally belong to one of the preconquest clans; and the final ritual, after the fees have been paid to the ruler, is held not at the ruler's village but at the home of the master.

Further important evidence is to be found in the distinction between the "puberty" school for daughters of the ruling clans (*vhusha ha vhakololo*), for which there is no music whatsoever, and that for commoners (*vhusha ha vhasiwana*), which is saturated with music and dancing.[17] The chief ritual song of the commoners' school differs in rhythm from that of *domba,* but its style is similar and it is not impossible that they should belong to the same musical tradition.

There is more evidence, which cannot be discussed here, and it all suggests that, prior to the invasion of the ancestors of the present rulers, Vendaland was populated by a loose

17. See John Blacking, "Songs, Dances, Mimes and Symbolism of Venda Girls' Initiation Schools: Part 1," *African Studies,* XXVIII, no. 1 (1969), 1–35; see also parts 2–4 in nos. 2–4.

federation of mutually dependent but politically autonomous units, with a rich and varied culture and a lively interest in magic, religion, and rain-making. Their music was predominantly heptatonic, and there was a considerable variety of styles. The hexatonic music may have been a separate stream or merely part of the heptatonic tradition.

These peoples were invaded by clans who were culturally "poor" but politically and militarily strong, and whose music was almost certainly pentatonic. They imposed their elaborate rituals of chieftainship on the local inhabitants and patronized their customs. Initiation schools were taken over, but were never run by the men of the ruling clans who, to this day, rarely participate in musical performances. The current interest of noblewomen in the girls' initiation schools may be partly due to the influence of their mothers or co-mothers; the rulers have always been very careful to select wives from the "aboriginal" clans, in order to remain on good terms with the confidants of the spirits who "owned" the land before they came. (This reconstruction of the Venda past would, incidentally, support the hypothesis that little musical variety and originality is to be expected in a society with a unified, hierarchical political system, but considerable variety can be expected in a segmented society. A further example, from more sophisticated cultures, is provided by the contrast between the degree of creative musical activity in unified, empire-building England and in segmented Germany in the eighteenth and nineteenth centuries.)

This interpretation of Venda musical history seems to be open to one serious objection. It is generally accepted that the ancestors of the present ruling clans brought with them a remarkable drum called *ngoma lugundu*, which helped them to rout their enemies. Following this, it is assumed that the present Venda drums were originally brought by these people. But even if the conquerors did introduce the shape of the drums, as Kirby has implied, this does not necessarily mean that they also introduced the social and musical uses of them. Besides, the evidence strongly favors the original existence of *two* drum cults, which have now been amalgamated into one. The drum cult of the original inhabitants of Vendaland was

like that of the Lovedu,[18] concerned with magic, rain-making,
and the use of drums in initiation; whereas the drum cult of
the conquerors was related to the political power of the chief.
It is probable that the conquerors, like the Ankole of Uganda,[19]
used drums not for music but as symbols of power and as
signals for rallying people in time of war. Thus the *ngoma
lungundu* story [20] may refer only to the sacred drum or drums
of a drumless people and not to the prototype of the much
used, sacred drums of the original inhabitants of Vendaland,
models of which are now kept in the village of any self-
respecting ruler.

I hope that the brief outline I have presented of some events
in Venda musical history is substantially correct, and that
subsequent research will confirm it. Nonetheless, even if some
of my field material is unbalanced and has distorted the
ethnographic picture, and even if my particular conclusions
are proved wrong, the main purpose of this paper will not
have been defeated. I have tried to demonstrate why ethnomusicologists—those in Africa, at any rate—must pay careful
attention to exact details of performance and to the cultural
background of music before they can compare musical styles,
and how the results of their analyses may assist ethno-
historians in reconstructing the history of Africa. I hope I
have shown how the historical process may have affected the
growth and creation of music in Vendaland, and how the different styles of Venda music are in turn a reflection of historical events.

18. See E. J. and J. D. Krige, *The Realm of a Rain-Queen* (London:
Oxford University Press, 1943), esp. pp. 126–40.
19. John Roscoe, *The Banyankole* (London: Oxford University Press,
1923), pp. 44 ff.
20. E. Mudau, *"Ngoma Lungundu,"* in *The Copper Miners of Musina
and the Early History of the Zoutpansberg*, ed. N. J. van Warmelo,
Ethnological Publications, no. 8 (Pretoria: Government Printer, 1940),
pp. 8–32, 109–32; see also H. von Sicard, *Ngoma Lungundu: Eine
afrikanische Bundeslade*, Studia Ethnographica Upsaliensia, no. 5
(Uppsala: University of Uppsala, 1952).

10.

Stylistic Evidence
in Nguni Song

DAVID K. RYCROFT

Editor's Note: One of the chief raw materials of music history is stylistic evidence, and the collection, analysis, and evaluation of such evidence by the musicologist is a preliminary to the work of the historian. In making his study, the musicologist legitimately tries to catch a glimpse of historical events or of an "evolutionary" sequence. With this in mind, David Rycroft here surveys the musical style of those southern Bantu peoples that are collectively referred to as the Nguni language group, singling out songs from the Zulu, Swazi, and Xhosa.

GENERAL FEATURES OF NGUNI MUSIC

IT MAY CERTAINLY BE STATED of all Nguni peoples that their music is predominantly vocal rather than instrumental. There is no evidence that elaborate drums and percussion ensembles like those found elsewhere in Africa have ever held a place in their communal dance music. They frequently dance or perform the actions of some common task accompanied only by their own antiphonal singing. At weddings and important ceremonial occasions, ankle rattles, hand-clapping, or the brandishing of weapons, shields, sticks, or implements may enhance their rhythmic expression, but singing is always paramount. Hand-clapping is done only by women. It is normally performed with flat palms and with the fingertips meeting. For Zulu girls' coming-of-age ceremonies, however, there used to be a distinctive style of clapping with hollowed palms or sometimes with a stone held in each palm.

Earlier writers have referred to an Nguni practice of beating upon war shields for ceremonial purposes, and Kirby describes a survival of this as Xhosa young peoples' dances.[1] At Xhosa circumcision ceremonies an even more rudimentary form of percussion accompaniment, known as the *ingqongqo*, is employed. A plain oxhide, hand-held or suspended above the ground on poles, is beaten by several participants.[2] To other Nguni this practice is unknown. They do not hold such ceremonies, though they may have done so formerly, before the time of Shaka.[3]

Among the Zulu, an instrument used exclusively as an accompaniment for female initiation songs was the *ingungu*, friction drum, adapted—sometimes temporarily—from a milk pail or beer pot.[4] The ceremony and the instrument are rarely found today, however.

Instead of the ancient practice of beating on a hide,[5] small drums are now often used by Nguni doctors for exorcism, and numerous separatist religious sects nowadays employ drums in their services. But these instruments have no standardized

1. Percival R. Kirby, *The Musical Instruments of the Native Races of South Africa* (London: Oxford University Press, 1934; reprint ed., Johannesburg: Witwatersrand University Press, 1953), pp. 23–24.
2. *Ibid.*, pp. 20–23.
3. E. J. Krige, *The Social System of the Zulus* (London: Longmans, 1936; new ed., Pietermaritzburg, South Africa: Shuter & Shooter, 1962), pp. 116–17.
4. *Ibid.*, pp. 102, 336; Kirby, *Musical Instruments*, pp. 26–28.
5. Krige, *Social System of the Zulus*, p. 336.

form and are evidently borrowings or innovations, as are also those made from metal oil drums, used for modern Zulu *ingoma* dancing, which is largely a town art-form.

Personal instruments, however, such as several types of flutes and musical bows, held an important place in private Nguni music-making in earlier times.[6] Reference will be made later to the most important of these instruments. They are rarely found today, except in remote areas, where the players are mostly women and children. Men, since they have more direct contact with Westernized town life, have come to adopt nonindigenous instruments such as the "German" concertina and, especially, the guitar. Some interesting hybrid local styles have emerged.

Organized arm gestures and body postures, accompanied by stepping or stamping, at various tempi, are typical of all Nguni dancing styles.[7] It is asserted by the Zulu that their solemn *amahubo* (singular: *ihubo*), ceremonial anthems, are performed without dancing. Certainly little leg movement takes place, but there are obligatory arm gestures, particularly that of pointing, *ukukhomba*, which is also an important action in some of their acknowledged dances.

A distinctive muscle-quivering dance is peculiar to certain Xhosa tribes. The Xhosa appear to be distinct in other respects too, including language and customs. Linguistic evidence suggests that there may have been greater Hottentot influence upon the Xhosa than upon other Nguni. The Xhosa settled farther south and were probably the first to encounter the Hottentots. All other Nguni peoples seem to have more in common with one another than with the Xhosa.

TONALITY IN NGUNI MUSIC

At the present stage of our knowledge, it is difficult or perhaps impossible to offer all-embracing generalizations about music of the Nguni peoples as a whole, particularly on the

6. Kirby, *Musical Instruments,* see Index under Swazi, Xhosa, and Zulu.
7. H. T. Tracey, *African Dances of the Witwatersrand Gold Mines* (Johannesburg: African Music Society, 1952) ; Krige, *Social System of the Zulus,* pp. 340–44.

subject of tonality. Assertions that the tonality is exclusively pentatonic, however, are certainly inaccurate. Even within a single tribe or family, a variety of "scales" may be found, and there are differences of style associated with the execution of different types of song. Evidence of this is available from a study of published recordings of music of the Zulu Buthelezi tribe and of Swazi and Xhosa items.[8]

Earlier claims by some writers that Nguni music was pentatonic were no doubt based upon limited experience, perhaps of only one type of Nguni music—those high-spirited *indlamu* or *ingoma* dance-songs of a comparatively light nature, performed by young people for general merrymaking. Even among these songs, however, many will be found to be hexatonic, resembling our own diatonic but without the seventh degree. These light dance-songs are the most frequently heard items of Nguni music, particularly in towns, mining compounds, and the like, where they may also often be adapted for use as work songs. Before the advent of Hugh Tracey's ILAM recordings, which cover a wide range of Nguni music, this style of song made up the bulk of the commercially recorded Nguni repertoire, apart from hybrid varieties of town music. Nguni light dance-songs, as distinct from Europeanized town products, still follow tribal conventions regarding the observance of speech-tones and are basically traditional in style. While the Xhosa may again be counted out in this respect, this type of light dance-song seems to be readily acceptable and transmissible between one Nguni tribe and another and might thus be said to possess something of a common Nguni style, though local shadings are observable. A simple representative (Example 1) is the Zulu wedding song or children's song from Ifafa, Natal: *"Aline lona nini makoti?"* "When will the rain come, O

8. LP discs issued by the International Library of African Music (ILAM), Roodepoort, South Africa, in a series entitled The Music of Africa. Since this paper was prepared, some additional field recordings have been made by the author and published on two LP discs (with accompanying brochures), *Swazi Music* and *Zulu, Swazi and Xhosa Instrumental and Vocal Music*, issued as numbers 1 and 3 (1968 and 1969) in a series of African musical recordings published by the Musée Royale de l'Afrique Centrale, Tervuren, in collaboration with Belgian Radio and Television, Brussels.

EXAMPLE 1. Zulu Light Dance-Song

bride?" [9] (Rain on the wedding day is said to be lucky.) It is possible that the Mpondo, the most northerly of the Xhosa tribes, or the Bhaca, also in the eastern Cape Province, were originally responsible for this style of music.

Besides a body of light dance music that has something like a common Nguni style, there remains, nevertheless, a great deal of music that has more individual national, tribal, clan, or local distinctiveness.

In ceremonial music and communal dance-songs an "open" voice quality seems common to all Nguni, and there is a tendency among old men toward a tremulous vibrato, which may be unintentional. But in young men's songs there is greater tribal diversity. In many Xhosa young men's songs a tense voice quality is cultivated, and sometimes an extremely low, forced bass. Young Swazi men employ portamento and sudden crescendi and diminuendi in their regimental songs. Some explosive fortissimo yells occur in Zulu regimental chants and war cries (izaga). All Nguni employ portamento, but in different degrees. The Zulu probably use it the most extensively and the Xhosa the least.

As an optional variant to what we should regard as true song, one type of Zulu recreational and wedding dance of long standing, the isigekle, may be performed against "choral recitation." [10] Here there is regular rhythm but parlando voice

9. Unpublished recording made by the author in 1961. The singer is Victor Mcunu.
10. ILAM AMA TR 12.

quality and no fixed musical notes.[11] I have encountered a similar practice among other Nguni. Contrary to Western standards, this still qualifies as "song," while their *izibongo*, "praises," do not. The latter use fixed musical pitches but are unmetrical.[12] It appears, therefore, that the Nguni distinguish music from other forms of expression on rhythmic rather than tonal criteria.

Rhythmically, the dance-songs of some Xhosa tribes display considerably greater subtlety than those of other Nguni, which might be called stodgy by comparison. Zulu dance-songs have perhaps the greatest virility and fire, however, if not so much rhythmic finesse.

Within the Zulu repertoire of reputedly archaic *amahubo* anthems and ceremonial dance-songs, some employ a rudimentary three-note "scale" comprising two conjunct fourths. But others, also of great age, contain chromaticism, though the fourth is still an important structural interval. Much Swazi ceremonial music, including ritual anthems, contains similar semitone progressions, with structural fourths and fifths. There seems to be less chromaticism in Xhosa ceremonial music.

Regarding the occurrence of semitone progressions in genuinely old music that cannot have come under Western influence, two possible sources suggest themselves, though neither of these is altogether conclusive. One is the influence of speech-tones on melody. I think it improbable that any exact musical interval could arise from Nguni speech-tone progressions, but the subject will be pursued at a later point. The other possible factor is the unbraced musical bow, the classic Nguni instrument for solo song accompaniment. Among the Zulu and Swazi this is traditionally played in such a way as to yield an interval that roughly approximates a semitone. Several ceremonial dance-songs of the Zulu Buthelezi tribe employ semitones and are reputed to have been composed by

11. David K. Rycroft, "Linguistic and Melodic Interaction in Zulu Song," in *Akten des XXIV Internationalen Orientalistenkongresses, München* (Wiesbaden: Deutsche Morgenländische Gesellschaft, 1957), pp. 726–29.
12. David K. Rycroft, "Melodic Features in Zulu Eulogistic Recitation," *African Language Studies*, I (1960), 60–78.

one or another ancestor who "sang it to the accompaniment of his *ugubhu* bow."

Kirby posited the origin of certain South African vocal scales from harmonics of a single instrumental note, but he stopped short on the subject of possible derivation from two fundamentals and their overtones.[13] I feel, however, that the latter possibility warrants consideration in the case of our present material.

BOW-SONGS

Musical bows of various types, both mouth-resonated and with attached gourd resonator, are widely distributed in central and southern Africa.[14] But customs as to whether bows of one or another variety are played either by men or women, by the young or by the old, vary from tribe to tribe.

Though it is rarely found today, the classic form of gourd-bow among the Nguni is the simple, unbraced variety (Zulu: *ugubhu;* Swazi: *ligubhu;* Xhosa: *uhadi*) with a calabash resonator attached near the lower end of the stave. The instrument is played by either men or women. It is held vertically by the left hand, near the bottom, with the opening in the calabash facing the left breast and the string facing away from the player. The string, of twisted sinew or of oxtail or horsetail hair, is beaten with a stalk of thatching grass or a thin reed and yields one open, low-pitched note. A second note is produced by finger-stopping or, to be more precise about Zulu technique, by pinching the string near its lower end, between the left thumbnail and index finger. Among the Zulu and Swazi this stopped note is generally roughly a semitone (90 to 150 cents) higher than the open note. Among the Xhosa a larger interval, loosely approximating a whole tone, is usually preferred.

In addition to the unbraced type of bow, the Zulu and Swazi (but not the Xhosa) have a braced gourd-bow, with

13. Kirby, *Musical Instruments*, p. 240.
14. C. M. Camp and B. Nettle, "The Musical Bow in Southern Africa," *Anthropos*, L (1955), 65; David K. Rycroft, "Friction Chordophones in South-Eastern Africa," *Galpin Society Journal*, XIX (1966), 84–100; Kirby, *Musical Instruments*, pp. 193–245.

divided string, from which three notes can be obtained. It is used for accompanying less serious music than that which is sung with the unbraced bow, and it is said to have been imported from the Tsonga, of Mozambique, probably early in the nineteenth century. The commonest among several names for this instrument are (Zulu) *umakhweyana,* and (Swazi) *makhweyane.* The string is usually of brass or copper wire, and this is tied back by a loop near its center. It is played in such a way as to yield three fundamental pitches: two open notes (one from each segment of the string) which may be tuned roughly anywhere between a whole tone to a minor third apart, and a third note, usually about a semitone above the higher of the former two. This is produced by stopping the string near the restraining loop with the knuckle of the left index or middle finger. The calabash resonator, which is attached to the restraining loop, rests against the outer curve of the bow stave, but it is insulated from the stave (as is also the case with the resonator of the unbraced bow) by a soft "washer" of cloth or fiber. For both types of bow, the orifice in the calabash is usually relatively small compared with gourd-bows from elsewhere, measuring about six or seven centimeters in diameter. Gourd-bows observed among non-Nguni peoples (in southern, central, and eastern Africa, generally) seem mostly to have a much larger orifice to the resonator.

For southern Africa, Kirby has described both these types of bow in detail, as well as various mouth-resonated forms of bow formerly used by the Nguni and their neighbors.[15] Certain of the simpler types of bow might possibly have been adopted from the Bushmen or Hottentots, but the gourd-bow, braced or unbraced, seems to have been unknown to both of these southern precursors of the Bantu.

Playing technique for both types of gourd-bow includes deliberate amplification of harmonics, mostly the third, fourth, and fifth partials of the two or three fundamentals. Selective resonance of one or another of these partials is obtained by moving the mouth of the resonator closer to or farther from

15. Kirby, *Musical Instruments,* pp. 193 ff.

the player's chest, thus varying the size of the opening and altering its resonant frequency. Absolute precision of intervals between the two or three fundamentals seems not to be regarded as particularly important. What is more important is that the string tension should be adjusted so as to allow the calabash to resonate the required range of harmonics.

Vocal style in bow-songs tends to be very quiet and relaxed, probably to avoid drowning the pure, soft fanfare melody of the resonated harmonics, which is at best a private tune, scarcely audible to anyone but the player. Previous writers, and also those taking sound recordings, have, I think, overlooked the importance attached to this aspect of bow playing, though with respect to other, mouth-resonated instruments, Kirby's descriptions are excellent.[16]

In songs accompanied on the braced bow, the selectively resonated harmonics certainly appear to directly influence the singer's choice of vocal scale, which commonly matches the fundamental notes of the bowstring (or their octaves) plus the resonated third partials of these, i.e., notes an octave and a fifth above the fundamentals. In ten recorded bow-songs by Zulu Buthelezi women, in which the braced *umakhweyana* is used, the fundamental notes yielded by the bow could be transposed as D, E, and F.[17] Tones employed in the vocal line consist of no more than these same three notes (or their octaves) plus A, B, and C, which are fifths (i.e., third harmonics) above these. The middle bow note, E, usually serves as tonal center. Here we have a hexa mode with two semitone intervals. The latter present no difficulty to the singers, who make frequent melodic use of them, though almost always as descending intervals. It should be noted that the main semitone interval normally lies between the tonal center and the note above it—never in the position of lower, leading note to tonal center like the Western relation of leading note to the tonic. In passing, it might be added that Christianized Nguni have been criticized by missionaries, no less than have other

16. *Ibid.*, pp. 199–241.
17. On ILAM AMA TR 10, side A.

Bantu, for rendering semitone steps inaccurately in Western hymn tunes.

Whether the braced bow's rising whole-tone-plus-semitone sequence has actually given rise to a hexatonic scale or whether it is played this way in order to fit in with an established vocal scale cannot, however, be determined. And, in any event, the braced *umakhweyana* cannot be considered as the source of chromaticism in very old ceremonial music if, as is claimed, it is a relatively recent borrowing. The classic, unbraced bow has, on the other hand, allegedly inspired earlier Nguni composers. What is the pitch relation between instrument and voice when these two-note bows are employed?

In several recorded songs from the Xhosa Ngqika tribe, accompanied on the unbraced bow, the bow notes lie approximately a whole tone apart.[18] The singers employ hexa modes, transposable as D–C–B–A–G–F, which could be viewed as arising from two interlocking major triads based on the bow's notes—i.e., related to their third, fourth, and fifth partials, all of which are clearly audible (see Figure 25).

FIGURE 25
Bow Notes and Vocal Tones, I

	Bow fundamentals	Vocal tones
	F	C F A
	G	D G B
Bow partials	1	3 4 5

The occurrence of the C–B semitone in a vocal mode such as this may thus stem directly from bow technique. But the evolution of just such a hexa mode from a rudimentary chain of fourths *without* instrumental intervention is perhaps equally possible, as will be considered later.

A more direct connection between vocal semitones and the two instrumental notes can be seen in some Swazi and Zulu

18. On ILAM AMA TR 13, side B, bands 1–5.

items where the bow notes lie approximately a semitone instead of a whole tone apart. In her rendering of the traditional Zulu narrative song entitled *"uNomagundwane,"* Princess Constance Magogo (mother of Chief Gatsha Buthelezi and daughter of King Dinizulu) employs a penta mode containing two semitone intervals.[19] If the fundamental notes of the ugubhu bow are transposed as F♯ and F, the vocal notes would be F♯, F, C♯, C, and A. Vocal notes C♯ and C yield, of course, a transposed semitone step analogous to F♯ and F, and they strongly suggest the third partials of these bow notes as their source (see Figure 26).

FIGURE 26
Bow Notes and Vocal Tones, II

	Bow fundamentals		Vocal tones		
	F		C	F	A
	F♯		C♯	F♯	—
Bow partials	1		3	4	5

Although an unrelated note or two are occasionally found in some songs with the unbraced bow (Xhosa and Swazi as well as Zulu), I do not think these "odd men out" necessarily negate the likelihood that the others are derived from bow harmonics.[20] What cannot be clearly ascertained, however, is whether the various local modes used in bow-songs all actually took their birth from the bow or whether styles of bow tuning were not dictated by the requirements of one or more known, pre-existing vocal scales—to which the addition of new notes may have been inspired by bow technique.

SPEECH-TONES AND TONALITY

In many Nguni bow-songs, the overall flow of vocal melody follows the pitch contours of speech more closely than is the case with group songs, where more melodic stylization

19. On *Zulu, Swazi and Xhosa Instrumental and Vocal Music,* side A, band 4.
20. On ILAM AMA TR 13, 72, and 10, respectively.

often overlays the text. This distinction between speech-tone treatment in solos, as against group songs, has been discussed in an earlier paper.[21] In spoken Nguni—generally, Zulu, Xhosa, and Swazi—two tonal registers, or "levels" of *relative* pitch, are observed, and certain syllables may glide from one to the other. The term "relative" is used here because a syllable sequence such as high-low-high-low is normally realized in speech not as an alternation of two fixed pitches, like sol-do-sol-do, but as something more like sol-mi-fa-do. Both the high and the low speech-tones in an utterance tend progressively to drop in pitch. This overall descending pitch contour, which affects the *absolute* pitch at which speech-tones are realized but does not obliterate their high-low contrast, is technically known as sentence intonation. The rate of descent is different in the case of questions, and in long statements it may be broken up into several shorter descending contours.

In solo bow-songs, this descending sentence-intonation contour seems to be faithfully followed. Text and melody are an artistic whole. It is as if the singer were enhancing a spoken utterance by rendering it musically. In most group songs, on the other hand, there seems to be more melodic latitude. The relative speech-tone rise and fall within individual words is generally observed, but not necessarily the sentence intonation. It seems permissible for a high syllable at various points in the phrase to be realized on almost any note, provided that one or more lower notes are available for intervening low syllables.

While speech-tones can be credited with determining to a large extent the syllable-to-syllable rise or fall in the melodic line of a song, they cannot, by reason of the relative and variable nature of spoken pitch in Nguni languages, be said to determine the exact intervals employed in song. It would be fruitless to seek in speech the source of exact semitones or minor thirds. In fact, a considerable number of old songs, particularly ceremonial anthems of the Swazi and Zulu, employ semitones even when the text is wordless—and hence devoid of any obligatory speech-tone sequence.

21. Rycroft, "Linguistic and Melodic Interaction."

WORDLESS SONG TEXTS

Callaway quotes the following text for what he claims to have been "Utshaka's Rain Song": [22]

1. I–ya–wu.	Awu, o–ye–i–ye.
2. (Response)	I–ya–wo.

To this he adds the footnote, "this song consists of musical sounds merely, but imperfectly represented above, without any meaning." One may speculate that the purpose of using expressive but lexically meaningless lines, as well as fa-la-la-type interpolations in dance-songs, may have been in order to allow greater melodic freedom, unbound by the speech-tone limitations of words. But there are also grounds for suspecting that in earlier times considerable emotional content may have been vested in these particular sounds, especially in the context of religious or ritual functions that are no longer observed today.

Songs with texts partly or wholly of this kind are still sung today. Among Tracey's Buthelezi recordings there occurs the following *ihubo* attributed to King Cetshwayo (b. 1829), sung by villagers led by the present chief of the Buthelezi clan, who is a grandson of Cetshwayo.[23]

Call:	Siwahlula ngemi-khonto.	We overcome them with spears.
	E–ya–ye.	— — —
Response:	Ho–ho.	— —
Text:	Sinik' abafo!	Give us the enemies!
	Bamqal' okandaba.	They provoke the son of Ndaba.[24]
	Kaqali muntu.	He provokes no one.
	Sinik' abafo!	Give us the enemies!
	Uzithulele.	He is silent.
	Kaqali muntu.	He provokes no one.
	Sidedele siminye!	Let us drain the beer pot!

22. H. Callaway, *The Religious System of the AmaZulu* (1870; rev. ed., ed. W. Wanger, Mariannhill, South Africa: Mariannhill Mission Press, 1913), pt. 1, p. 97.
23. On ILAM AMA TR 12, side A, band 5. For elucidation of the text, acknowledgment is due to S. S. Ngubane.
24. Ndaba, born in 1680, was the great-grandfather of Shaka and the great-great-grandfather of Cetshwayo.

This is sung with great solemnity, accompanied with slow arm gestures but no dance steps. The mode used is hemitonic penta, transposable as E–C–B–G–F. The C–B interval varies between a semitone and rather less, but otherwise the notes tally fairly closely with those of Princess Magogo's bow-song cited earlier. There is considerable use of portamento in this, as in all such ceremonial songs of the Zulu. Pitch fluctuates a good deal, and there is a gradual overall pitch rise of about a whole tone between the beginning and end of the song.

Another Zulu *ihubo*, which is treasured by the Buthelezi as their own particular tribal anthem,[25] is attributed to Ngqengelele (b. 1790), great-great-grandfather of the present chief. The gist of the text, interspersed with lines such as *"he–ya! he–yi!"* is as follows:

> We are now cast away
> From our father Shenge's place of olden time;
> What ails you, people?
> Do you not know we were founded in olden days?
> Now we are seated near the doorway.

(The doorway is the place of honor—referring here to finding favor with the ruling Zulu tribe.) (See Example 2.)

CHAINS OF FOURTHS

Only three notes, G, D, and C, and their octaves are employed in the above song. This rudimentary scale occurs in many more of the Buthelezi ceremonial songs [26] and also in some of their reputedly very ancient dance-songs.[27] Often, as in the next example, the arrangement of the notes is that of two conjunct fourths (though octave separation may be occasioned by male and female voices). A whole-tone step below the lower fourth then completes the octave. The full compass is not used outright, but the leading and the responsive phrases are confined, respectively, to the upper fourth and to the lower fourth plus a whole tone. The Buthelezi war song

25. On ILAM AMA TR 9, side B, band 3.
26. *Ibid.*, bands 3–6.
27. On ILAM AMA TR 12, side A, bands 1–5.

EXAMPLE 2. Zulu Buthelezi Tribal Anthem

"Yindlwan' embana! Ake siwashise!" [28] "It Is the Hated House! Let Us Burn Them!" illustrates this point. It is attributed to Mnyamana, a great-grandfather of the present chief. (See Example 3.)

The prevalence of fourths in this music, as elsewhere among Bantu tribes, belies Sachs's rather surprising generalizations that Black Africa is "nearly devoid of fourths" and that "the third appears to have almost the monopoly in Black Africa." [29]

Several other *amahubo* and ancient dance-songs of the Zulu use this rudimentary three-tone scale in exactly the

28. On ILAM AMA TR 9, side B, band 4.
29. Curt Sachs, *The Wellsprings of Music* (The Hague: Martinus Nijhoff, 1962), p. 63.

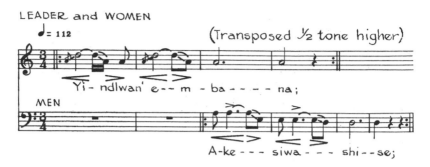

EXAMPLE 3. Mnyamana's War Song

same way. Many more of their songs, however, employ four, five, or six tones. But in a large number of these, the same rudimentary three tones appear to be structurally prominent, either as two conjunct fourths again, transposable as C–G–D (–C), or in inverted, disjunct form: G–D–C–G. Hornbostel's theory that the prevalence of fourths "as a frame for melodic phrases" and the use of intermediate notes for melodic steps produce "melodic forms known as pentatonic" would seem to be particularly apt here.[30] Example 4 is a Zulu regimental song, "Do You See the 'Star and Sun'? [probably the name of a regiment] Look Out! We Shall Overcome Them All!" [31]

In other Nguni songs based on structural fourths, it is not

EXAMPLE 4. Zulu Regimental Song

30. Erich M. von Hornbostel, "African Negro Music," *Africa*, I, no. 1 (1928), 30.
31. Unpublished recording made by the author in 1961. The singer is Victor Mcunu.

always B and F that serve as intermediate notes in a C–G–D frame. B and F♯, each a semitone below C and G, respectively, are the ones used in the Cetshwayo *ihubo* cited earlier—if we transpose the tone series to permit comparisons. In several Swazi songs the intermediate notes are a semitone *above* two of the structural notes. This is immediately suggestive of bow technique, such as that of Princess Magogo's bow-song, though it is not known whether songs such as that of Example 5 are actually of bow-song origin. Example 5 is a generalized

EXAMPLE 5. Swazi Girls' Ceremonial Reed-Cutting Song

extract from a Swazi women's song entitled *"Lezontaba,"* "Yonder mountains." [32] The structurally important notes are A, G, D, and low A. If these are transposed as D, C, G, and low D, for comparison with the old fourths structure, the passing notes (transposable as A♭ and E♭) can then be seen to lie a semitone above G and D, respectively. This pentatonic series seems to resemble precisely the "exceptional Japanese pentatonic" pattern referred to by Hornbostel.[33] In the absence of other evidence it seems possible that bow technique might here again be responsible for the introduction of semitone steps in Swazi music of this kind.

In Nguni light dance-songs the conjunct or disjunct fourths structure is again frequently evident, and in many five-note examples the intermediate notes are transposable as A and E within a C–G–D frame. This of course resembles our familiar "common" pentatonic series. Either C or G most commonly serves as finalis in these songs. The Zulu song *"Aline lona nini . . ."* (Example 1) serves as a representative.

32. On ILAM AMA TR 68, side B, band 3; on *Swazi Music*, side B, band 6.
33. Hornbostel, "African Negro Music."

More commonly, however, Nguni light dance-songs use *six* notes—those of the above pentatonic series plus the note F, i.e., an almost fully diatonic scale but with the seventh degree missing. In some Xhosa Mpondo songs in this category, a cycle of fifths is suggested rather than a structure of fourths, as for instance in the Mpondo men's song of Example 6.[34]

This song gives the impression of making an excursion through three fifths, from G down through C and F to B♭, but may alternatively be seen as an extended descending chain of disjunct fourths, G–D, C–G, F–C, B♭, with A as intermediate note in the second fourth. A chain structure extended as far as this is rare in Nguni light dance-songs.

EXAMPLE 6. Mpondo Men's Song

34. On Gallotone GALP 1033, side 1, band 6.

More usually the hexatonic songs operate within an upper fifth, transposable as G–C, with diatonic steps, and descend to the G below, B being absent, as in the Zulu work song, *"Bayasibopha,"* "They Arrest Us" [35] (Example 7).

Frequent use of E in relations with G and C in such songs (transposed to "C-major" tonality) gives the impression of common chord progression and, since the familiar diatonic notes C, D, E, F, and G are used, European influence might be suspected. The teaching of the missionaries and the singing of

EXAMPLE 7. Topical Zulu Work Song

church hymns may well have inspired greater use of such features, but it is open to argument whether they inaugurated them among the Nguni. Alternatively, one could speculate upon an evolutionary development of this hexatonic series from the early Zulu three-tone series, even without, for the moment, considering possible instrumental influences.

We have seen in the three-note Zulu war song, Example 3, a contrasting use of the upper *vis-à-vis* the lower fourth and the downward extension of the latter by a whole-tone step to complete the octave. For present purposes, A–E–B–A serves as a convenient transposition of these notes, in descending order of pitch. If the whole-tone step B–A below the lower fourth were duplicated below the *upper* fourth, by analogy the note D, a whole tone below E, would result. Extension of the process of adding analogous whole tones below other notes could produce scales that are either "common pentatonic,"

35. Unpublished recording made by the author in 1960. The singer is Raymond Kunene.

or hexatonic of the common Nguni variety and, finally, a fully diatonic heptatonic series. This analysis does not conflict with Hornbostel's theory of fourths filled in by intermediate notes; rather, it suggests a means by which these, rather than other intermediate notes, should have found a place in Nguni pentatonic songs. Figure 27 illustrates the above working hypothesis. The early Zulu three-tone series is represented as stage 1. Completion of the octave by the whole-tone step B–A is indicated by a circle, as are also the analogous whole-tone steps between other notes in stages

FIGURE 27

The Evolution of Scale in Nguni Music by Accretion
of Analogous Whole Tones:

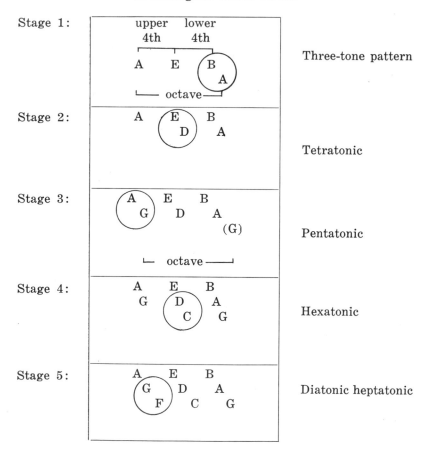

Stage 1:   Three-tone pattern

Stage 2:

          Tetratonic

Stage 3:

          Pentatonic

Stage 4:

          Hexatonic

Stage 5:

          Diatonic heptatonic

2, 3, 4, and 5. These analogous steps could give rise to other series in the manner indicated.

Four-tone "missing links" seem rare among available material, but the *ihubo* anthem of the Zulu Ngcobo tribe, *"Thuthuka Ngonyama!"* "Increase, O Lion!" [36] is of interest as a possible example of stage 2. Of the four tones, the leading phrase employs E, B, and A (in a manner similar to the *responsive* phrase of the three-tone war song, Example 3) followed by an almost exact, lower transposition of this sequence, so that the B–A whole-tone step appears to be duplicated below a low E to yield D. For comparison, the structure of the phrases in the three-tone war song and the four-tone anthem can be represented as in Figure 28.

FIGURE 28
Tonal Structure of Two Zulu Songs

Three-tone war song	
Leading phrase	A–E
Responsive phrase	E–B–A
Four-tone anthem	
Leading phrase	E–B–A
Responsive phrase	A–E–D

The light dance-song previously shown as Example 1 is pentatonic, using the notes of stage 3 in rearranged order, though in the melodic configuration of this particular song only the lowest part of the compass displays a prominent fourths' structure.

The hexatonic Xhosa Mpondo song of Example 6 may be viewed as an instance of stage 4, with the compass extended nearly two octaves, as was mentioned earlier. Heptatonic series are not as common in Nguni music as hexa and penta, but they certainly do occur, as in the Swazi lullaby (Example 8) recorded by Tracey.[37] The tone series here is exactly the diatonic hepta of Figure 27: that is, if it were transposed as B, A, G, F, E, D, C.

36. *Ibid.* The singer here is John Ngcobo.
37. ILAM AMA TR 68, side A, band 6; *Swazi Music*, side B, band 1.

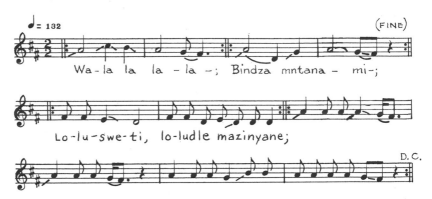

Wa-la la la -la -; Bindza mntana - mi-;

Lo-lu-swe-ti, lo-ludle mazinyane;

EXAMPLE 8. Swazi Lullaby

CHROMATICISM AND CONTRASTING TONALITY

Among the Zulu and Swazi, as was considered earlier, much use is made of chromaticism, and one gains the impression that a contrast of tonality is often deliberately cultivated. A score is offered (Example 9) as an impressionistic transcription of the beginning of a Swazi national *lihubo* anthem recorded by Tracey.[38] Two contrasting tonalities seem to be employed here: D′, C′, A, G, F, D—which is a version of "common" pentatonic—and (G♯′), F♯′, D′, C♯′, A♯, G♯, F♯ (D, C♯). The second series is something like a replica of the first, in which every note except D is a semitone sharper. Sequences D′–C′–A–G–F (phrase I) and D′–C♯′–A♯–G♯–F♯ (phrases VI and VIII) give the impression of providing intentional contrast, as do also the A–G–F–D (part of phrase I) and A–G♯–F♯–D (phrase IV). For the present, the practice of contrasting tonalities in this way, within one and the same tune, must remain an unresolved puzzle—unless bow technique is perhaps again responsible. There seems no question of Western influence here.[39]

38. *Ibid.*
39. Since the preparation of this paper, the subject has been treated at greater depth in David K. Rycroft, "Nguni Vocal Polyphony," *Journal of the International Folk Music Council*, XIX (1967), 88–103; and Rycroft, "Zulu and Swazi Music," in *South African Music Encyclopedia*, ed. J. P. Malan (Pretoria: Human Sciences Research Council, forthcoming).

EXAMPLE 9. Swazi National *Lihubo* Anthem

Obvious instances of Western influence can be seen where clear tonic-dominant or tonic-subdominant harmony has been attempted, but they should not be confused with the "tonality shift" or "tonality contrast" that is an essential feature of much of the truly indigenous music of southern Africa. This was pointed out in 1959 by Blacking,[40] and it is also evident, in embryo, even in the Zulu three-tone songs, in which an upper fourth and a lower fourth are contrasted. Other features, like rhythmic stolidity or, at the other extreme, stereotyped anticipatory syncopation in modern "town" songs and a disregard for speech-tones, can be blamed on the West.

THE PITCH-LOWERING EFFECT
OF VOICED CONSONANTS

A typical Nguni speech feature seems to persist, however, in all their singing—whether traditional, missionized, or

---

40. John Blacking, "Problems of Pitch, Pattern and Harmony in the Ocarina Music of the Venda," *African Music*, II, no. 2 (1959), 23.

modern, and even when Nguni speakers sing in English. This is the pitch-lowering effect of most of their "voiced" consonants—*bh, d, g, z,* etc.—on higher notes or on high speech-tones. High syllables that commence or end with such a consonant have a brief rising portamento on-glide, or a falling off-glide, respectively.[41] The phenomenon possibly arises out of a particular manner in which the voiced consonants are enunciated. This feature, either in speech or in song, is not known to occur in any Bantu languages other than those of the Nguni group. Neither is it found in Bushman or Hottentot singing. It is, however, said to occur in speech in Chinese, in several other Far Eastern languages, and in German. In a treatise on singing, by J. and V. Forchhammer, the German pupil is given exercises to overcome this "undesirable feature"; [42] among the Nguni, however, it is accepted as natural and correct in both speech and song.

In traditional Nguni singing, most of all among the Zulu, a special feature is made of portamento pitch-glides. These are mainly descending and may cover as much as a sixth or an octave, either with clear onset and end pitches (but frequently without the stepwise recognition of intermediate notes as in Western melisma) or with the onset or the end of the glide being indeterminate in pitch. Where this occurs at the end, the effect might be described as "pitch fade." These glides have a definite foundation in Nguni speech, partly in the brief consonantal on-glides and off-glides to otherwise level speech-tones, and partly in true falling-pitch speech-tones—in which both a high and a low speech-tone, connected by portamento, are realized in speech on one and the same syllable. In song these features often seem to be exaggerated and are sometimes applied at points where they would seldom occur in speech, except perhaps when calling at a distance. Exaggerated down-glides are also used as a cadence feature in *izibongo* praise poetry, an art-form

41. For a fuller description, see Rycroft, "Linguistic and Melodic Interaction" and "Melodic Features in Zulu Recitation"; see also "Speechtone/Melody Relationships in Southern African Vocal Music," in *South African Music Encyclopedia.*
42. J. and V. Forchhammer, *Theorie und Technik des Singens und Sprechens* (Leipzig, 1921), pp. 526 ff.

which, among the Zulu, has melodic characteristics but is clearly distinguishable from song.[43]

OFFBEAT PLACEMENT OF STRESS
AND THE DISTORTION OF SYLLABLE LENGTH

Of Nguni peoples it seems to be the Zulu who favor the most extreme forms of word distortion regarding syllable length and stress placement. This occurs very noticeably in some of the oldest and apparently most respectable items of the Buthelezi clan's repertoire. In song, the duration given to the longer and shorter syllables of spoken Zulu is frequently directly reversed, and stressed syllables are placed on off-beats.[44] Example 10 is a line from an item of choral recitation—a drawled, singsong form of choral speaking without fixed musical pitches—which may be used among the Buthelezi as a basis for the *isigekle* wedding or recreational dance as an alternative to song.[45] Above the line of text I have indicated the approximate arrangement of syllable lengths and stresses in a normally spoken version of the line. Below the text is shown the rhythmic distortion to which syllables are subjected during choral recitation. A translation of the line is "They have tight hold of me like a young buck." It is significant to note that speech-tones are faithfully followed during this recitation but that syllable lengths are distorted. Stress is given to the correct syllables, but these frequently do not fall on the strong beats of the dance steps. The latter coincide in the dance with the long syllables.

A similar practice is common in true dance-songs among the Zulu. Distortions of syllable length and offbeat placement of word stresses in the downbeat of the dance steps or body meter thus reflect true tribal practice, and such mutilations of speech should not be blamed on the earlier, "misguided" hymn writers who have lately been taken to task. Older hymn writers or translators often seem to have fallen un-

43. Rycroft, "Melodic Features in Zulu Recitation."
44. Rycroft, "Linguistic and Melodic Interaction."
45. Unpublished ILAM tape, HID 19 (1955).

EXAMPLE 10. Excerpt from *"Sebeng'phethe!"*
—Choral Speech for Zulu *Isigekle* Dancing

wittingly somewhere between the subtleties of Nguni tribal
convention in this respect and the unsubtlety of Western
tradition. The new tendency, which is to set all the word
stresses decently *on* the beat, is often in fact even further
from true Nguni tribal practices.

The habit of placing word stresses *off* the beat in relation
to the downbeats of the body meter is of course not restricted
to the Zulu but is widespread in Africa. Waterman has referred to "offbeat phrasing of melodic accents" in West
Africa and listed it as a basic African trait.[46] In connection
with this phenomenon, a possible and quite natural physiological foundation, which I have not seen mentioned elsewhere, springs to mind. It is offered here as a working
hypothesis.

In strenuous physical activity, such as heavy manual work
or acrobatic dancing, it appears to be instinctive in human
beings to tense the diaphram and *close the glottis* at the actual moment of maximum exertion—in fact, babies do so in
defecation. When singing takes place as an accompaniment
to violent exertion, the emission of vocal sound of any kind
is of course impossible at the actual moment of this glottal closure during pushing, lifting, leaping, and the like.
But immediately before or after the moment of exertion (or
both before and after it: "Huk——Aaaahh!") it is not only
possible but highly natural that it should occur. It seems
conceivable that this procedure could be incorporated, with-

46. Richard Waterman, "African Influence on the Music of the
Americas," in *Acculturation in the Americas*, ed. Sol Tax (Chicago:
University of Chicago Press, 1952), p. 213.

out undue mental effort, into vocal syncopation or offbeating against any repetitive, strongly felt physical tension—and this is surely a natural "main beat," whether or not it becomes audibly expressed as such.

The Zulu work song *"Bayasibopha,"* which was cited earlier, demonstrates this point. The downbeat of the physical meter here manifests audibly as a heavy thud—of pickaxes striking home or of any other violent action—providing the downbeat of the musical meter in every alternate bar. Whenever it occurs there is momentary vocal silence, and the vocal phrase begins immediately *after* it—commencing, appropriately perhaps, with the release of a plosive consonant. Hornbostel, too, sought the reason for the apparent uniqueness in the conception of African rhythm in physiological processes.[47] He distinguished between an *acoustically stressed time-unit* and the pattern of *motor accent:* "We proceed from hearing, they from motion."

Among Nguni peoples it is the Xhosa, however, who seem to achieve the greatest subtleties of offbeat and "near miss" word phrasing. While the Zulu tolerate considerable distortions of syllable length for musical ends, the Xhosa seem to prefer to render words more correctly, but this is done at the expense of regular time-values in the melodic line, and the phrasing bears an exceedingly loose relationship to the body meter. Hand-clapping commonly provides a metrical foundation in Nguni light dance-songs, but the general mood of Xhosa songs is one of lively neatness and precision, in comparison with the high-spirited and more vehement forms of expression of other Nguni—especially the Zulu. A significant feature of all the Nguni dance-songs I have so far studied is the even-spaced regularity of the hand-clapping. This stands in complete contrast to the more intricate hand-clap patterns of Bushman dance-songs and of so much of the music of Central and West Africa.[48]

Among the Nguni it seems to be particularly a Xhosa refinement for the words of dance-songs to pursue a largely

47. Hornbostel, "African Negro Music."
48. Cf., among others, A. M. Jones, "African Rhythm," *Africa,* XXIV (1954), 26–47.

independent phrasing of their own. On first hearing, it is easy to attend fully either to the words or to the claps, but it is difficult to grasp a connection between the two. One's first impression is that stressed syllables are placed on off-beats, between the hand-claps, and unstressed syllables *on* the beat. But it soon becomes apparent that word syllables seldom coincide exactly with any clap, or with any convenient sub-divisions of the hand-clap meter—that is, if, as a Westerner, one expects the onset of the vowel to be the coincident feature. This seemingly "near miss" placement is not hap-hazard, however, but is likely to be repeated with exactitude by the singer with each repetition. Example 11, "Luckily

EXAMPLE 11. Xhosa Dance-Song

I'm Not Married: I Can Still Do As I Please!" is one of a dozen such dance-songs I was able to study.[49]

By careful imitation, the Westerner may be able to ac-quire the Xhosa "near missing" technique. If he succeeds, and submits his actions to self-examination, I suggest that he may become aware of a certain correlation between the hand-claps and his *consonantal* articulation. This, too, is a working hypothesis, whose usefulness requires further testing. It will be appreciated that in producing consonants, par-ticularly plosives (*p, t, k, b, d, g,* etc.), the mechanics of pro-duction are twofold. There is an initial closure of the lips, or a thrust by some portion of the tongue, followed by a release and the emission of a vowel—unless the consonant is final,

49. Unpublished recording made by the author in 1957. The singer is Mrs. L. Nongobo Whyman.

which is unusual in a Bantu language. The initial thrusting movement is of course a direct physical parallel, on a microcosmic scale, of outward limb movements such as stamping the foot, clapping, and the like—gestures of tension through which the metrical beats in music are frequently expressed. The final release of the consonant into a vowel is, on the other hand, an act of relaxation for the speech organs. Upon consideration, it seems natural that the two gestures of tension, inward and outward, in speech and in outer movement, should coincide rather than follow each other.

Western practice runs quite counter to this in song: the onset of the *vowel* is calculated to coincide with the beat. Silent mechanical preparations, although these require tension gestures by the speech organs, seem to be deliberately disregarded—as in the wind player's preparatory "tonguing" in order to sound his note on the beat when required. The Xhosa "near miss" songs with which I am familiar seem, conversely, to require coincidence between the initial thrusting tension gesture of the beginning of the consonant and either the hand-clap itself or a convenient subdivision of the metrical pattern it expresses. This would serve to explain why the onset of the vowel, which takes place only after consonantal relaxation, occurs as a "near miss" in most cases. It is to be noted, however, that not all consonants are plosive.

Offbeating, and also deliberately loose word-phrasing, which together seem intended to give the impression of something resembling natural speech rhythms, happen to be stylistic features that have come into vogue in Western popular music during the past few decades. These practices are natural in blues and calypso, and the idea may well have come into popular music from these two sources. But it is interesting to note that one of the most greatly admired exponents of this "natural speech rhythm" style of singing is Miriam Makeba, who is of Xhosa descent.

There is evidence of a two-way traffic between African music and the music of the rest of the world. It is probable that such traffic will increasingly occupy the attention of music historians.

11.

The Changing Face
of African Music
South of the Zambezi

PERCIVAL R. KIRBY

AN EXTENSIVE STUDY of the literature dealing with South Africa, Rhodesia, and Zambia has led me to realize that the Bushman, Hottentot, and Bantu aborigines have largely escaped the overwhelming influences of the great Eastern civilizations that have for so long dominated the more northerly areas of the continent. This is particularly true south of the Vaal River, for, although Indonesian influences are detectable among the Venda people of the northern Transvaal, such influences are practically nonexistent elsewhere in southern Africa. The musical evidence for this suggestion is, I venture to think, conclusive.

BUSHMAN MUSIC

The Bushmen, a race of nomadic hunters, are, so far as I have been able to judge, still living a life analogous to, if not practically identical with, that of their prehistoric ancestors. Curt Sachs drew attention to the fact that at that early stage in the world's history two types of dancing were practiced, which he distinguished as extrovert and introvert.[1] The first of these embraced four features: "cultivation of animal dances, outstanding dance talent, body-conscious loose dancing, and choral dance"; he emphasized the fact that this kind of dancing is typical of the Pygmies of Africa, who have preserved it up to the present time. He might have added that it is also typical of the Bushmen, several thousand of whom still live in and near the Kalahari Desert.

This retention of ancient practices is particularly noticeable in Bushman music. When I first heard it, in July, 1936, I was forcibly struck by several curious phenomena. The first was that in their choral songs the women yodeled, and, as far as I know, my paper of 1936 was the first in which this feature was recorded.[2] The second was that the yodeling in question, as well as the scale used in these choral songs, was based exclusively upon partials of the harmonic series, including the seventh. That this could not have been accidental was, I think, proved by the fact that melodies similarly based on precisely the same partials of the harmonic series were played by the men when using their shooting bows as musical instruments.[3]

I also noticed that the form of Bushman choral song consists of a single phrase in what we might describe as triple rhythm. Such a phrase would be repeated again and again until, for no apparent reason except possibly for the sake of variety, another would replace it, this being in turn replaced

1. Curt Sachs, *The World History of the Dance* (New York: Norton, 1937), pp. 209–10.
2. Percival R. Kirby, "The Musical Practices of the ?auni and ǂkhomani Bushmen," *Bantu Studies*, X, no. 4 (1936), 390 ff.
3. Percival R. Kirby, "Primitive Music," in *Dictionary of Music and Musicians*, ed. George Grove, 5th ed., 15 vols. (New York: St. Martin's Press, 1954), V, 923.

by a third, and so on. At times the earlier phrases would reappear, but, so far as I could discover, there was no system underlying their arrangement; the repetitions were apparently haphazard. Unity, of course, was preserved by the phrases all being built upon the half-dozen or so partials of the harmonic series.

On the other hand, certain of their stringed instruments had manifestly been acquired from neighboring Hottentots, and polyphonic tunes in two parts were executed on these, with the fundamental sounds elicited from the string furnishing a bass part while harmonics selected by various methods formed a melody. The intervals between the bass and the melody were generally octaves and fifths, though occasionally a third was introduced. Moreover it appeared to me that in many cases the two sections forming the phrase were brought about by opposed fingering patterns.

The most striking feature of all, however, was that Bushman girls could imitate European music with simple harmonies that they had in all likelihood heard on farms and outside the church at the Kuruman mission. And they were able to sing in the European diatonic scale without prejudice to their own very different mode. In fact, they kept the two styles completely distinct.

HOTTENTOT MUSIC

Regarding the Hottentots it is less easy to be precise, since so few of them are to be found today; and these have in general been profoundly influenced by neighboring and more sophisticated civilizations, although they were originally seminomadic pastoralists armed only with clubs and spears.

I myself have only been able to study the remnants of the Korana, scattered along the upper reaches of the Orange River and the lower reaches of the Vaal, and a group of Namaqua in Windhoek, South-West Africa. The Gonaqua of the "Eastern Province" have now entirely disappeared. But fortunately the early travelers have left a few accounts of Hottentot music, and, in addition, certain of the Tswana peoples long ago adopted some of the Hottentot instrumental practices when they came into contact with them in the late eighteenth century.

On December 2, 1497, Vasco da Gama met what I consider to have been the Korana at Mossel Bay, where he heard them perform upon "four or five" reed-flutes *in harmony*, each man playing but one note. Though da Gama did not write down in musical notation what he had heard, the four-note scale to which the flutes were tuned has come down to us, having been preserved both by the Korana, from whom certain Tswana acquired it in the late eighteenth century, and by the Nama. In 1932 I listened to a reed-flute ensemble, tuned to that same four-note scale, played by the Bamalete, a Tswana tribe, at Ramutsa in British Bechuanaland (now Botswana); [4] in 1937 I heard a similar ensemble played by Namaqua Hottentots at Windhoek in South-West Africa. But whereas the Bamalete had retained the original tuning and methods of performance, the Nama had added to the four original flutes a whole series of instruments of higher pitch, fastened together after the manner of panpipes. They affirmed that this had been done in imitation of the concertina—that is, combining many notes in one instrument—and thus this change must have been made subsequent to 1829. The original four-note scale of the Hottentot reed-flutes, played by four Nama musicians under my direction in 1937, has been preserved in a recording. [5]

The famous Hottentot stringed-wind instrument known as the *gora*, which appears to have been their own invention, was first noted by Dapper in 1668; [6] as the first mention of the use of a shooting bow by the Hottentots was made by de Beaulieu in 1620, [7] it would seem that they, a race of flute players, discovered a method of sounding a string by wind sometime

4. Percival R. Kirby, "The Reed-Flute Ensembles of South Africa," *Journal of the Royal Anthropological Institute*, LXIII (July–December, 1933), 373–77.
5. *Hottentot Reed-Flutes*, University of the Witwatersrand; also available on Gallotone GE 994 T, side A.
6. Otto Dapper, *Naukeurige Beschrijvinge der Afrikaansche Gewensten* (Amsterdam, 1668), p. 653b.
7. A. de Beaulieu, *Memoires du voyage aux Indes Orientales du Général Beaulieu* (Paris, 1664), p. 8.

during the forty-eight years between these two dates. And the sounds produced by the vibrating string of the *gora* when it is set in motion by the flattened quill (which is the soul of the instrument) are, as would be expected, partials of the harmonic series, the same sounds elicited by the Bushmen from their shooting bows.

But the advent of the missionaries in their midst caused the Hottentots to abandon their own musical practices and to imitate those of their mentors with more or less success, though the missionary influence apparently did not last long. In February, 1932, at Bloemhof in the Transvaal, I interviewed a number of Korana and there heard young women singing what were obviously the two upper parts of a European hymn, which they had converted into a lullaby. (The words were Korana, and meant "Give me, give me! We have taken the honey out. This is my soul. Amen.") The music of this hymn, both melody and harmony, was in the European diatonic scale, but the rendering of it was lazy and drawling. Only one aged man, who was well over a hundred years old, could sing to me genuine Korana melodies,[8] though I later heard others at Bloemfontein in the Orange Free State.

BANTU MUSIC

It is among the Bantu peoples of South Africa that I have been able to observe within the past half-century a rapid transition from their original music-making to that of Europe and America. Unfortunately the various cylinder recordings which I made many years ago, and which on my retirement I left in Johannesburg to be preserved, have disappeared. [*In September, 1964, a considerable number of these recordings were discovered and an attempt will be made to rerecord them on tapes.*] However, it is possible to illustrate most of the points that I wish to make from a collection of commercial discs which I got together some time ago. They include old-time practices as well as those of more recent times.

8. Percival R. Kirby, "The Music and Musical Instruments of the Korana," *Bantu Studies*, VI, no. 2 (1932), 195–200, 203–4.

My first introduction to Bantu music occurred in 1914 when, as music organizer to the Natal Education Department, I found myself responsible for directing the musical education of African, Coloured, European, and Indian children and student-teachers. At that time all African education was in the hands of missionaries of various denominations, who expected the young people under their charge to aim at European ideals and to follow European methods. In music, which was almost exclusively vocal, this was the desideratum, for the singing of hymns in four-part harmony had been insisted upon throughout Natal for many years, even in African primary schools, and I found that it would be quite impossible to eradicate the practice.[9]

Ecclesiastical influences were, indeed, so strong that a prolific group of would-be composers sprang up and turned out sheaves of simple musical works in imitation of the acquired idiom—all the compositions being, of course, in four-part harmony. But the harmonies used were invariably rudimentary, and inversions of chords were at first rigidly eschewed, as were chromatically altered notes. Also, the natural accentuation of the vernacular was frequently completely disturbed.

In considering this last defect, it did not take me long to discover that the languages of the southern Bantu peoples all displayed the phenomenon of speech-tone, whereby words pronounced alike but intoned differently had entirely different meanings. I soon came to the conclusion that this phenomenon must have profoundly affected the music of these peoples, and I eventually summarized my views on the subject by stating what I believe to have been true for the greater part of mankind in the early stages of development: Whenever a number of individuals who spoke a language in which speech-tone determined meaning simultaneously voiced common sentiment by means of a common verbal formula, their voices perforce had to proceed *in parallel,* rising and falling together, even if they did not begin or end in unison.[10] A scien-

9. Percival R. Kirby, "Annual Report," in *Report of the Superintendent of Education of Natal* (Pietermaritzburg, South Africa, 1919, 1920).
10. Percival R. Kirby, "Some Problems of Primitive Harmony and Polyphony, with Special Reference to Bantu Practice," *South African Journal of Science*, XXIII (1926), 963.

tific study of this phenomenon, as observed among the Xhosa peoples some thirty years ago, was made by a South African, Amy Starke.[11] Under such circumstances, harmony as it is known in Europe could not arise; it did not develop until speech-tone ceased to be the dominant factor in language and stress took its place.

Unfortunately, European manners and customs, as well as musical and linguistic practices, have for nearly a century and a half been influencing and even replacing those of the aborigines who inhabit the southeastern parts of South Africa, so that nowadays it is sometimes far from easy to determine with any degree of certainty what is truly aboriginal and what has been borrowed. But there still remain traces of practices that at one time were practically universal, and by comparing these with performances of more recent music we can paint a picture of the gradual change that has taken place as a result of what might be called musical integration.

It is, of course, impossible here to go into details regarding the transition from indigenous, aboriginal music to that practiced by the Westernized African population today. What I shall do is to discuss in succession a number of examples of recorded music that illustrate the way in which the Bantu have gradually abandoned their own musical techniques in favor of those of the Europeans. While a qualitative and quantitative analysis of these recordings would be desirable, here I can only draw attention to the most outstanding features.

One result of the activities of missionaries in South Africa has been the creation of almost innumerable native religious sects. In fact, I think that today there are well over a thousand of them. Among these "Separatists," as most of them call themselves, the principal group, known as "Nazarites," was founded in 1911 by a Zulu named Isaiah Shembe, who endeavored to adapt the Christian religion to Zulu customs and art. There is no doubt that in Shembe's hymn *"Lalela Zulu"* we have authentic Zulu choral music, such as the early pi-

11. A. Starke, "The Relation between the Intonation of Song and Speech of the Amaxosa" (Ph.D. diss., University of Cape Town, 1930).

oneers in Natal must have heard.[12] This hymn is of great interest, for its music dates back at least to the days of Chief
Mpande (1840–72). The words of the hymn mean: "Listen, ye
Zulus, to the people talking about your country." And it is
particularly interesting that in this hymn loyalty to Christ is
implied by the expressed loyalty to the old Zulu king Dingane
(reigned 1828–40), whose name actually occurs in the text.

The main melody is pentatonic, as might be expected, and
it is executed by baritone voices. But at times, deeper voices,
which normally sing in parallel with the others, double the
melody in the lower octave. The "embroideries" sung by the
women are of a comparatively free nature.

Next in the sequence is a song composed in a pentatonic
mode, with occasional added parts. According to the label on
the record, the singers are said to be Pondo, but the music
is typically Zulu. Attention should be drawn to the intonation
of the notes of the mode, particularly to what we should
call the sixth of the scale. This note tends to sound sharp to
the European ear, and it suggests most strongly the seventh
partial of the harmonic series, especially when heard unac-
companied by other sounds in simple polyphony. This song
is entitled "Hemba," and there is no European influence
observable in it.[13]

A second example sung by the same group also has a pentatonic melody, sung in the baritone register, or *vuma*, as it
is called in Zulu and Xhosa, and it is accompanied by a lower
part that moves in parallel with it. The parallelism within the
pentatonic scale involves the use of the interval of the third
(and its inversion, the sixth). The rhythm is basically duple,
though not metronomically so, just as the scale intervals are
by no means mathematically accurate. Yet the underlying
scheme of the whole is quite clear. The title of this song is
"*Leziya nkomo*," "Those Cattle Yonder." [14]

I have long maintained that probably the pentatonic scale
was originally derived from certain partials of the harmonic

12. Gallotone GE 996 T, side A.
13. Gallotone GE 997, side B.
14. Gallotone GE 997, side A.

series, as seen in Bushman song and instrumental music. If this suggestion is correct, the fact that the sixth of the scale heard on the record referred to above does not sound like the seventh harmonic seems to me to require explanation. This I find in the "pull" of the perfect fourth and fifth, when parallel voices sing these intervals within a pentatonic scale derived from the harmonic series. The harmonic seventh tends to be lowered in pitch so as to make a perfect concord with the second degree of the scale, whether above or below it. In other words, we have here what might be called a Bantu *musica ficta*. It is well known that in early European polyphony the diminished interval between the notes F and B was regarded as inharmonious, and the B was altered to B♭. I would suggest that in this song there is a similar phenomenon.

Another scale is demonstrated by a recording made at least forty-five years ago.[15] It is a Swazi translation of the familiar hymn "What a Friend We Have in Jesus," *"Kwa kade inhliziyo yami,"* and it was sung by an alleged Swazi chief to the accompaniment of a piano. The Swazi words are not a literal translation of the English text, but that does not matter for our present purpose. What is important is that here the vernacular language is forced into the procrustean bed of European hymnology, and the scale in which the melody is written is foreign to the Swazi singer. He certainly does his best to sing it, but he has difficulty in accommodating his voice to the equal temperament of the piano and also in singing the seventh, or leading note, of the diatonic scale. I myself have found several tribes in which no distinction was made between tone and semitone. Perhaps this phenomenon is analogous to the fact that in Zulu and Xhosa the same word, *uhlaza,* is used for both blue and green; indeed, the old German missionary, Kropf, stated in his dictionary that in his day the Xhosa did not distinguish between these colors.[16]

The first hymn ever to be composed by a southern Bantu

15. Zonophone 4021, side B.
16. Albert Kropf, *A Kaffir-English Dictionary*, ed. Robert Godfrey, 2d ed. (Lovedale, South Africa: Lovedale Mission Press, 1915).

was written by a member of the Xhosa tribe, a petty chief named Ntsikana, who was the first convert to Christianity in the eastern Cape Province. Since he was completely illiterate he could not write it down, and so we only know its music from the recollections of John Knox Bokwe (1855–1922).

Bokwe, trained at the Lovedale Mission, began to compose in 1875. He has described his aims in these words:

The author's knowledge of music was self-acquired. Departing from the usage his own people had grown accustomed to in their religious hymn singing, he composed his tunes so as to preserve in *singing* the correct accentuation followed in speaking the Xosa language. The practice in church praise had hitherto been to adapt English tunes to Kaffir words, but the different usage of the two languages in placing the accent made the accentuation fall quite out of place on the Kaffir words in most of the hymns.[17]

One of Bokwe's earliest works is the hymn *"Msindisi wa boni,"* "Savior of Sinners." [18] I possess a copy of this hymn in Bokwe's own handwriting, as well as a recent recording of it. Curiously enough, in the recording the upper parts are inverted, with the melody sung by one of the middle voices. Again, where the composer wrote the flatted seventh in his tune, the singers give us the unaltered leading note. The choir that performed this hymn in the recording is that of St. Peter's Hostel, and its members had been trained to control their voices in the European manner.

I would like to mention here still another choral work, by Foley, the late Xhosa composer. In this song Foley has actually used inversions and even some chromatic harmony, and he has done it quite successfully. The singers render it with considerable effect. In this performance a Bantu musician is attempting with increasing success to bridge the gulf between his music and that of Europe. The song, *"Untshangase,"* describes the assumption by Xhosa women of the long skirt, which is today the emblem of the married woman.[19]

17. John Knox Bokwe, *Amaculo ase Lovedale* (Lovedale, South Africa: Lovedale Mission Press, 1910), p. iii.
18. Columbia YE 117 WLA 152.
19. His Master's Voice JP 523, side B.

MUSIC IN JOHANNESBURG

On the Rand, in the mine compounds, almost every type of South African indigenous music may be heard; but in Johannesburg the tendency has long been for the urbanized Bantu to imitate what they have been able to hear of European popular music. Church choirs, of course, are numerous, and a large Bantu choral society, directed by a European, has from time to time given creditable performances of such works as Handel's *Messiah*.

But the influence of the dance band and of recordings of dance music has been very great, and numerous imitations of European and American dance bands have been formed, which have regaled their Bantu patrons for many years. I will discuss briefly two examples to show how the American idiom has been appropriated.

The first of these is a little dance tune, called *"Izono zam,"* which is based upon a harmonic formula of only three chords—the familiar tonic, dominant, and subdominant.[20] Above this formula the women singers intone a commonplace melody (which is not African at all), while an inner part is sung by a lonely male voice which blithely ignores the harmonic progressions going on around it.

The whole is quite unsatisfactory from both the African and the European points of view, if regarded as a musical composition. The mere fact that it consists of a single musical sentence, unrelieved by any contrast whatever, is sufficient to prove this. But if the tune is regarded as a specimen of the transition from African idioms to those of Europe and, perhaps, America, it is of considerable interest to the musicologist.

The second example of urbanized Bantu dance music, a tune called *"Pesheya kweye ntaba,"* is much more sophisticated and far more satisfactory than the previous one.[21] It is performed by a group called the Manhattan Brothers accompanied by the Merry Blackbirds Orchestra. This, in my

20. His Master's Voice GU 96, side B.
21. Gallotone GE 973, side A.

opinion, is a very remarkable imitation of American dance music. The group has mastered the art of simple modulation, something unheard of in old tribal music, and indeed impossible to it. The instrumentalists, too, have learned their lesson, especially the pianist and the trumpeter, although the saxophonist holds on to his "blue" notes, whether they fit or not. The music remains an imitation, though not a bad one.

Finally, what about the musical play, *King Kong?* Well, there you have music which has retained very little of the African idiom, however much of Africa there may be in the libretto of the work. The idiom of the music is essentially Western, and, although the melodies may have been devised by an African, the harmonic background and the scoring for the accompanying instruments is undoubtedly European.

I may be quite wrong, but I see little future in this kind of thing, although it will no doubt serve its purpose.

LARGE-SCALE COMPOSITION

In the past I have had as students in my department at the University of the Witwatersrand only two African musicians who wished to take the degree of Bachelor of Music under my guidance. As far as I know, one African, Michael M. Moerane, has composed a work for modern orchestra, under the expert supervision of a distinguished European musician. His work, a tone poem called "My Country," was performed by the BBC Symphony Orchestra in London,[22] and also, I understand, in New York. It is unlikely to be heard in South Africa, although the full score and parts are in the country. The composer has, apparently, written nothing more on a similar scale.

I hope that I have been able to demonstrate that in the southern parts of Africa an almost complete chronology of aboriginal musical practices still exists, and that those practices, though they contain features that are also to be found in the music of the more northerly parts of the continent, represent a series of far simpler artistic cultures than those to be found today among many of the peoples in the north.

22. Broadcast on BBC African and Home services, November 17, 1944.

Music
and History

12.

Music and History:

A Historian's View

of the African Picture

JOHN D. FAGE

IT IS ONLY since about 1950 that historians have really begun
to engage in coherent study of the history of Africa and its
peoples. Before, insofar as professional historians concerned
themselves with Africa at all, their interest rarely extended
beyond the study of the activities of European and Asian in-
truders in that continent. Such activities, though no doubt a
part *of* African history, are very far from being the same
thing *as* African history. One result of this slowness in attempting to see the history of Africa as a whole is that over
a considerable part of the continent, especially in Black
Africa, much of the energy of historians is still devoted to
the search for clues of any kind which may help to illuminate
the long periods for which written evidence, let alone written
records, is scanty or nonexistent. Under these circumstances,
any attempt at an overall historical synthesis would prob-

ably be out of place here.[1] It is perhaps best to begin with a
few words about the kinds of evidence that those historians
of Africa who are rash enough to attempt general syntheses
are apt to be considering.

We are now generally agreed, I think, that the oral traditions of many African states can be used and treated as the
equivalent of written chronicles, provided that they are used
with due care and circumspection.[2] But the time-depth of
even the best of these is limited. We are doing very well indeed if we can follow them back for as much as five hundred
years or so. Moreover, oral traditions are not *record* material;
they are not absolute data. They are *ex parte* statements
which must be subjected to careful checking and cross-
checking.

The next recourse of the historian in Africa—as anywhere
else, for that matter—is to archaeology. But many areas of
Africa have scarcely even been explored by archaeologists.
Even in those favored parts of the continent where archaeologists have been systematically at work for a generation or
so, there is still usually room for argument about the interpretation of their findings—and not only for the remoter
periods. In these circumstances, the would-be historian of
Africa often finds himself looking for whatever historical
clues he may glean from workers in such abstruse disciplines
as comparative linguistics, ethnobotany, or even serology. A
glance at the issue of the *Journal of African History* which
reported the 1961 Conference on African History and Archaeology at the School of Oriental and African Studies will show
something of the value to the historian of work in fields such
as these in Africa.[3]

Indeed all is grist for the mill of the historian seeking to
recover Africa's precolonial past, and the historian may have
more to learn from the ethnomusicologist than vice versa.

1. Those interested will find such an attempt in Roland Oliver and
John D. Fage, *A Short History of Africa* (Baltimore: Penguin, 1966).
2. The basic discussion of this subject is in Jan Vansina, *De la
tradition orale: Essai de methode historique*, Annales de la Musée Royale
de l'Afrique Centrale, no. 36 (Tervuren, 1961); *Oral Tradition: A Study
in Historical Methodology*, trans. H. M. Wright (Chicago: Aldine, 1965).
3. *Journal of African History*, Vol. III, no. 2 (1962).

However, as a professional historian who has been faced for some years with the interpretation and presentation of the African past, perhaps the following remarks may at least serve to stimulate discussion.

The first point that strikes me is that these papers and discussions represent approaches to Africa's past at two quite distinct levels. The first of these is well exemplified by the papers of Nketia on Ghana and of Wachsmann on Buganda (Chapters 1 and 5).

Both these scholars, albeit by rather different methods—the one mainly through the evidence of musical styles, and the other principally through the evidence of musical instruments—have produced pictures of the musical past of certain well-defined and fairly small areas with which they are very familiar. These pictures are perfectly intelligible in broader historical terms. Indeed, they have not told me very much about the general history of their two areas that I did not already know (in the case of Ghana) or that I probably could not discover for myself from more or less accepted historical accounts (in the case of Buganda).

Such an observation is not in any way intended to belittle what Nketia and Wachsmann have done. Just as the history of Tudor England is not only the history of the English Reformation, the dissolution of the monasteries, the rise of a new middle class, and so forth, but is also the history of a period of lively literary and musical experimentation, so too an understanding of the musical history of Ghana and of Buganda is important if we are to gain a full, rounded, and balanced apprehension of their past.

A number of points arise in connection with this geographically specific kind of musicology in Africa. The first is that its time-depth seems to be very much the same as that which can be achieved for more general history by the study of formal state traditions. This similarity is not, I think, mere coincidence. There is, I would say, a very close connection between the maintenance of formal oral tradition and the existence of a formal state (or mode of government). For a state to continue to be a state—to know who should rule and how, and how it stands in relation to its neighbors

—it must maintain a generally accepted account of its origins and development (however much this account may from time to time need to be twisted or slanted to meet new needs). Equally, it seems to me, so long as the community of such a state remains in existence, it must be constantly developing its music. Indeed music is inevitably a part, and often in Africa an important formal part, of that oneness which state traditions seek to perpetuate. One conclusion about this kind of musicology must therefore be that, although it can enrich—greatly enrich—our understanding of the past, it is not likely to extend the time-depth obtainable from oral tradition. This may be expected to extend back to the declared origins of current states, which are seldom more than about five centuries old.

Second, it is worth noting that Nketia, Wachsmann, and also Blacking (Chapter 9) have strongly stressed for musical traditions what the historian working on formal oral tradition must also always remember: Tradition cannot be properly understood without a full comprehension of its social environment. The musicologist in Africa (like the historian) cannot meaningfully operate without knowing the society whose music (or history) he is studying.

There is yet another common ground between the musicologist and the historian in Africa. The authors I have mentioned show how the music history of an area with well-developed political and commercial systems is accretive, how it tends to absorb and to transform for its own purposes elements coming from outside. This too is common historical experience.

A fourth point, which has been stressed by Rouget (Chapter 2), is that song texts are not automatically good, unequivocal, generally valid historical source material. He has suggested that they are often allusive and difficult to pin down, both in meaning and in time. This again accords with general historical experience. One might illustrate this, perhaps, from English nursery rhymes. The significance of the Noble Duke of York or of Little Jack Horner is lost unless we already know a good deal of history. And when we do know the relevant history, what the rhymes tell us may not be very new.

Nevertheless Rouget performs a very valuable service by suggesting that there may be criteria of style by which the historicity of song texts could be assessed, and it is important that this tentative conclusion from Dahomey should be tested in other areas. Rouget, Nketia, and Wachsmann, of course, have all worked in societies which have long histories of organized monarchical government, and where consequently there are also formal state traditions to provide a sound starting point for historical investigation. Is it possible therefore that song texts may be more valuable as historical sources in those parts of Africa where there were no strong state systems? Miss Anderson's section on Mauritanian music does not hold out much hope. Indeed there is little evidence in her contribution as a whole that music, musical styles or instruments, or song texts afford historical information that is not available from more usual historical sources. Often, in fact, she needs to use historical knowledge to enable her to interpret her musical data. What is interesting, however, is the suggestion that Saharan musical styles can be related to the different strata of its mixed society. Although it is no part of a historian's function to distinguish between musical styles, such distinctions must be of value to him if indeed they can be correlated with ethnic or sociological data. It may be of interest to add that such examples of Hottentot and of southern Bantu music as I have heard have struck my ill-trained ear as being much less complex in form than the West African music which is more familiar to me. If this is really so, then once again it would seem that music is corroborating history, for in general terms one might say that the history of these southern peoples has been less stable, and so less accretive, than that of many peoples of West Africa or of the Great Lakes region of East Africa.

This dangerous and doubtless ill-judged incursion into matters of musical style brings me naturally enough to the second level of musicological investigation that has been touched upon. Here conceivably what the musicologist has to offer may be of much greater value to the historian. For if we go back more than about five centuries into the African past, where there is virtually no oral tradition, no European and few Arabic written sources, and often very little firm archaeology, then the historian is often in the position of trying to make do with the interpretation of any straws which may be blown his way by scholars of other disciplines.

It is very doubtful, however, whether musicology could ever throw any useful light on a question such as that of the origins of the Yoruba. Akin Euba, who raises this question, himself comes to this conclusion, saying that greater knowledge of Yoruba cultural history would be needed before one could assess whether any elements of Yoruba music were "pre-Islamic Arab in origin." His chapter makes it obvious enough that such an assessment would be bound to be confused by the musical consequences of the advance of Islam into Yorubaland during the last two centuries or so. But even so, it is not clear whether he has appreciated the historical magnitude of the question. We now know, for example, from archaeological sources, that Ife, the traditional dispersion center of the Yoruba, must have existed on its present site for at least a thousand years. Linguists have no doubt that the Yoruba language is a West African Negro language, and that it must have been developing more or less *in situ* for many thousands of years more. If there were an immigrant element in the pre-nineteenth-century Yoruba monarchies, it seems most likely that—as with some other West African kingdoms—it must have been that of a small minority (which was presumably largely acculturated into existing society).[4]

However, the history of Bantu Africa does not seem to go anything like as far back into the mists of time as does that of the Negroes of West Africa. Of particular interest here is

4. See J. Vansina, R. Mauny, and L. V. Thomas, *The Historian in Tropical Africa* (London: Oxford University Press for International African Institute, 1964), and esp. chap. 2 by R. G. Armstrong. On the antiquity of Ife, see Brian M. Fagan, "Radiocarbon Dates for Sub-Saharan Africa, VI," *J. Afr. Hist.*, X, no. 1 (1969), 154; and Frank Willett, "Survey of Recent Results in the Radiocarbon Chronology of Western and Northern Africa," *J. Afr. Hist.*, Vol. XII, no. 3 (1971).

Jones's thesis, based essentially on his interpretation of musical data, of a prehistoric Indonesian colonization of Africa (see Chapter 4). This is a fascinating thesis, and one which historians have been discussing for some years now. As historians, we can hardly question Jones's basic data,[5] but it is important to us to know how far these data are acceptable to other musicologists. My impression from listening to discussions of this is that there are some fundamental technical issues yet to be settled. Nevertheless there are questions which the historian may rightly ask. For example, granting that Africa's xylophones originated in Indonesia, it is necessary to postulate Indonesian *colonization* in Africa to account for their distribution there? We can be sure about Indonesian colonization in Madagascar, but the evidence that has been suggested for it in Africa proper is meager in the extreme. I would certainly say that colonization was not necessary, that trading contacts with the east coast would be sufficient. After all, the fact that both Chinese and Japanese have been known to play pianos (and to play Western music on them) is not in any way proof of European colonization in their countries. Nor is it proof even when, for example, modern Japan has a flourishing piano-making industry and tunes its pianos to the European scale.

However, the issue on which Jones touches is by no means as simple as this. Among other things, we need to try to account for the wide distribution in Africa of crops of Southeast Asian origin. This has led to a good deal of argument in recent years, especially since the publication of G. P. Murdock's book.[6] Here I must observe that, stimulating though Murdock's synthesis is, much of what he has to say on this and other matters, including the very fundamental and related question of the how, when, and why of the Bantu expansion, is far from being generally accepted. I have else-

5. The full statement is in A. M. Jones, *Africa and Indonesia: The Evidence of the Xylophone and Other Musical and Cultural Factors* (Leiden: E. J. Brill, 1964).

6. George Peter Murdock, *Africa: Its Peoples and Their Culture History* (New York: McGraw-Hill, 1959).

where tried to suggest some of the weaknesses in Murdock's arguments.[7] Here I should perhaps try to be constructive and briefly sketch what I think may have happened in this vital phase of African prehistory. In so doing I lean heavily on contributions to the African history seminar at the School of Oriental and African Studies and on discussions with my colleague Roland Oliver, as well as on papers presented to the 1961 S.O.A.S. conference.

Something like 7,000 years ago it would seem that the ancestors of today's African Negroes were inhabiting the Sudan from West Africa to Ethiopia. The rest of the continent was peopled, north and east, by Caucasoids (whose languages used to be termed Hamito-Semitic, but which J. H. Greenberg prefers to call Afro-Asiatic, and Tucker and M. A. Bryan call Erythraean). In East Africa, these people reached appreciably farther south than they now do. To the south of them were the progenitors of the modern Bushmen and Hottentots. Between the limits of approximately 5000 B.C. and 2000 B.C., these Negroes began to experience the "Neolithic Revolution" and to develop agriculture. It doesn't matter for our purposes whether they conceived of this independently (as Murdock thinks, and as is also argued, albeit on different grounds, by Roland Portères),[8] or whether it came to them from the Nile Valley (as archaeologists such as Desmond Clark maintain).[9] What does matter is that this great development in food production led to a growth of population and so to expansion.

The Sahara was at this time becoming more arid, so the expansion was essentially southward. Here the Negroes faced the great obstacle of the tropical forest. For any large number of people to live in the forest, two things may have been necessary: iron tools and suitable food crops (vegetables rather than the grains of savanna agriculture). It seems likely that the second of these was more vital than the first,

7. "Anthropology, Botany, and the History of Africa," *Journal of African History*, II, no. 2 (1961), 299–309.

8. See his summary, "Papers Relating to the History of Food Crops in Africa," *ibid.*, III, no. 2 (1962), 195–210.

9. See, for example, "The Spread of Food Production in Sub-Saharan Africa," *ibid.*, pp. 211–28.

and that one of the first reactions of the migrants to the forest was to pass quickly through it until they found, to the south, woodland and savanna not unlike those of their homeland. The argument for this starts from linguistic considerations which were first presented by Malcolm Guthrie.[10] The consequence was the emergence of a "Bantu nucleus" running across Africa south of the forest at about latitude 12° south. From this nucleus, the Bantu later spread out both northward and southward. Since the modern Bantu Negro languages are much more closely related to each other than are the Sudanic Negro languages, it is suggested that this secondary expansion may have been a relatively swift process. It is therefore not unreasonable to argue that the Bantu expansion northward into the forest only became possible after the acquisition, some time in the first millennium A.D., of Southeast Asian food crops suited to forest living. On the other hand, Negroes who speak Sudanic languages, which are much more differentiated from one another, are today forest dwellers as well as savanna dwellers. It seems quite as reasonable to argue that their penetration of the forest was a more gradual advance by people who initially did not have the Southeast Asian plants but who adapted their agriculture and developed their own forest foods as they went.

Any reconstruction of this kind must have large areas of doubt in it, and the historian needs as much established data as he can get. If the hypothesis which Jones has developed from his interpretation of musical data is correct, then the other hypothesis about the significance of Southeast Asian food-crops for the Negro peopling of Africa would undoubtedly be strengthened. In particular, perhaps, it might be much more clearly applicable to West Africa than it now is.

10. "Some Developments in the Prehistory of the Bantu Languages," *ibid.*, pp. 273–82. For the continuing debate on the problem of the Bantu expansion, the following articles in the *Journal of African History* may be consulted: Roland Oliver, "The Problem of the Bantu Expansion," VII, no. 3 (1966), 361–76; M. Posnansky, "Bantu Genesis—Archaeological Reflections," IX, no. 1 (1968), 1–11; and Jean Hiernaux, "Bantu Expansion: The Evidence from Physical Anthropology Confronted with Linguistic and Archaeological Evidence," IX, no. 4 (1968), 505–15. Guthrie's full data may be examined in his *Comparative Bantu* (Upper Saddle River, N.J.: Gregg Press, forthcoming).

But the musical data involved must first be generally accepted by musicologists (and the extrapolations from these data into other fields of culture history also need to be more generally confirmed by the relevant specialists). It is to be hoped, therefore, that one of the outcomes of this volume will be to clarify, or at least to better illumine, some of the more open theories about the remoter past of African music.

The Contributors

LOIS ANN ANDERSON is Assistant Professor at the School of Music of the University of Wisconsin.

JOHN BLACKING, Professor of Anthropology at Western Michigan University, was formerly chairman of the African Studies Programme at the University of the Witwatersrand, Johannesburg, South Africa.

PHILIP J. C. DARK is Professor of Anthropology at Southern Illinois University and Research Associate in African Ethnology at the Field Museum of Natural History in Chicago.

DAVID M. DIXON is Lecturer in Egyptology at University College London.

AKIN EUBA is Senior Research Fellow in Musicology at the Institute for African Studies, the University of Ife, Ile-Ife, Nigeria.

JOHN D. FAGE is Director of the Centre of West African Studies and Professor of African History at the University of Birmingham, England.

MATTHEW HILL, Assistant Professor of Anthropology at the University of Waterloo, Ontario, was a Visiting Research Fellow at Fourah Bay College, Freetown, Sierra Leone, during 1967/68.

A. M. JONES is Lecturer in African Music, with special reference to oral literature, at the School of Oriental and African Studies, University of London.

PERCIVAL R. KIRBY was Professor Emeritus in Music and

[267]

History at the University of the Witwatersrand, Johannesburg, South Africa, until his death in 1970.

J. H. KWABENA NKETIA is Professor of Music and Director of the Institute of African Studies at the University of Ghana.

GILBERT ROUGET is head of research at the Centre National de la Recherche Scientifique and head of the Department of Ethnomusicology of the Musée de l'Homme, Paris.

DAVID K. RYCROFT is Lecturer in Bantu Languages at the School of Oriental and African Studies, University of London.

KLAUS P. WACHSMANN is Professor in the School of Music and the Department of Linguistics at Northwestern University.